UNBOUND

GROWING EVER-FREER IN CHRIST

Jesus said, "Unbind him, set him free, and let him go."

John 11:44b

This edition of the *Truth in Love Biblical Counseling's "Unbound: Growing Ever-freer in Christ"* curriculum contains many additions and modifications to the original 1990 version of "S.A.F.E.," by Troy Smith., and subsequent revised *Truth in Love Ministries'* versions of *A Journey to Freedom*, and the First Edition of *Unbound* in several ways:

4. Any personal stories used from the original materials created by Pastor Troy Smith, the founder of SAFE, have been generalized for clearer reading and broader application.

5. The original material this is derived from consisted of seventeen weeks; our version has twenty-six.

Cover Photo: AdobeStock_105721975; ©kasto

ISBN: 979-8-708-53061-5

TRUTH IN LOVE
BIBLICAL COUNSELING
TM

TILBCC

Truth in Love Biblical Counseling & Training Center
An Auxiliary Ministry of
Truth in Love Fellowship
PO Box 5281
Vancouver, WA

Printed and bound in
The United States of America

TABLE OF CONTENTS

PREFACE TO THE SECOND EDITION

The impact of *Unbound: Growing Ever-freer in Christ* has been remarkable over the last several years, and many changes have taken place in our society and in the needs of those who come for help to our ministry.

From the input of the many pastors, biblical counselors, disciplers, and hundreds of participants in the *Unbound* program, it was clear that this amazing tool God has provided us with needed to be updated.

There is not anything new under the sun (Ecclesiastes 1:9). Yet some of the ways we address the age-old problems and the way they show up in the culture and climate of today has changed and *Unbound* needed to be adapted and updated as a result.

We have reformatted the entire workbook in several ways:

- The text has been edited to flow better and to provide updated examples and word-pictures.
- Different fonts have been used that are more appealing to the screen-trained eye.
- Two-column pages are standard throughout, with the columns separated by a line – for the same reason.
- Artwork has been added to adjust for the visually-stimulated brains of many living in the times we live in.
- Formatting changes have been made to break-up the information and create pauses – like in music.
- Key items (such as "Anchor Points") have been highlighted throughout so that they are easier to note and remember.
- The have introduced the saturation verse for each lesson at the beginning of each lesson.
- We have done so with a large page that the participant can capture with their camera phone and have handy whenever they need it.

A number of other changes have been made that those familiar with the First Edition will notice and appreciate. A great many of those folks have contributed suggestions (and more) to create this "Unbound Reboot."

As always, our prayer is that each and all who are introduced to *Unbound* will find useful tools for developing their personal relationship with Jesus Christ and for finding ever-increasing freedom from the death and decay of their past.

May God richly bless all who have contributed in any and all ways to this material.

Soli Deo Gloria

August 2020

PREFACE TO THE FIRST EDITION

The materials in your hands or on your screen make up the basic tools for **Unbound**. *Unbound* is one of the *Truth in Love Biblical Counseling Center's* programs for providing solid Biblical counsel and discipleship to those in bondage to the death and decay of the lies they've believed, the sins they've committed, and the evils they have suffered. Unresolved and unhealed brokenness in our lives keeps us in bondage to the past and robs us of the freedom that Christ died to give us all (Galatians 5:1).

Unbound is the result of decades of Biblical counseling experience from a variety of people, coupled with an expansion of two programs: the first was a program once known as *S.A.F.E. (Setting Addicts Free Eternally)*. That program has been repackaged as "The Transformation Principle," and is currently published by Thomas Nelson Publishers. The second was Truth in Love's, *A Journey to Freedom*. The material you are reading through right now includes that curriculum.

A little history: The S.A.F.E Program began in the mid-1980's when Pastor Troy Smith felt called to minister in Portland, Oregon, and discovered that nothing being used, inside or outside the church, really worked to help those in bondage to addiction. He had been working with people from all walks of life who were overcome by drug, alcohol, and other addictions.

He had come face to face with the reality that, although a person had entered into a personal relationship with Jesus Christ, too often that same person was still being controlled by destructive habits, unruly emotions, and addicted behaviors.

Those things were still destroying these people's lives even though they had surrendered their lives to Christ. They prayed; they read their Bibles; they went to church; they had been baptized; but try as they might, they could not break free and stay free from the bondage they had been in for so long.

After an exceptionally significant defeat through the death of a woman who seemed to be making remarkable progress, Pastor Troy took to heart what he had recognized full well: The 12-Step Model does not work beyond an initial interruption of behaviors and that only God could supply him with a program that does.

After a period of concentrated prayer, God helped him pull together the basic principles and practices that formed the heart of the S.A.F.E. Program, and others that have flowed from it.

The S.A.F.E. Program and S.A.F.E. Ministries went through many changes over the years, eventually arriving at the place where Pastor Troy handed over the reins of leadership to another man. That gentleman faced the task of tying up several loose ends and, after a couple of years of diligence and faithful stewardship, shutting down the ministry. What was once known as "S.A.F.E Ministries" and "S.A.F.E. International" had been dissolved and the curriculum reformatted.

When the hand-off took place, Pastor Troy Smith (who held the copyright for the S.A.F.E. curriculum) worked with Thomas Nelson Publishers and republished the material under his own name with the title, *The Transformation Principle: Journey to Freedom*. Pastor Troy now leads a similar ministry to S.A.F.E. that goes by the name "The Transformation Principle Ministries."

Over the course of many years, while using the materials in many different settings under many different circumstances and addressing more and more diverse patterns of besetting sin and brokenness, the Truth in Love team saw an increasing need for a number of adjustments to be made to that basic program. As society deteriorates the scope and range of sin and brokenness in people's lives has dramatically and exponentially increases.

In order to meet the growing need for deeper and more foundational matters to be addressed—even for those who have been part of the church for many years—there were obvious changes that were needed. Gradually, prayerfully, all of those changes were made by the *Truth in Love Biblical Counseling* team. A lot of supplementary material has been developed and added, and a great deal of updating and fine-tuning has taken place. The result? The *Unbound* program you are reading right now.

For those who are interested in examining the "roots" of *Unbound*, we highly recommend *The Transformation Principle*, by Pastor Troy Smith. The basic building blocks provided in that material have impacted thousands of lives.

VIII

The ebb and flow of the original cannot be replaced: it has proven over and over again to truly be by God's providence that the order of the lessons follow a dynamic pattern that one cannot help but see God's mind behind.

We have done all we can to ensure that proper credit has been given where credit is due throughout *Unbound*. Yet we may have missed something. So, if anyone discovers a lack in that regard, we ask that they notify us via email at tilc@live.com, so that we can get the mistake corrected.

All Scripture quotations designated "Lamb," are personal renderings of the original language text by Pastor Warren G. Lamb (Ph.D., Th.M., M.A., M.S.). Some minor changes in grammar and sentence structure have been made in an effort to make the meaning of the text being quoted clearer for today's readers.

While our materials are available through Amazon (a division of which serves as our publisher), we do not make any profit from them. Instead, we make them available for the minimum price that the publisher will allow. When possible, we make our materials available simply for the asking. This is a ministry that is supported through donations alone.

Our goal and intent are to provide the best resources we can to help those living in bondage to lies, sin, and evil find true freedom in Christ and be "unbound, set free, and let go."

Our prayer is that each and all who are introduced to *Unbound* will find useful tools for developing their personal relationship with Jesus Christ and for finding ever-increasing freedom from the death and decay of their past.

May God richly bless all who have contributed in any and all ways to this material.

Soli Deo Gloria

x

ACKNOWLEDGEMENTS

There have been many people involved in the development of *Unbound: Growing Ever-freer in Christ* over the years. In fact, there has not been a single person that has spoken with us about the curriculum whose input has not been invaluable.

It has been my practice to make clear that *Unbound* is the result of the collaborative efforts of countless individuals over a great many years. This is why speaking of myself in the first-person will only be found here, in the "Acknowledgements."

As was mentioned in the Preface to the First Edition, the foundational principles and many of the key lessons in *Unbound* trace back to Pastor Troy Smith and the SAFE Program God led him to develop in the mid-1980s. Without that base, *Unbound* would not exist. Countless thousands of lives have been introduced to and transformed by the powerful dynamic of Scripture saturation. Our deepest gratitude goes out to Pastor Troy for his faithful obedience when God called him to develop the SAFE Program, and his decades of faithfully teaching these principles.

With that said, there are a couple of people whose efforts over the last two years have made this "reboot" what it is.

For over a year, Pastor P.J. Davis reworked the wording of the lessons to get them to flow better and to not sound like our main contributor's (my) "voice." He helped make sure that footnotes were added where they would be helpful in providing background or explanatory information. Pastor Davis also helped restructure some of the lessons so that the different ways that people learn were taken into consideration and adjusted for. Thank you, PJ!

Two of the ladies impacted and helped in their relationships with Christ through the *Unbound* curriculum have shared their creative talents to produce the "Verse Plates" at the beginning of each lesson. Betty Ann White and Mariah Hatfield know the importance of visual prompts in learning. They understand that most of us find learning easier when a picture is connected with information. Introducing the saturation verse for each lesson at the beginning of each lesson needed an approach that was not dry and boring. For you doodlers, you will find lots of room for doodling. We are grateful that they shared their talent with us and pray you are blessed by their offerings!

There are a handful of people who support and challenge me in the background that God uses regularly to keep me encouraged and motivated. Their input — in the big and the small ways, the formal and informal conversations — helped ensure that the refining and fine-tuning of *Unbound: Growing Ever-freer in Christ* became what you have in front of you today. Their support and encouragement have been priceless!

One of those people is one that serves on our counseling team and who is almost as familiar with this material as I am. Her name is Kelli Russell and she uses *Unbound* daily as a counseling and discipling tool. Kelli has been one of the key contributors to the refining of *Unbound* for a long time. Her interactions with the material as a participant and as a counselor produced insights that were greatly needed. In fact, being a creative person and being a visual-learner herself, her input was the main catalyst for the addition and inclusion of much of the artwork and other visuals — especially the Verse Plates. We all owe her our thanks for her contribution to making this revised and updated version of *Unbound* what it is. Thank you, Kelli!

There are three women who are daily encouragement and support for me in more ways than I can count: my wife and two daughters. Their influence can be seen and felt in the soft and gentle places in *Unbound*. Their inspiration can be heard in the word-pictures that are utilized to bring clear understanding of and connection to important concepts and truths on a personal level. And their unflagging support has helped me keep pressing on when I have wondered if the work is going to matter. Thank you, ladies!

It almost seems cliché to thank my Lord and Savior Jesus Christ, but without His relentless grace, none of this would have happened on any level. It is His love that has drawn me and everyone who has ever been impacted by this material to Himself and to His Word. It is His sacrifice that has made reconciliation with God and with anyone else possible. And it is His strength that keeps us in the battles when quitting seems so much easier. May He be honored by what we have done here.

One final note of thanks: To each and every person who delves into the pages of *Unbound*, thank you for being willing to entrust part of your journey to us. Our greatest desire is for you to gain a solid grasp on your identity in Christ; to develop a solid understanding of the nature and character of God; and to have a solid confidence in the nature and character of God and how that all intersects with your life. It is in those three areas that we all find the truth of who God is, who He created us to be, and what that means for time and eternity.

May this curriculum help you find rest for your souls and hope for your hearts in Christ.

Soli Deo Gloria
Warren Lamb
Tustin, California

PHOTO AND ART CREDITS

INTRODUCTION

Jesus had a friend named Lazarus, and Lazarus had died. In fact, he had been dead for four days when Jesus arrived at the tomb of his friend. Jesus did not leave His friend that way but raised him back to life!

Interestingly, immediately after Jesus raised Lazarus from the dead, He turned to those standing nearby and said, "*Unbind him; set him free; let him go*" (John 11:44b). If you are not familiar with the story of Jesus raising Lazarus from the dead, you can read the entire account in your Bible in John 11:1-44.

One of the most amazing aspects of Jesus' life and ministry while He was here on earth was His tendency to disrupt funerals. The most powerful and intriguing of those stories is this one, where Jesus raises His friend Lazarus from the dead and restores him to his family. While we will not go into great detail now, there are several aspects of this incident that wonderfully illustrate both the goals of *Unbound: Growing Ever-freer in Christ*, and our way of working to reach those goals.

As previously mentioned, Jesus did not arrive at Lazarus' tomb until the fourth day following the burial of his friend. Imagine the condition of Lazarus' body at that point. He did not smell particularly good. Decay had set in. He was getting "gooey." Oddly enough, Lazarus' sisters (Mary and Martha) sent for Jesus even before their brother died, but Jesus delayed coming to them.

At first look, Jesus' delay in coming seems hard-hearted and cold. But Jesus knew full well what His Heavenly Father had in store for Lazarus and the others. He meant for them to see this man resurrected from the dead through the powerful word of Jesus himself. He meant for them, and for us, to catch a glimpse of the future God has arranged for all who follow Jesus, namely freedom from death itself.

When Lazarus walked out of that tomb after four days, there could have been no doubt in *anyone's* mind that Jesus had truly raised him from the dead. It was not a rumor, a fable, a myth, or a legend. It was a very real event, recorded by a personal witness and attested to by hundreds of other witnesses.

Now, many people know of the "biggest-little-verse" in the Bible: "Jesus wept" (John 11:35). What we often miss is that Jesus' sadness over what happened to this man He loved appears sandwiched between two significant statements: "...He was deeply indignant...," (verse 33) and, "Jesus, deeply indignant again... (verse 38)."[1]

In his dealings with the death of Lazarus, Jesus comes face-to-face with the most overwhelming evidence of Satan's reign of evil and devastation. He confronts the temporary domain of Satan, represented by death and sorrow — things God never intended for us to experience — and He is indignant.

Wonderfully, death and everything that goes with it *never* defeats the indignant Son of God! In fact, quite the contrary. As demonstrated so dramatically at the tomb of Lazarus, Jesus has won full victory over sin, death, condemnation, and evil. What is more, that victory also belongs to any and all who would believe and trust Him for it.

When Lazarus comes out of the tomb, still shrouded in the heavy mantle of thick strips of cloth they

wrapped dead folks in during those days, Jesus makes a very important statement to the onlookers. This is where *our* story, the story of *Unbound*, interweaves with who Jesus is and why He came.

Jesus said to those with Him, *"Unbind him, set him free, and let him go"* (John 11:44b). Think about that for a moment: Dead...Decaying...Foul-smelling...Putrid. Lazarus emerged from that tomb in the same state our lives do when we become bound up in the death and decay of lies we have believed, sins we've committed, and evils we have suffered. But our bondage is no more the *final* answer than Lazarus' burial wrappings were for him.

Just as Jesus brought Lazarus back to life in the physical realm, so also He gives each of us a brand new, born-again life when we place our faith and

---

[1] Some translations render the original Greek word here as "deeply moved in spirit" or "he groaned in the spirit."

While this is technically correct, we believe a better way to render the original is "deeply indignant."

trust in Him, and surrender our lives to Him (see 2 Corinthians 5:17-19; Ephesians 2:1-7). And, just as Jesus charged the living to help unbind Lazarus from the remnants and relics of his death and burial for the purpose of freedom and life, so also He charges His people today.

He instructs we who have found freedom and new life in Christ to help unbind and set free those who still live in bondage to the death and decay of their former lives. _This_ is why _Unbound_ exists! It is a powerful tool that God has used in one form or another for a great many years to help people find true freedom in Christ. Every lesson can be viewed as further "unbinding," as a further unwrapping of the layers of bondage that you have been prisoner to for so long.

Whatever it is that keeps you from the full and healthy, vibrant relationship with God that He created you to have — whether it is drugs, alcohol, pornography, disordered eating, one bad relationship after another, work, shopping, shame of the past, or whatever else is in the way — know this: There is hope. There are answers.

You may have a new life in Christ, yet you may also be buried under layer upon layer of "burial rags"; residue and the after-effects of the rot and corruption of sins committed, and evils suffered. _Unbound_ can help peel away all of it, allowing more and more living truth to take its place. This is where we find the freedom in Christ that He died to give us (Galatians 5:1-2); this is where we change the deadness of our old life for new life in Christ (John 8:31-32); this is where we are made truly free, once and for all (John 8:36).

KEYS TO THE PROGRAM

There are several specific things to know as you embark on this journey. There is work to do. All of it is essential and helpful, and your faithfulness will reap the most amazing blessings:

1. There is **homework** to do **every day**, six days a week, for the **entirety of the program**. Start right now, _believing_ you are worth the investment. We promise you; you are!

3

2. There is a specific Bible verse to saturate on with every lesson. You will be introduced to the lesson's verse on the page facing the first page of the lesson. This is also found at the top of the "Study Sheet" at the end of each lesson.[2]

   a. When we speak of "Scripture saturation," we are using "technical language": It means "To **read out loud** at least (hopefully) 100 times per day" (except for the pre-meal saturation verses from the "Restore" section that you will be introduced to in Lesson 3).

   b. Do the best you can, asking God to help you become more consistent each day. It will not take long for you to experience and see the amazing effects in your own life.

3. The goal is not to memorize, which is an intellectual exercise. The goal is to *saturate* ourselves so that the truth penetrates to the depths of our heart and our soul and does not just become lodged in our minds.

   a. "Meditating" on the Word of God (Psalm 1:1-2) means to quietly recite, ponder, and reflect on, like cattle chewing the cud.

4. For the "Daily Reflections," (found at the end of each lesson) there is no right or wrong answer. There are no grades. The daily investment you make will bear fruit in due season, just like any healthy fruit tree does. As you progress, you will understand the truth you are saturating on more and more. As you do, the truth will transform you on a heart and soul level. Only that kind of change is real, *authentic*, transformational change.

   a. Using a journal to record your responses is one of the best ways to process through the Reflections. If you are working with a discipler or counselor, this is helpful for your meetings together. If you are not, you are welcome to connect with the Truth in Love Counseling Team via email at tilbcc@outlook.com.

5. There is no "fail." We set goals, and we may exceed those goals or fall

---

[2] This concept and approach were at the heart of the SAFE Program from the beginning. We have found nothing that works as effectively for bringing life transformation.

short of them. But falling short is *not* failing. Nowhere in God's Word is "failure" associated with any person (except for one "could-be-better-rendered" passage found in some English translations of Numbers). Faith fails, strength fails, hope fails, courage fails, plans fail, other things fail, but nowhere does it say that God fails, and nowhere does it say that people fail — or that people are failures.

a. Here is a word-picture that may help: Being fearful of being a failure is like being fearful you are going to wake up tomorrow as a Leprechaun. It simply *cannot* happen!

6. Be honest and authentic — there is no judgment, no condemnation, and no criticism. The more honest and authentic you are, the more the truth will overtake your life, and the more successful you will be at breaking free from the bondage that besets (plagues, torments, harasses, overwhelms, troubles you). You will become more and more **unbound** every day.

7. Keep honest records of your progress each week (there is a Progress Record form next to each lesson's Study Sheet for you to use if you desire). Doing so will help you discover where to seek adjustments in schedule, desire, dedication, and commitment.

8. The "Restore" book at the back is a "secondary saturation tool," an "emotional first-aid kit," that needs to be incorporated into your routine as early and as often as possible (we formally introduce it in Lesson 3). There are daily challenges we face on the battlefield of our emotions and our thought-life, and this resource provides many saturation passages to help fight and win those battles.

9. Learning to pray is going to be invaluable to you. There are not any formulized prayers to pray. Just like any other skill, it takes time and practice. Jesus gave us a model to follow in Matthew 6:9-14, but He did not say, "Pray this prayer." Keep in mind that God already knows your thoughts and emotions, your desires and fears, and He is always waiting to talk with you about them (Philippians 4:6-7).

a. To get you started in prayer, you will find a one-page help in the Supplemental Materials section titled, "A Pattern for Developing Your Prayer-Life."

Always remember that there are people praying for you and available to you to help along the way. This is a discipleship program, which means that no one takes this journey alone. You can always reach someone by email using the Contact Us page on our counseling website at www.TILBCC.com.

Pay attention to and stay mindful of the **Anchor Points** (look for an anchor ⚓) scattered throughout the material. They will become powerful tools in your toolbox as you walk the path of freedom in Christ.

Our prayer is that as you learn, grow, transform, and experience freedom, you will look for at least one thing to be thankful for each and every day. As you learn to be thankful, you will discover that your focus on "lack" disappears, and your ability to see and enjoy God's personal, kind affection toward you blossoms.

May God richly bless you and help you as you partner with Him:

"Come to me, all you who are weary and burdened, and I will give you rest. Take my yoke on you and learn from me, because I am gentle and humble in heart, and you will find rest for your souls. For my yoke is easy to bear, and my load is not hard to carry." (Jesus, in Matthew 11:28-30)

The Power of Our Thinking[3]
Cultivate a thought, reap an action . . .
Cultivate an action, reap a habit . . .
Cultivate a habit, reap a behavior . . .
Cultivate a behavior, reap a character . . .
Cultivate a character, reap a destiny!

---

[3] Original source unknown

GOAL

SET A SOLID FOUNDATION

7

Lesson One	*Worthy*
Lesson Two	*Our Base*
Lesson Three	*The Basics*

SET A SOLID FOUNDATION

The first priority when building anything is to lay a good foundation. When our foundation is weak, fragile, cracked, missing pieces, and sits on a weak base, nothing we build on it will be solid or will last--especially when the pressure is on (Matthew 7:24-27).

God tells us in many places in His Word (1 Corinthians 3:11, et al.) that the only secure foundation is Jesus Christ. He is the Cornerstone that the whole thing stands on. If we try to build on anything else, disaster is the only thing we can expect.

We were created to be in loving fellowship with God Almighty, Creator and Sustainer of all things. The only way that sinful humans can have friendship and fellowship with the Holy and Righteous God is through His Son, Jesus Christ. How does that happen? How can we be sure?

As we surrender to Jesus Christ, who is Himself the Truth (John 14:6), and as we saturate our minds with His truth as revealed in His Word, we learn to trust in, and live by, the solid and sure truth of His Word. The fruit of that is a person transformed into the amazing Masterpiece He always intended each of us to be.

Here is a word picture that will be helpful to keep in mind as you progress through this curriculum: The healthy life and the freedom you long for are like a safety deposit box. The two keys that unlock the box are labeled "Surrender to Christ" and "Saturation on the Truth."

The more we **surrender** to Jesus Christ, and the more we **saturate** on the Truth of His Word, the more we are able to walk in true wholeness and in true freedom from the lies and bondage we have been living/dying in. The result will be each of us growing closer and closer to becoming the healthy, vibrant, fruitful, godly person that our Creator always intended for each of us to be.

"For we are HIS Masterpiece created anew in Christ Jesus so the good things HE planned for us long ago would be OUR WAY of LIFE."

Ephesians 2:10, Lamb, NLT

mariahhatfield
2020

10

LESSON ONE
WORTHY

"I just feel so worthless!" Have you ever said those words? Have you ever *believed* those words?

Perhaps the deepest, **most malicious lie** many people believe is that they are "worthless." A comparison of dictionaries shows worthless defined as, "lacking worth; of no use, importance, or value; despicable; good-for-nothing." These are pretty apt descriptions of what "worthless" feels like, right?

Alternative words often used include contemptible, shameful, ugly, vile, useless, insignificant, pointless. Anyone who has carried around the burden of "being worthless" has felt all these things and more. But no matter which synonym you choose, all of these words are lies when it comes to *any* person, *any* human being! While we may be *undeserving* of any good thing, deserving and worthy are two vastly different realities.

To "be deserving" means to have earned something and it points to the value of an action that we have performed—a *functional* or *doing* value. Worth, on the other hand, is not about "doing" but about "being," and refers to the inherent essence of something.

For example, suppose you have a block of gold sitting on the table in front of you. That block of gold, being gold, has an inherent (fundamental and built-in) worth no matter what form or shape it is in. If it is melted down and shaped into a doorstop, its worth is still the same; but its functional and aesthetic value have changed.

That same block of gold melted down into a creamery to use with Grandma's fine-china tea service will have a different functional and aesthetic value, but it is still gold and still worth what it was before anything was done to alter it. Now, we can add gemstones and fashion that gold into a magnificent jewelry ensemble, greatly increasing its functional and aesthetic value; or we can leave it in its rawest form and stuff it under a manure pile. The one thing that *does not* and *will not* change is its INHERENT WORTH.

In like manner, when we consider each and every human being on planet Earth, we find that each and every person – no matter what they have done or have not done—has inherent worth, because each and every one of us is created in God's image (*imago dei*).

This concept of us humans as bearers of the *imago dei* goes all the way back to the earliest chapters of the Book of Genesis in the Bible. Genesis uses the phrase "*imago dei*" three times, and each time it refers to God's view of mankind, not mankind's view of himself.

First, we see God creating man in His image (Genesis 1:26-27). Then we see that the children born to the first man and woman are also "in the image of God" (Genesis 5:1-3, with 1:26-27 revisited).

The third time Genesis uses the phrase *imago dei* is highly significant and points to the sanctity of all human life — again from God's perspective — when God institutes capital punishment for murder.

Here is what we see: Noah and his family have just departed the ark following the flood and God gives them the basic laws they are to live by. Two laws are brand new: first, from this point on you will be eating meat, and do not eat it alive or raw; second, "Whoever sheds human blood, by other humans must his blood be shed; for in God's image God has made humankind" (Genesis 9:6, NET).

Scripture's emphasis on the *imago dei* does not end with Genesis 9. In the New Testament, Jesus' half-brother James revisits and intensifies how we are to regard one another when he says, "But no human being can subdue the tongue; it is a restless evil, full of deadly poison. With it we bless the Lord and Father, and with it we curse people **made in God's image**" (James 3:8-9, emphasis added).

Now, in reality, this idea of bearing the *imago dei* is only the beginning of how we are to understand our inherent worth and value. In Psalm 8, David ponders over how it could possibly be that the Divine Creator of all that exists would have regard for mankind, and — even more significantly — would place His creation in the hands of mankind to steward and to manage.

Or consider Jesus, who, in Matthew 6, invests quite a few moments charging His listeners not to be anxious about any of their needs. Their Heavenly Father knows all of their needs, just as He does the needs of the birds He provides for, and "you are of far more value than they." God also provides beautifully for the grass and flowers, even though, once again, humankind is worth far more than any plant (Matthew 6:28-29). We can rest assured then, says Jesus, that God will provide for the humans He has created in His image even more than he does for the grass and flowers (Matthew 6:30-33).

Later in Matthew, Jesus again says something else significant for our understanding of human value and worth. In Matthew 16:26, He asks, "For what will it profit a man if he gains the whole world and forfeits his soul? Or what will a man give in exchange for his soul?" As far as Jesus is concerned, one person (and that means YOU!) is of FAR more WORTH than the created universe!

In Luke 12:6-7, Jesus declares, "Are not five sparrows sold for two cents? Yet not one of them is forgotten before God. Indeed, the very hairs of your head are all numbered. Do not fear; **you are more valuable than many sparrows**" (emphasis added).

The list goes on and on, including how there is rejoicing in heaven when ONE sinner turns from their sinfulness and surrenders to Christ as Savior (Luke 15:7, 10). This rejoicing comes as a result of the restoration of a lost loved one to their rightful and intended place as a future co-inheritor with Jesus, one who will be glorified right along beside Him (Romans 5:1-2, 6, 8, 10; Romans 8:16-17, 28-29).

Remember that block of gold? When we have turned from our own sinful, selfish ways and surrendered to Him, another change takes place (more in Lesson 2). Our inherent worth is still there, but there is a change in our *functional* value (the "new creation" of 2 Corinthians 5:17). When a person is converted, it is like being the block of gold taken out from under the manure pile, being cleaned up, and now available for God to "tap" and put in the game.

In Ephesians 2:10, we find one of the most beautiful word-pictures in all of Scripture regarding worth: "For we are His **masterpiece, created anew** in Christ Jesus so the good things He planned for us long ago would be our way of life."

Think of a master artisan, like Michelangelo, crafting a magnificent statue out of a clump of marble. It does not start out very pretty at all, but the end result is a magnificent piece of art. You see, in Ephesus, the home of the Temple of Diana (or Temple of Artemis)

– one of the Seven Wonders of the Ancient Word – the city was full of artisans: sculptors, carvers, potters, silversmiths and goldsmiths, jewel faceters, and the like.

What they created were called *poiema* (think "work of art," not "craftsmanship"). "Work of art, masterpiece": That is the way the word *poiema* can be best understood. It is pronounced "poh-EE-ma" and is an ancient Greek term for "visible expression," and it is where our English word "poem" comes from.

You, according to Scripture, are God's "poem," a masterpiece from the Hand of the Creator. Just as the artisan seeks to express his heart and mind through his work, so the Creator seeks to express His heart and mind through you.

There is inherent worth and honor in being His *poiema*, yet there is responsibility as well. Being His "visible expression" means we need to prayerfully seek to have a solid hold on our inherent worth, on our identity in Christ (for those who are believers), and to more and more fully "express" His will and His ways, His heart and His mind.

All of this means that, instead of getting our sense of worth and value from what we do and how flawlessly (or poorly) we do it, we focus on being who He created us to be in Christ, and allow the "doing" to flow naturally from the "being" - like ripe fruit falling from a tree. A peach tree does not have to sit out in the orchard and focus all of its attention on growing peaches ("I've gotta grow *peaches*; I've gotta grow *peaches*...")—it simply grows peaches because it IS a peach tree and that's what peach trees DO...the "doing" flows naturally from the "being." We were created as human "beings," not human "doings."

God created us worthy of love, worthy of dignity, worthy of His very best: the sacrifice of His Son in our place. We cannot change that any more than we can change our eye color, our gender (XX and XY chromosome structures cannot be changed), or our DNA from human to something else.

Our inherent worth is just as much a part of us as our humanity and it cannot be taken from us. And even if there are those in our life who now deny or have denied us that dignity and worth, it does NOT change the fact that we are inherently worthy of it.

There is more to be said about this further on, but please hold on to this truth: While we are not *deserving* of any good thing (it cannot be earned), we are *fully worthy* of God's BEST—we were *created* that way!

ဆ • ဗ

WORD-PICTURE

Imagine walking through the garage with a box full of Fiestaware – those brightly colored ceramic dishes that immediately catch your eye when you walk into the dishware section of a department store. Now, imagine that the bottom of the box splits open and the entire contents of the box *crashes* onto the concrete floor. *CRASH!!*

Shattered pieces of bright red and blue and green and yellow and orange and purple ceramic are in a pile at your feet. Hundreds of pieces – their bright white insides showing along the edges – lay scattered across the floor.

What do you do?

Most of us – after our shock and confusion subside – will start cleaning up the mess and throwing away what has now become trash. Even if we consider trying to glue some of the bigger pieces back together, we will realize that the effort would be futile, at best.

But when God – our Creator and Heavenly Father – sees the wreckage and shattered pieces of our life, He does *not see trash*; He sees *TREASURE*. God, the Master Artisan, takes all of those broken pieces and begins putting them together into a mosaic – a work of art that did not exist before, and one that

14

could *not* exist WITHOUT THE BROKEN PIECES!

Ask God to help you see the Masterpiece He originally created you to be, and that He is even now transforming you into being. Ask Him to help you trust Him to mold and shape you into the beautifully unique work-of-art He intends for You to be. Ask Him to help you accept His acceptance of you because you are His in Christ.

DAILY PRACTICES	DAY 1	DAY 2	DAY 3	DAY 4	DAY 5	DAY 6	"REST" DAY
SATURATION VERSE ___	More □ 100 □ Less □	More □ 100 □ Less □	More □ 100 □ Less □	More □ 100 □ Less □	More □ 100 □ Less □	More □ 100 □ Less □	More □ 100 □ Less □
BIBLE READING	Chapters ___	Chapters ___	Chapters ___	Chapters ___	Chapters ___	Chapters ___	
STUDY MANUAL LESSON # ___	Read Today's Lesson Today Yes □ No □	Read Today's Lesson Today Yes □ No □	Read Today's Lesson Today Yes □ No □	Read Today's Lesson Today Yes □ No □	Read Today's Lesson Today Yes □ No □	Read Today's Lesson Today Yes □ No □	
DAILY REFLECTION	Completed Today's Lesson Today Yes □ No □	Completed Today's Lesson Today Yes □ No □	Completed Today's Lesson Today Yes □ No □	Completed Today's Lesson Today Yes □ No □	Completed Today's Lesson Today Yes □ No □	Completed Today's Lesson Today Yes □ No □	
USED "RESTORE" BOOK	Yes □ No □	Yes □ No □	Yes □ No □	Yes □ No □	Yes □ No □	Yes □ No □	Yes □ No □
PRE-MEAL SATURATION VERSE	Breakfast □ Lunch □ Dinner □	Breakfast □ Lunch □ Dinner □	Breakfast □ Lunch □ Dinner □	Breakfast □ Lunch □ Dinner □	Breakfast □ Lunch □ Dinner □	Breakfast □ Lunch □ Dinner □	Breakfast □ Lunch □ Dinner □
SPECIAL ITEMS	Yes □ No □	Yes □ No □	Yes □ No □	Yes □ No □	Yes □ No □	Yes □ No □	Yes □ No □
PRIVATE PRAYER	Time Spent ___	Time Spent ___	Time Spent ___	Time Spent ___	Time Spent ___	Time Spent ___	Time Spent ___
TODAY, I AM THANKFUL FOR...							

Lesson 1 Study Sheet

Each day review the lesson for that week.
Record one thing you are grateful for each day on your Progress Record.

This Lesson's Verse:

"For we are His masterpiece, created anew in Christ Jesus so the good He planned for us long ago would be our way of life." (Ephesians 2:10, Lamb)

Day 1 Reflection

What thoughts and emotions did you experience as you read through this lesson? *Additional study passage: Psalm 139:14*

Day 2 Reflection

How much or how often have you felt worthless in your life? What is the worst it got? *Additional study passage: Psalm 88:15*

Day 3 Reflection

Can you look back to a time, a person, or a situation where you were shown or were able to see a worthiness you didn't normally feel? Describe that. What did you do with that at the time? *Additional study passage: Philippians 4:8*

Day 4 Reflection

What other effects has a sense of worthlessness had in your life? What are your thoughts on that now? *Additional study passage: Romans 8:5-6*

Day 5 Reflection

What do you think the effect will be in your life when you are able to fully believe the message from this lesson? *Additional study passages: Psalm 25:2; Psalm 91:2*

Day 6 Reflection

What difference do you think it would make in the world if more people understood and believed this "inherent worth" message? *Additional study passages: Ecclesiastes 9:18; John 14:27*

'For I *know* the plans
I have for you,'
declares the LORD,
'plans for

and not for
calamity
to give you a future
and a HOPE.'

Jeremiah 29:11 (NASB)

LESSON TWO
OUR BASE

[This lesson is the longest one, but it is important for you to have this information as clear as possible in your mind — a great deal depends on it.[4]]

The foundation we build our life on will determine the outcome — and that includes how we deal with what others bring to our life that is bad, wrong, or difficult. Our foundation and the materials we use to build our life — if not solid and pure—will result in sinful choices, broken relationships, and lousy outcomes. It only makes sense to choose the best foundation we can find, right?

Scripture tells us, *"For no man can lay a foundation other than the one which is laid, which is Jesus Christ"* (1 Corinthians 3:11). Most of us have invested a great deal of time, effort, and resources into building our lives on a foundation crammed with cracks, broken and missing pieces, resting on a base that is unstable and unreliable. It is *impossible* for us to rebuild our lives until we first lay a new and solidly sure foundation. Just as the key to building a strong and sturdy house begins with a solid foundation, so it is when we are attempting to build a solid life.

The most crucial and essential key to success in our journey to wholeness is this: We <u>must</u> replace our shoddy, defective, and broken foundation with the only one provided by and guaranteed by God Himself. The only *sure* foundation for a sound, solid, fruitful life is Jesus Christ. Only a life founded and grounded on Him can be full, rich, vibrant, and whole.

So, how do we get from "here" to "there;" from a broken foundation to one that is solid? We have to start by understanding some foundational, fundamental truths, a few of which we looked at in Lesson One. This lesson, and every lesson, we will "build" on what we have learned so far, strengthening the foundation and adding more truth as we go along. The goal is to faithfully work on engrafting these things into our hearts, our minds, and our souls so that the trash gets taken out and the treasure of Truth replaces it.

TRUTH #1: GOD DESIRES A WHOLE, HEALTHY, VIBRANT, AND LOVING RELATIONSHIP WITH US

---

[4] Our goal is to present the Gospel from God's perspective and design instead of from the perspective of our need.

21

God created us for the purpose of loving us and one day inviting us to share in His glory. Many people think God created us to glorify Him. In a manner of speaking, that is true. But, on the other hand, we have to be careful not to adopt defective thinking here.

What do we mean by "glorify God?" God has always had all the glory there is: He has never had any need for anyone or anything to "glorify" Him. We may reflect his glory, we may make it clearer to someone else (magnify His glory) , but we can never add to His glory (Note: There are translations of the Bible that say, "Glorify the Lord with me," Psalm 34:3, but a better rendering of that would be, "Proclaim the Lord's greatness with me.").

We have several passages of Scripture from one end of the Bible to the other which reinforce the idea that God created us for our good, not His. In Psalm 8, David first marvels at how the power and majesty of the One who created the universe is obvious in creation. Then, his mind turns and he wonders at how special mankind must be because God created us "a little lower than the heavenly beings," and put all of His creation in our care.

Indeed, from the very beginning of Scripture (Genesis 1:26-27) we are told that God created mankind in His own image.

It is only of humankind that the Bible says this. In Genesis 9, after Noah and his family come off of the ark following the flood, God instructs them to be fruitful and multiply (just as He did with Adam and Eve), and then adds two commands. The second of these establishes the fact that God holds every human life to be sacred, and that He expects us to hold one another in high esteem (Genesis 9:6).

In Matthew 6:25-35, when Jesus teaches those who follow Him not to be anxious and tells them why not to be, He points out that God takes care of the birds, who contribute nothing to their own nourishment (other than eating), and that we are "of far more value" than they are.

Later, Jesus remarks, "For what good does it do a person to gain the whole world (Bible language for "whole created universe") but to forfeit his soul?" (Mark 8:36). He also says, "...I tell you, there is joy in the presence of God's angels over one sinner who repents" (Luke 15:10, NET).

The point is this: As far as God is concerned, one soul — you — is worth more than the created universe. God created us for the purpose of loving us and one day inviting us to share in His glory (Romans 5:1-2, Galatians 4:7; Romans 8:15-17; and others). He delights when any one of us turns from our sinful and rebellious ways and surrenders to Him.

Tragically, God's original design and created intent was broken long ago. And, for many of us, it remains broken in varying degrees. The brokenness we live and experience in our homes, in our relationships, in our own minds, and in every aspect of our lives is a reflection of that "Original Design Brokenness" — all because we believe and live out lies.

TRUTH #2: GOD'S DESIRE IS THAT EVERYONE WOULD FREELY ACCEPT HIS LOVE AND BE RECONCILED TO HIM, BUT HE KNOWS THAT EVERYONE WILL NOT

Probably the most famous verse in the entire Bible is John 3:16: *"For this is the way God loved the world: He gave his one and only Son, so that **everyone** who believes in Him will not perish but have everlasting life (emphasis added)."*

The next two verses are very important as well: *"For God did not send his Son into the world to condemn the world but that the world should be saved through Him. The one who believes in Him is not condemned. The one who does not believe has been condemned already, because he has not believed in the name of the one and only Son of God"* (John 3:17-18).

Based on these passages and others, we can clearly see that God's desire is for all people to believe and surrender to Jesus (verse 16). But He also knows that some will, and some will not (verse 18). The real question is, "Will I follow Jesus or not?" God calls me to make a choice.

In 2 Peter 3:9, the Apostle Peter states, *"He does not wish for any to perish but for all to come to repentance."* Then we see in 1 Timothy 2:(3)4, "(Such prayer for all is good and welcomed before God our Savior,) *since He [God] wants all people to be saved and to come to a knowledge of the truth."* And all the way back in Ezekiel 18:23 we read, *"'Do I have any pleasure in the death of the wicked,' declares the Lord GOD, 'rather than that he should turn from his ways and live'?"*

Here again, we see sown throughout the Scriptures God's desire for everyone to come to know, accept, and love Him. This same idea is reinforced in the Bible's very last "invitation," offered in Revelation 22:17: *"And the Spirit and the bride say, 'Come!' And let the one who hears say: 'Come!' And let the one who is thirsty come; let the one who wants it take the water of life free of charge"* (In the King James this reads, *"whosoever will, let him take the water of life freely."*).

Such is the heart of God. But again, we are faced with a tragic reality: Rather than respond to His love and agree to follow Him, we all choose instead to go our own way and to reject Him, and then we defiantly stay that course as our life disintegrates around us more and more.

TRUTH #3: GOD'S ORIGINAL DESIGN, HIS CREATED ORDER, WAS WILLFULLY BROKEN BY HUMANKIND

Once we realize that God loves us and wants us to be in a whole, healthy, vibrant, and loving relationship with Him, we also realize that something is wrong. Because of our sinfulness — by nature and by choice — His created purpose for us is far out of our reach. God is good, righteous, just, and holy, and He cannot have friendship or companionship with sin.

Regardless of how much God desires a relationship with us, it cannot happen as long as we love sin more than we love Him, and as long as sin remains unconfessed and unrepented of in our life. That does not necessarily mean we have to know and confess *every* sin because it is impossible for us to know them all. But, what we know, we are to confess and repent of. That is His expectation of us.

The first man and woman enjoyed a daily fellowship with God that was drastically severed all in one day by their own rebellion. The break has lasted from then up through this very moment. Their rebellion began when they believed a lie; a lie that was in direct contradiction to the truth that God had proclaimed to be so. That same pattern has been repeated every day throughout human history — admittedly in our own lives. We are all given the same opportunities to choose truth over lies, and we often choose lies, for selfish reasons, just like Adam and Eve did.

(Study Note: You can see an interesting parallel story in Matthew 4:1-11, where Satan personally tempted Jesus in the wilderness: same three lies, same goals. Thankfully, they did not work!)

The sin that separated Adam and Eve from God was their disobedience to God's command to not eat fruit from a particular tree in the Garden of Eden. Sound harsh? "They ate fruit! *Really!* Is THAT all?!"

No, indeed it was not really about the fruit. Eating the fruit was not the basic problem. Adam and Eve sinned by eating the fruit because they believed a lie. They willfully disobeyed God because they chose to believe the Serpent. The alternative truth presented by the Serpent was more desirable and preferable than obeying what God had said.

Of course, we have all done that and worse, haven't we? Today we lie, steal, get jealous over what others have, misuse and mistreat other people for our own pleasure — the list goes on and on. We do all this because we believe that what sin offers is more desirable and preferable than God's will and God's plan. Do you understand? It is disobedience built on lies.

24

Unless and until God intervenes, we have no hope of remedying the shattered connection between Him and us. There is nothing that rebellious mankind can do to restore God's original design and be reconciled to Him.

TRUTH #4: GOD HIMSELF HAS PROVIDED THE WAY OF RESTORATION AND RECONCILIATION

Because the due penalty for sin is eternal separation from God ("Death": Genesis 2:16-17; Romans 6:23), paying that due penalty, the "sin-debt," for even one lie or one selfish act would require eternal spiritual death (separation from God) for every perpetrator. This is because God and sin can have **no affiliation**, let alone a mutually loving and caring relationship. Mankind is surely lost and without any hope apart from God's intervention and help.

God's answer to the sin problem is Jesus Christ. Jesus said, *"I am the Way, the Truth, and the Life; no one comes to the Father except through me"* (John 14:6). Jesus is the *only one* who can reconcile us to God. There is no other way. **He IS the Way.** In fact, the heart of the Gospel is spelled out in 2 Corinthians 5:19, which says, in part, "in Christ God was reconciling the world to Himself, not counting people's trespasses against them..."

How did God work this out? Jesus is fully God and became a man (see John 1:1, 14; Philippians 2:5-11). God the Son existed with God the Father before there was a "beginning."

At the incarnation (His conception by the Holy Spirit in the womb of His mother Mary), Jesus took on humanity. He is fully God and fully man (don't try to figure this out right now, you don't need to).

As the GOD-man, Jesus was, and is, without any sin at all. He lived a fully righteous life, was tempted in every way that we are, and yet *still* He did not sin. He truly is "God with Us," the meaning of the name Emanuel (also spelled Immanuel, Matthew 1:23).

Just as the First Adam represented us in God's Court in "The Rebellion" (Genesis 3), the sinless Jesus, the GOD-man, is the only one who could be our holy and righteous representative in God's Court *after* The Rebellion. He is the Second Adam. [4]

God's righteous, fair, and unbiased response to *all* sin is His full and pure wrath. Yet, out of His love for us, and out of His commitment to our one day

---

[4] For a fuller understanding of this, read Romans 5, especially Romans 5:12-20.

sharing His glory (knowing that we could never ourselves pay the debt for our sin), He made Himself the only fit sacrifice able to deal finally and fully with sin.

When Jesus (God the Son) died on the cross, He took on the Father's full wrath for our sins in our place. That means God Himself took the punishment we deserve so that we would never have to face it ourselves. Now THAT is good news!

THAT is the kind of love God has for everyone that He created in His image — and that includes you!

God's Word says, "...Christ also suffered once for sins, the just for the unjust, to bring you to God" (1 Peter 3:18, NET). Because our sins separate us from God and keep us separated from Him, and because the penalty for sin is death (eternal separation from God), Jesus willingly died our death for us.

Because Christ paid our sin-debt, Holy God can now have intimate fellowship with once sinful man. The only provision for forgiveness of sin that God has made is Christ's death. There is salvation in no one else (see John 14:6; Acts 4:12). He died that we might live with God ever-after. This is what is known as "redemption."

Yes, Jesus is the answer to the problem of our separation from God because of sin. However, His work has no effect on our lives unless we receive and surrender to Him (John 1:12) as the one and only Savior. This is the essential ingredient to everlasting life, and to living in freedom and wholeness.

Every time we look to ourselves, or to someone or something else to save us, we fall into the trap the Bible calls "idolatry." (More later.)

TRUTH #5: GOD SAYS IT IS UP TO US TO ACCEPT OR REFUSE HIS GIFT OF REDEMPTION — AND THE CONSEQUENCES ARE FULLY OURS

God's offer to each of us is found in one of the best known verses in the Bible that we looked at a little earlier (John 3:16, NET), *"For this is the way God loved the world: He gave his one and only Son,* *so that everyone who believes in him will not perish but have everlasting life."*

Here we find that God's gift is everlasting life *in place of* what we actually deserve (Romans 6:23). It cannot be earned; it cannot be bought. It is a gift God freely gives to all who will believe (totally trust in, depend on, rely upon) His Son, Jesus Christ.

In God's economy, though we are *undeserving* of this gift, we are *fully worthy* of this gift, because that is how God created us.

As we receive everlasting life, God also promises, *"But to all who have received Him — those who believe in His name — He has given the right to become God's children"* (John 1:12, NET). In Bible times, to receive someone was to welcome them into your home and to make everything you owned available to them for their use, however they wished.

Once we "receive" Jesus, once we have surrendered who we are and what we have to Him (as much as we are able to at the time), God gives the gift of redemption. The essence of redemption is us being reconciled to God, restored to the relationship He created us to enjoy.

That translates to us having an everlasting life that is not just future, it actually starts TODAY! It actually begins when we willingly surrender our lives to Jesus Christ. Jesus said, *"I came that they may have life, and have it abundantly."* (John 10:10).

Abundant life means life that is far more than we would ever expect or anticipate. It is not a life filled with all of the earthly pleasures we can imagine, but a life filled with a sense of God's peace and God's presence, no matter where we are or what we face.

God grants us a new identity and a new citizenship **as His adopted children** (Romans 8:15-17). We are "created anew" (2 Corinthians 5:17), and our new life in Christ begins.

Very often, however, because of difficult and troubling circumstances in life or ongoing consequences of choices we have made in the past, we feel that the benefits of being the redeemed of God will have to wait until we get to Heaven. That may be what we feel, but it isn't what's true! God truly has prepared an abundant and fruitful life for us here — now. This abundant life is ours as we walk daily with Him.

Sure, we will experience trials and troubles. But, when trials and troubles come, we can rest in the sure knowledge that God is right there with us, every step of the way, and that He will never let anyone or anything separate us from Him again (John 10:27-30; Romans 8:38-39). No matter our circumstances now, they are only temporary — and we are not alone in them because "God with Us" is *with* us!

TRUTH #6: GOD INVITES YOU TO MAKE A CHOICE

Now, the choice as to whether or not you will cooperate with God's desire and have a life in and with Christ is yours to make. The choice as to whether you will know you will spend eternity with God or be everlastingly separated from Him is also yours. No one can make that decision for you. This one is between you and God.

If we choose to receive Christ, we must be willing to turn away from our sinful patterns and sinful desires, and instead turn ourselves over to Him completely. This is both an "in-the-moment" decision and act, and a "day-after-day" decision and act. Wherever you are in response to Jesus at the moment is the perfect place to be RIGHT NOW to surrender.

If you never have, now is the time (2 Corinthians 6:2: *"For he says, 'I heard you at the acceptable time, and in the day of salvation I helped you.' Look, now is the acceptable time; look, now is the day of salvation!"*). If you have surrendered to him at some point in the past but need to come clean and surrender more, now is also the time for that.

Before any of us meet and learn about Jesus Christ, we are all going our own way, doing what we believe is best. If our idea of "best" is rooted in lies and sin, we get carried further-and-further away from Him and the life He desires for us. We get carried further-and-further into the death and decay of the sin and sinfulness that separate us from Him. The joy of salvation is that we do not have to continue on such a path.

The day we invite Jesus to be Master of our life and surrender ourselves to Him, that is the day we begin our turn from sin and death to a life of light and hope in Christ.

In the Bible, this turning is called "repentance." Repentance is turning around and going in the completely opposite direction. It is a one-time event (when we first trust Jesus) and an ongoing event (as we turn from self to him each day). We need a willing heart to continue to give Jesus control of our life on a day-by-day (sometimes moment-by-moment) basis.

He certainly knows better than we do what is best, and His idea of "best" is rooted and grounded in the pure, righteous Truth. Our trust must be in Him and Him alone; both for everlasting life, as well as every-day life.

For those who wonder, "How do I trust Jesus for every-day life?" the answer begins when you surrender to Him and then ask Him to help you *keep* surrendered to Him. As you do so, He will help you to know and understand (as much as you can, when you can) what needs to happen every step of the way.

Do you feel a bit overwhelmed at this point? If so, please know this: Everything said in this lesson will become more and more clear and better understood as you continue to be **unbound** on this journey to wholeness.

As you start to learn what it is that has been keeping you in bondage and why, and how and what to do about it in your new life in Christ, things become clearer and you become more like the person God created you to be. This is called "abiding," and it is a concept we will revisit often throughout the program (In fact, there is a brief mini-lesson "On Abiding" right after Lesson 7). And don't worry — He wants this for you even more than you want it for yourself.

Have you surrendered your life to Jesus Christ? Are you convinced that you need to? Have you invited Him to be Master of your life? Have you invited Him to have full reign in your life? If not, why not do so now? If you have, perhaps this is the perfect opportunity to surrender whatever it is you have been holding back from Him. He will do a much better job with it than you ever could.

TRUTH #1: GOD DESIRES A WHOLE, HEALTHY, VIBRANT, AND LOVING RELATIONSHIP WITH US

TRUTH #2: GOD'S DESIRE IS THAT EVERYONE WOULD FREELY ACCEPT HIS LOVE AND BE RECONCILED TO HIM, BUT HE KNOWS THAT THEY WILL NOT

TRUTH #3: GOD'S ORIGINAL DESIGN, HIS CREATED ORDER, WAS WILLFULLY BROKEN BY HUMANKIND

TRUTH #4: GOD HIMSELF HAS PROVIDED THE WAY OF RESTORATION AND RECONCILIATION

TRUTH #5: GOD SAYS IT IS UP TO US TO ACCEPT OR REFUSE HIS GIFT OF REDEMPTION — AND THE CONSEQUENCES ARE FULLY OURS

TRUTH #6: GOD INVITES YOU TO MAKE A CHOICE

6
T
R
U
T
H
S

The following prayer contains a summary of the truths we have covered so far in our lessons. Wherever you are in your relationship with God, please consider using this <u>as a guide</u> to help you become reconciled to and united with God in the only authentic way there is: fully surrendered to Christ.

A PRAYER OF SURRENDER

"Almighty God, I know and am fully convinced that I have sinned against You, and that I deserve Your wrath. I also know and am fully convinced that, because of what Jesus did out of His love for me, I do not have to face that wrath.

I have chosen more than once to be the master of my own life and to live in ways I know are wrong. Please forgive me and help me forsake that way of life. I know that Christ died for my sin, taking Your wrath for my sin on Himself so that I would never have to bear it. Thank you for offering that gift of mercy and grace.

I also know that Jesus rose from death and wants to be Master of my life. I invite Him to take charge of my life and surrender it completely to You. In exchange, I gratefully receive Your gift of everlasting life. My desire is to live for You and to serve You, no matter what.

I know, too, that every area of my life now belongs to Jesus. Help me surrender more and more Each day bringing every thought, word, and deed into obedience to the truth that is in Him.

You are preparing a place for me with You and I will one day be with You for the rest of eternity. Thank You for that wonderful promise and hope. In Jesus' name. Amen."

(<u>Please note</u>: Sometimes people talk about "inviting Jesus into your heart." That is not a Biblical concept. It is not taught anywhere in Scripture. It is only by way of authentic conversion [a change in fundamental beliefs that drive one's life] that we are saved. A good indicator is this: *"The God that you hated is now the God that you love; the sin you loved is now the sin that you hate."* – Paul Washer)

NOTES

DAILY PRACTICES	DAY 1	DAY 2	DAY 3	DAY 4	DAY 5	DAY 6	"REST" DAY
SATURATION VERSE ___	More ☐ 100 ☐ Less ☐	More ☐ 100 ☐ Less ☐	More ☐ 100 ☐ Less ☐	More ☐ 100 ☐ Less ☐	More ☐ 100 ☐ Less ☐	More ☐ 100 ☐ Less ☐	More ☐ 100 ☐ Less ☐
BIBLE READING	Chapters ___	Chapters ___	Chapters ___	Chapters ___	Chapters ___	Chapters ___	
STUDY MANUAL LESSON # ___	Read Today's Lesson Today Yes ☐ No ☐	Read Today's Lesson Today Yes ☐ No ☐	Read Today's Lesson Today Yes ☐ No ☐	Read Today's Lesson Today Yes ☐ No ☐	Read Today's Lesson Today Yes ☐ No ☐	Read Today's Lesson Today Yes ☐ No ☐	
DAILY REFLECTION	Completed Today's Lesson Today Yes ☐ No ☐	Completed Today's Lesson Today Yes ☐ No ☐	Completed Today's Lesson Today Yes ☐ No ☐	Completed Today's Lesson Today Yes ☐ No ☐	Completed Today's Lesson Today Yes ☐ No ☐	Completed Today's Lesson Today Yes ☐ No ☐	
USED "RESTORE" BOOK	Yes ☐ No ☐	Yes ☐ No ☐	Yes ☐ No ☐	Yes ☐ No ☐	Yes ☐ No ☐	Yes ☐ No ☐	Yes ☐ No ☐
PRE-MEAL SATURATION VERSE	Breakfast ☐ Lunch ☐ Dinner ☐	Breakfast ☐ Lunch ☐ Dinner ☐	Breakfast ☐ Lunch ☐ Dinner ☐	Breakfast ☐ Lunch ☐ Dinner ☐	Breakfast ☐ Lunch ☐ Dinner ☐	Breakfast ☐ Lunch ☐ Dinner ☐	Breakfast ☐ Lunch ☐ Dinner ☐
SPECIAL ITEMS	Yes ☐ No ☐	Yes ☐ No ☐	Yes ☐ No ☐	Yes ☐ No ☐	Yes ☐ No ☐	Yes ☐ No ☐	Yes ☐ No ☐
PRIVATE PRAYER	Time Spent ___	Time Spent ___	Time Spent ___	Time Spent ___	Time Spent ___	Time Spent ___	Time Spent ___
TODAY, I AM THANKFUL FOR...							

Lesson 2 Study Sheet
Each day review the lesson for that week.
Record one thing you are grateful for each day on your Progress Record.

This Lesson's Verse:

"'For I know the plans that I have for you,' declares the LORD, 'plans for welfare and not for calamity to give you a future and a hope.'" Jeremiah 29:11 (NASB)

Day 1 Reflection

What picture do you have in your mind of what your life will look like when it has been built on the sure foundation discussed in this lesson? *Additional study passage: 1 Corinthians 3:11-15*

Day 2 Reflection

What is your understanding of the encouragement and counsel to "receive Christ?" *Additional study passages: John 1:12-14; John 3:36*

Day 3 Reflection

How do you deal with feelings of guilt and shame in your life? *Additional study passage: 2 Corinthians 7:9-10*

Day 4 Reflection

When you think about repentance, describe what comes to mind. What do you think a life given to repentance would look like? *Additional study passages: Matthew 3:7-8; Acts 26:19-20; Ephesians 5:8-20*

Day 5 Reflection

As you have read through the lesson, what did you decide to do with the counsel to "receive Jesus" and surrender to God? What do you think the result of that decision will be? *Additional study passages: John 8:31-32, 36; 1 John 1:5-9*

Day 6 Reflection

In applying the Gospel every day to your life, how do you think you will be able to know how you are doing as time goes on? What do you think is the best way for you to manage that? *Additional study passage: Galatians 5:13-24*

For the
Word of God
is LIVING and ACTIVE
and SHARPER than *any*
double-edged sword,
PIERCING *even* to the
point of
SEPARATING *soul*
from *spirit*,
and *joints*
from *marrow*;
it is able to JUDGE the
desires and thoughts
of the heart.

Hebrews 4:12 (NET)

On the following page is a tool we call the "**SPECTRUM OF EMOTIONS**".

You will note that there are seven columns of words. Each column has a main a category word at the top. These category words help us start to develop a more comprehensive understanding of and connection to the legitimate emotional content of our lives.

Using the chart is straightforward. Go down each column of words and circle/underline/highlight, or in some way mark the words that "resonate" with you — the words that make you go, *"Yeah...That's it!"*.

While you may not be able to provide a technical definition of a word, there will be something about that word that strikes a chord with you. This can help you better understand and describe what it is you are "feeling"; what emotions you are experiencing.

Once you do this, you can look at the word at the top of the column and see what basic category that emotion fits under. Having these labels helps us identify and understand what it is we need to take to God, surrender to Him, and seek His help with. It helps us better articulate the truth about what is going on with us.

It is in these honest, open, authentic conversations with God that we are finally able to find His peace (Philippians 4:6-7) and to discover and walk through His solutions.

As always in *Unbound*, there is no "right" or "wrong" in how you use this tool. It is simply here to be an aid in helping you connect with the reality of your thoughts and emotions and have those honest conversations with God that you need.

Some folks make a number of copies and keep them handy. Others laminate a copy and use a wet-erase marker to mark the chart.

However you find that works for you, that is the way you use it. No right or wrong, remember?

We pray you find this useful throughout your time in *Unbound*.

Romans 12:2

SPECTRUM OF EMOTIONS

MAD	SAD	GLAD	AFRAID	CONFUSED	ASHAMED	LONELY
Bothered	Down	At ease	Uneasy	Curious	Uncomfortable	Out-of-place
Ruffled	Blue	Comfortable	Apprehensive	Uncertain	Awkward	Left out
Irritated	Somber	Relaxed	Careful	Ambivalent	Clumsy	Lonesome
Displeased	Low	Content	Cautious	Doubtful	Self-conscious	Disconnected
Annoyed	Hurt	Optimistic	Hesitant	Unsettled	Disconcerted	Insecure
Steamed	Disappointed	Satisfied	Tense	Tentative	Chagrined	Unappreciated
Irked	Worn out	Refreshed	Anxious	Perplexed	Abashed	Invisible
Perturbed	Melancholy	Grateful	Nervous	Puzzled	Embarrassed	Unwelcome
Frustrated	Downhearted	Pleased	Edgy	Muddled	Flustered	Discounted
Angry	Unhappy	Warm	Distressed	Distracted	Sorry	Misunderstood
Fed-up	Dissatisfied	Happy	Scared	Flustered	Apologetic	Excluded
Disgusted	Gloomy	Encouraged	Frightened	Jumbled	Guilty	Insignificant
Indignant	Mournful	Fulfilled	Vulnerable	Unfocused	Regretful	Ignored
Resentful	Grieved	Tickled	Repulsed	Fragmented	Remorseful	Neglected
Ticked off	Depressed	Proud	Agitated	Disheartened	Shamed	Removed
Jealous	Lousy	Hopeful	Shocked	Insecure	Disgusted	Disregarded
Fuming	Crushed	Cheerful	Alarmed	Dazed	Belittled	Isolated
Explosive	Miserable	Thrilled	Overwhelmed	Bewildered	Humiliated	Unwanted
Enraged	Defeated	Delighted	Frantic	Lost	Disregarded	Rejected
Irate	Dejected	Joyful	Panic-stricken	Stunned	Violated	Deserted
Incensed	Empty	Elated	Horrified	Chaotic	Dirty	Outcast
Burned	Wretched	Exhilarated	Petrified	Torn	Mortified	Abandoned
Outraged	Despondent	Overjoyed	Terrified	Baffled	Defiled	Withdrawn
Furious	Devastated	Ecstatic	Numb	Dumbfounded	Devastated	Forsaken
Raging	Embittered	Euphoric	Dead Inside	Speechless	Degraded	Desolate

LESSON THREE
THE BASICS

As mentioned in the "Introduction," the materials in your hands make up the basic tools for **Unbound**, one of the Truth in Love Biblical Counseling Center's programs for providing solid biblical counsel to those in bondage to unresolved and unhealed brokenness in their lives. This curriculum is the byproduct of decades of biblical counseling experience from a variety of people.

We have a firm belief that one of the promises made by Jesus is too often overlooked in society today (especially in the "Recovery Movement"). Jesus promised, *"So if the Son sets you free, you will be really free"* (John 8:36). Whether it is the aftereffects of sins committed or evils suffered, getting those matters resolved with God is how we walk in freedom. **Unbound** is an effective tool in one's pursuit of godly freedom in Christ.

Over the years, while using and expanding on the basic materials from a program once known as "S.A.F.E.: Setting Addicts Free Eternally," the Truth in Love Biblical Counseling team saw a need for adjustments, modifications, and improvements.

We found ourselves using variations of the S.A.F.E. materials in many different settings, under many different circumstances, and in addressing more and more diverse patterns of besetting sin and brokenness. We saw that there were layers of bondage in people's lives that needed to be addressed more foundationally and more concisely than the basic materials provided for. These realizations led us to rework S.A.F.E. into **Unbound**, the results of which you hold in your hand (or read on your screen) right now.

This program you have launched into truly is an "unbinding" process. As we have more and more layers of bondage removed, we gain greater and greater freedom from the sin and captivity of our lives, through the surrender of our hearts and minds to Jesus Christ.

By saturating our minds and hearts with the truth as stated so clearly in His Word, we learn to live life grounded in that truth. Then, more and more every day, we walk with Him in true freedom while the layers of rot and decay fall away.

Unbound **is a process, not an event**! It requires daily, intentional investment. There is homework every day, but that "homework" is actually "heart-and-mind-work." It is more than a bunch of stuff to do. Rather, it is a steady, systematic replacing of the lies with the truth. There is an admonition (warning) and a promise in Romans 12:2: *"And do not be conformed to this world, **but be transformed by the renewing of your mind,** so that you may prove what the will of God is, that which is good and acceptable and perfect (emphasis added)."*

Our part in this is the "renewing of your mind" part. We do this by discovering and saturating on the truth in God's Word. If you have ever had a driver license or student body card renewed, you know the process: walk in with your old one, walk out with a replacement. It has been "renewed." That is the same idea behind renewing the mind. We do not "freshen up the old;" instead, we "replace with new."

God's part in this enterprise is the "be transformed" part. You might find it interesting to know that the Bible's original language word for "transformed" is the same Greek word from which we get our word "metamorphosis" — the process that takes a caterpillar and turns it into a butterfly.

Also of interest, in the original language this word "transformed" is a "passive present" verb; meaning, it is something done *to* or *for* us, not something we do ourselves or for ourselves. It is God's part and is the *result* of us doing our part (which is, again, "renewing the mind") — the PERFECT partnership!

As we saturate our minds with the truths in God's Word, God takes those truths and replaces the old beliefs and behaviors, the old passions and desires, the old agenda and schemes, with ones that are filled with light and life and truth; ones that are in step, in tune, with His nature and character.

The basic dilemma with all besetting sin patterns is this: Man is in a natural state of rebellion against, and separation from, God. Our wrong beliefs, and our wrong behaviors based on those wrong beliefs — powered by vigorous emotions — keep us in bondage and far away from the only source of real help for our problems and troubled lives. All of this creates what is often a massive gap between what we feel, and what is actually true. It's a gap that needs resolution if we are to walk in freedom.

The reason bridging the gap between what we feel and what is true is so difficult is that there is no "feeling" to truth. Truth just "shows up." It simply "is." Truth plays no favorites, and it picks on no one. Emotions, on the other hand, get a great deal more attention because we "feel" them. While they may be *based* on the truth, emotions themselves are *not true*.

Real freedom can *only* occur when deep-rooted and false beliefs have been put off, and the truth as stated by God in His Word is put on in its place. We are then empowered to live that truth out vibrantly. Remember this antidote: "'That' is what I *feel*, but 'this' is what's *true*."

In order to use **Unbound** as a tool to root out false beliefs and narrow the gap between our emotions and the truth, we need to know, understand, and remember both some fundamental characteristics of ourselves as human beings, and the basic process of the program. These include the following:

I.   Our Wiring
II.   Our Problem
III. Our Solution

IV. Our Goal
V.   Our Method

I.   Our Wiring

Everyone lives their lives based on what they believe to be most true at any given moment. Keep in mind that when most of us say, "I believe...," we often refer to something we have intellectually acknowledged as true, and not, what we really stake our life on as true. To "believe" means, "to totally trust in, depend on, and rely upon as true." What we believe is what we live. A person can say all day long what they believe, but when you look at their life, you will be able to see what it is they *really* believe by how they live (For instance, if you "believe" there is black ice in the parking lot, no matter whether it is true or not, when you leave the building you will behave as if the ice is present).

On average, we make **90% or more** of our choices by what is commonly called our "subconscious mind," (the "heart," in the Bible) and it requires little or no intentional thought for us to carry out those choices. This non-intentional part of our mind makes choices based on what we believe to be most true and of greatest value in that moment. This choosing is rooted in the patterns we have developed over time — like brushing our teeth or flaring up in anger if someone crosses us.

The working of our non-conscious self is a beautiful, and sometimes treacherous, dance of the heart, mind, emotions, and body. The "heart" is the seat of our desires (see diagram, Page 48). The primary role of our mind is to find the most efficient way to satisfy the desires of our heart. The body is the part of us where all of this is carried out.

Our emotions fuel our drive to fulfill our heart's desires. Our bodies have appetites and patterns of behaving ("the flesh" in Scripture) that contribute to our habituated choices as well. This all flows together and is the seedbed that our problems arise from.

41

Left unchecked, these problems become "besetting."[5]

If the desires of our heart are rooted in us believing lies (lies which stand in direct opposition to what God declares to be true), we are driven to follow a path of sin and destruction. The more these patterns are saturated on and habituated, the more entrenched they become — to the point where, with little or no thought at all, they become a way of life.

Remember: What we believe and live is grounded in what we have saturated our minds with, whether true or false — our "mental diet *matters!*" Paul describes this principle in Romans 8:5-6, and it lies at the foundation of this program. This process of "saturate-and-produce" is how we all function. It is basic to the human experience, from the moment of birth forward. Because of that, in this natural process, the truth of something does not matter anywhere near as much as what we believe in determining how we live. We will believe as most true whatever it is that we consistently feed this unique creation called "the mind." Feed it lies and half-truths, it believes the lies and half-truths to be true. Feed it the truth, it will believe the truth. Whatever we feed our hearts and minds most is what we believe most.

Our drive to satisfy our deepest wants and longings surges out from the seat of our desires, which the Bible calls our heart (Matthew 15:18-20; Mark 7:20-23). Our heart works together with our mind to find what we believe at that point in time to be the "best" way to satisfy our desires, and our emotions fuel it and help us to be content with it — even if only for a moment.

Our mind's role is to satisfy the desires of the heart in the most expeditious way it can find; the body is a willing co-conspirator. This process usually happens very quickly, and often with little or no purposeful thought at all. Thus, the concept of the "subconscious." Once our mind is set on a course of action, the heart and mind work with the body to carry out the plan.

HOW OUR HEART CAN OVERRULE OUR RATIONAL MIND

How does our heart overrule our rational mind? Well, it all begins way back at the point where we discover that a certain activity or behavior delivers a high-impact reward. With the reward comes a compound chemical "rush" that

---

[5] Beset ("*euperistaton,*" Hebrews 12:1) means literally 'skillfully surround'; so, the image is of a particular sin that one is easily entangled in and overcome by — not as a victim, but as a collaborator and co-conspirator.

brings both sensual pleasure and emotional comfort at the same time. (This is the biological aspect of the process).

That is a powerful "lift" (think of how often we use terms like "I love the high"), and when a powerful lift is discovered by the brain, the mind files it away in the "solutions" file for future reference. The "solution" gets used again, the heart/mind/body comes to expect it, and the person is emotionally "hooked" before they even know what is happening. Our emotions get actively involved in this process to ensure that we respond to our mind's "best" suggestions as quickly as possible. We all know that emotions can be much stronger than reason.

Knowing this helps us understand that, since the majority of our decisions are made by our "subconscious," we will be able to affect significant change in our life only if we change the choices that are made at that level. Change the desires of the heart, and the motivations change. Our emotions will then motivate our minds to satisfy the desires of the *changed* heart, not the old one (Romans 6:6; Colossians 3:5-10).

And remember…Those decisions and choices are based on what we believe to be "best" at any given moment. So, we have to change what we believe in order to change what we choose. This regimen of this curriculum is a tool designed to help us do just that.

LET'S TALK ABOUT NEUROPLASTICITY[6]

Neuroplasticity has become quite the catchword in the last few years — not only in the realms of neurology and psychology but quite far afield from them these days.

More and more doctors, scientists, and even mental health professionals give us an increasing number of assurances that you can "re-wire" your brain. This has crossed over into holistic health, life coaching, mindfulness practices, and just about any other field that can be considered a "helping profession."

For generations, neuroscientists proclaimed that there were certain functions that are fixed or "hard-wired" into the brain and that any change was an anomaly. The man-on-the-street believed this, and we can often be heard saying things like, "I'm just wired that way," or "I've always been this way," or — perhaps the most common — "That's just my personality."

Since the 1970s, neuroplasticity has gained wider and wider acceptance throughout the scientific community as

---

[6] For an in-depth video presentation about neuroplasticity, go to https://www.authenticbiblicalcounseling.com/video_2018_1.html

a complex, multifaceted, and fundamental property of the brain.

Why ought we to care? What if there is a non-invasive, non-medication, God-given, natural way to improve everything from physical health and mental wellbeing to the overall quality of life? Would that seem like a viable option for a starting place in lieu of the plethora of psychoactive drugs and other radical treatments that are most common?

 So, what is neuroplasticity, how does it work, and what does it have to do with God and His Word?

Neuroplasticity is an umbrella term referring to the ability of our brain to reorganize and restructure itself, both physically and functionally, throughout our entire life. It is a natural and ongoing process that your brain is involved in all of the time, from the cradle to the grave.

In young and developing brains, this process is vigorous and dynamic. Even older and fully developed brains will retain neuroplasticity well into advanced years. In fact, studies combining stem cell protocols with specific repetitious activities are impacting Alzheimer's and dementia patients in powerful ways.

Neuroplasticity is how we learn new things, how we adjust to new circumstances, and how we maintain skill-sets for a lifetime.

Neuroplasticity is also how we develop idolatrous and besetting sin patterns that the world calls "addiction." Acute patterns of anxiety and depression, as well as severe conditions labeled narcissism, obsessive-compulsive disorder, and dissociative personality disorder, become entrenched as a way of life due to the dynamics of neuroplasticity. There is no neurological support for "personality disorders." What these are, in fact, are highly developed, deeply entrenched, powerfully habituated relational patterns. They are tried-and-true via neuroplasticity, not genetics or neurology.

It is the dynamics of neuroplasticity that makes finding freedom from these unyielding bondages possible. It is part of how God created us.

II.   Our Problem

In all of this, our problem is that our heart most often operates from a foundation of lies, false principles, selfish desires, and negative self-talk.

This is our nature as fallen human beings. As we deal with all the guilt, shame, fears, sense of entitlement, bitterness, unforgiveness, and frustrations of the past and of day-to-day life, those are the things our mind becomes saturated with.

In response to this burden, the world most often offers answers that contradict God's principles and plan. The more exposed we are to these counterfeit answers and "solutions," the more our minds learn to function based on those worldly principles.

One vital key to this destructive pattern becoming so easily entrenched is that we do not believe that we have an inherent worthiness rooted in being created in God's image (See Lesson One). In fact, the world around us denies that we are created at all, claiming we are simply an accident of the cosmos with no real purpose or meaning. The resulting feelings of worthlessness drive us *away* from God instead of *toward* God. As a result, we have developed unrighteous and sinful ways of coping with our problems and predicaments. We end up magnifying the breach between ourselves and the God who loves us and created us in His image.

Due to the fact that all of our worldly solutions to the problems of our heart are defective, deficient, and often lead to greater problems, we sink deeper and deeper into despair and hopelessness: "Pits of Gloom" (Lesson 6). We become enslaved in a destructive lifestyle and can find no way to break free. As we saturate our minds on our sense of failure and on the destructive cycles themselves, the bondage increases. As we struggle to tear ourselves from this quicksand, we are carried further and further down.

III. Our Solution

If we are to be successful in having and living a truly transformed life, we must change who we are at the heart level. Since we have spent a lifetime saturating our heart, mind, and soul with destructive thoughts, attitudes, beliefs, and behaviors, there is only one thing powerful enough to change us.

Our only source of real help is the Truth, which is **the Bible, God's Word.** There are many reasons that the Bible is such a powerful and effective tool. Here are just two:

A. THE WORD CLEANSES AND PURIFIES

Jesus, through the washing of the Word, cleanses all those who believe and trust in Him (Ephesians 5:25b-27). The truth that is in God's Word is the antidote for the lies and brokenness by which we have learned to live. Jesus tells us that if we "abide"[7] in His Word we are truly His, and that we will know the Truth and the truth will set us free (John 8:31-32)!

Knowing the truth is essential to having the freedom we long for. And, **God's Word** is the ultimate source of all truth (John 17:17).

B.   THE WORD IS ALIVE AND BRINGS CHANGE

As we saturate our minds with God's Word, the Holy Spirit takes that powerful weapon and uses it to transform our lives from within (Romans 12:2; 2 Timothy 3:16-17; Hebrews 4:12). This is not about behavior modification, but about authentic heart and life transformation — REAL change. It is a partnership between us and God. We do our part; He does His part (Romans 12:2). Freedom is ours (John 8:36; Galatians 5:1), and we no longer have to follow the destructive patterns we have lived for too long (Romans 6:17-18a).

IV.   *Our Goal*

Unbound is a tool designed to help us fill our hearts, minds, and souls with God's Word EVERY DAY, and thus serve as the catalyst for the transformation we seek. We foster this in three ways:

1. Regular Bible study to nourish the mind (Luke 4:4; 2 Timothy 3:16-17) and personal worship to invite Him close (Psalm 22:3; James 4:8).
2. By training our heart and mind (our "subconscious") to know, believe, and live out the truth taught in God's Word (Romans 12:2).
3. Saturating the mind with specific verses that teach a truth that combats a specific lie or a specific problem in our life, like the antidote to a poison (Joshua 1:8; Psalm 1:2-3). The "Restore" section at the back is FULL of these.

V.   *Our Method*

Unbound is designed to be followed systematically and consistently:

1. *Every day* (except your Sabbath/Rest Day), read the current lesson. We do this to ensure that the information in the lesson becomes part of our baseline thinking. We also do this at "the speed of life," so do not fret if you are not always at a place to finish one lesson every week or even read the lesson every day.

---

[7] See "A Word on Abiding," following Lesson 7.

2. Saturate with each "This Lesson's Verse" every day for the duration of the time you are working through the lesson, including on your Rest Day(s)—even if you are not able to get to the lesson itself.

  a. Remember that "to saturate" (usually) means to read aloud at least 100 times per day. Space it out through the day as needed. (NOTE: Some folks have an extremely difficult time keeping their thoughts focused when they read, even if they read out loud. Many have found help by recording their own voice reading the Scripture aloud, and then listening to the recording repeatedly and saying back what they hear. The point is, SATURATE!)

3. Answer the "Reflection" for that day

4. Be sure to record one thing you are grateful for each day (Philippians 4:8; 1 Thessalonians 5:16-18).

5. Take advantage of the saturation tools in the Restore book to combat special areas of trouble or difficulty. Think of it as an "Emotional First-Aid Kit."[8]

6. Read and complete "The Pledge," on the last page of the Restore section[9]. This is your personal pledge between you and the Lord, you and your Savior. Take a picture with your phone and keep it in your gallery where you can remind yourself of your commitment.

7. Do your Pre-Meal saturation verses (back of Restore section) 12 times before the specified meal. We have mentioned this tool before, and now it is time to start bringing it into use.

8. Do any other special exercises that are designated in the lesson or that you find helpful throughout the program. Not every lesson has additional exercises, but some do, and all of them are key tools you will use for many years to come.[10]

9. Be thankful for one thing every day and record it. This is because a heart that is thankful is more inclined toward worship, and

---

[8] "Restore" is in the very back of this workbook. There are "weapons" there for fighting and winning the battles of mind and emotions that most often plague us. The last page has "The Pledge." This is a personal commitment for you to make to help you gain the most out of this curriculum.

[9] We usually have no problem eating at least three times each day, yet we usually do not feed our souls anywhere near as often. In Matthew 4:4, Jesus declares to Satan, *"It is written, 'Man does not live by bread alone, but by every*

word that comes from the mouth of God.'" Our goal with the pre-meal saturation verses is to get in the habit of feeding our souls as readily as we will feed our bodies. The breakfast verse (Romans 12:1) is provided. You choose the ones you need for lunch and dinner. Use these as long as you need and switch them out as you feel God leading you to do so.

[10] Specific lessons with "Special Items" per the Progress record are 6, 7, 9, 10, 11, 12, 18, and 19.

personal worship is one of the key tools we need in order to have and maintain the transformed life we are pursuing.

 Keep this **Anchor Point** in mind: <u>While emotions are *real*, they are NOT the *truth*. Feelings change; facts do not.</u>

Our emotions are transient — they are undependable, unreliable, inconsistent, and they change from one moment to another, often rapidly. The truth is solid, sure, dependable, reliable, and consistent.

Making decisions based on our emotions is like allowing a drunk to get behind the wheel of a school bus — the bus will be all over the road and it is not going to turn out well for anyone. Emotions can have a "seat on the bus," just not the driver's seat. So, remember: the #1 antidote for living life based on the emotions we feel (usually rooted in lies) is to remind ourselves as often as we need to: "<u>Feelings are real; they just aren't fact. 'This' is what I **feel**, but 'this' is what's **true**.</u>"

⁍ • ⁎

EMOTIONS

| Seat of Desires | Mind | Body |

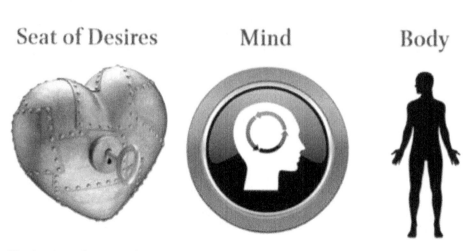

*Pastor Joey Carroll gets credit for the original design that led to this diagram.

All four major regions of the
brain are energized and engaged
SIMULTANEOUSLY when we
"saturate" with the Word of God!

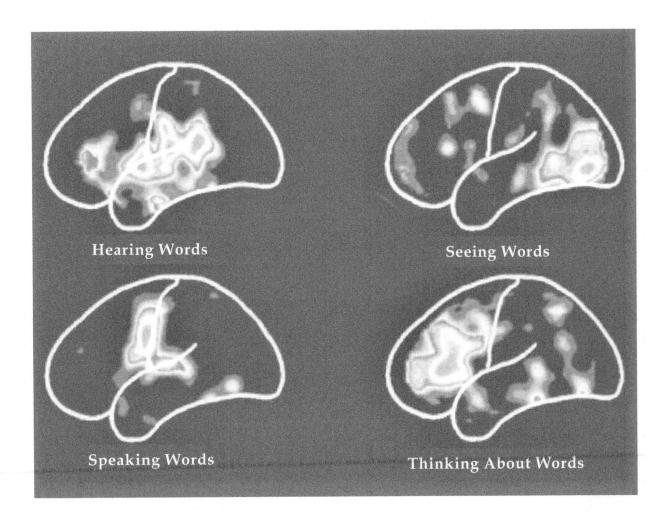

Hearing Words

Seeing Words

Speaking Words

Thinking About Words

DAILY PRACTICES	DAY 1	DAY 2	DAY 3	DAY 4	DAY 5	DAY 6	"REST" DAY
SATURATION VERSE ___	More ☐ 100 ☐ Less ☐	More ☐ 100 ☐ Less ☐	More ☐ 100 ☐ Less ☐	More ☐ 100 ☐ Less ☐	More ☐ 100 ☐ Less ☐	More ☐ 100 ☐ Less ☐	More ☐ 100 ☐ Less ☐
BIBLE READING	Chapters ___	Chapters ___	Chapters ___	Chapters ___	Chapters ___	Chapters ___	
STUDY MANUAL LESSON #___	Read Today's Lesson Today Yes ☐ No ☐	Read Today's Lesson Today Yes ☐ No ☐	Read Today's Lesson Today Yes ☐ No ☐	Read Today's Lesson Today Yes ☐ No ☐	Read Today's Lesson Today Yes ☐ No ☐	Read Today's Lesson Today Yes ☐ No ☐	
DAILY REFLECTION	Completed Today's Lesson Today Yes ☐ No ☐	Completed Today's Lesson Today Yes ☐ No ☐	Completed Today's Lesson Today Yes ☐ No ☐	Completed Today's Lesson Today Yes ☐ No ☐	Completed Today's Lesson Today Yes ☐ No ☐	Completed Today's Lesson Today Yes ☐ No ☐	
USED "RESTORE" BOOK	Yes ☐ No ☐	Yes ☐ No ☐	Yes ☐ No ☐	Yes ☐ No ☐	Yes ☐ No ☐	Yes ☐ No ☐	Yes ☐ No ☐
PRE-MEAL SATURATION VERSE	Breakfast ☐ Lunch ☐ Dinner ☐	Breakfast ☐ Lunch ☐ Dinner ☐	Breakfast ☐ Lunch ☐ Dinner ☐	Breakfast ☐ Lunch ☐ Dinner ☐	Breakfast ☐ Lunch ☐ Dinner ☐	Breakfast ☐ Lunch ☐ Dinner ☐	Breakfast ☐ Lunch ☐ Dinner ☐
SPECIAL ITEMS	Yes ☐ No ☐	Yes ☐ No ☐	Yes ☐ No ☐	Yes ☐ No ☐	Yes ☐ No ☐	Yes ☐ No ☐	Yes ☐ No ☐
PRIVATE PRAYER	Time Spent ___	Time Spent ___	Time Spent ___	Time Spent ___	Time Spent ___	Time Spent ___	Time Spent ___
TODAY, I AM THANKFUL FOR...							

This Lesson's Verse:

For the word of God is living and active and sharper than any double-edged sword, piercing even to the point of separating soul from spirit, and joints from marrow; it is able to judge the desires and thoughts of the heart. (Hebrews 4:12 NET)

Day 1 Reflection

Aside from examples like brushing your teeth or driving your car, what other instances are there in your life where you do things that are almost second-nature? *Additional study passage: Romans 8:5-6*

Day 2 Reflection

Explain why a person who lives by God's principles might expect to be successful in life. *Additional study passage: Psalm 15:1-5*

Day 3 Reflection

What is the one area in your life you would most like to change? Transformational change takes time and effort. Are you willing to do the work necessary to accomplish that change? *Additional study passage: Galatians 5:13-26*

Day 4 Reflection

Why would positive, healthy change be impossible without Christ's help? *Additional study passage: John 15:4-5*

Day 5 Reflection

Why is real and permanent change in our lives not likely to happen immediately and only happen over time, if we are willing to do the work change requires? *Additional study passage: Matthew 13:31-32*

Day 6 Reflection

Why would it be important during this season of life-change to saturate our mind with the affirmative, positive passages from God's Word, rather than the negative passages? *Additional study passage: Philippians 4:8*

GOAL

SECURE A RIGHT HEART

SECURE A RIGHT HEART

Having set and laid our foundation in Christ, we need to start building for the second phase of our transformation and establish a heart that is "right." By "right," we mean: *Established* in the truth, *pursuing* the truth, and *holding to* the truth as defined by God.

Our inability to know and trust the truth is rooted in the lies we have believed, and in our lack of accurately knowing what truth replaces them. We have already seen how the truth is a powerful antidote for deceptions and lies when it comes to our sense of worthlessness. We need to continue to clear away those things which are the greatest obstacles standing in the way of our knowing, pursuing, and holding to the truth.

The ability to see ourselves as we really are, and our ability to see God as He really is, will give us the clarity we need to move forward along this path to freedom and wholeness. Although the path may seem like a murky shadow right now, His Word will light our path and guide our steps (Psalm 119:105).

"But above ALL *pursue*

His Kingdom

and

Righteousness

since ALL
these things
will be provided
to you *as well.*"

Matthew 6:33 (Lamb)

LESSON FOUR
SEEING CLEARLY

It almost seems like the entire world conspires to get us to rigorously focus our attention and energy on our own wants, needs, and desires. Just about everyone seems to be trying to find out what will make them the most happy, and we are constantly being encouraged to do what we think is best for ourselves. The leading marketing strategies of successful companies focus on feeding the self-important, self-absorbed tendencies of our rebellious nature. And we seem to cooperate most willingly.

After all, we deserve to be happy, don't we? We deserve the very best, no matter what, isn't that true? There are innumerable self-help teachers, self-improvement trainings, psychologists, counselors, and untold spiritual guides willing to help us connect with our "inner-selves," to discover the "person within." Psychologists and mental health therapists encourage their clients to look deeply inside themselves in order to discover what went wrong on their journey to self-fulfillment and achieving their true potential. What's more, they then encourage those same clients to look inward once again in order to find their own solution to the problem within themselves.

This inward-directed focus is not only unhealthy, it is defective. It is, in essence, *self-focus*. Self-focus not only causes most of the problems we deal with already, it actually creates even more problems than we otherwise have. In this lesson we will uncover why this is so, and we will discover God's better method and plan.

THE PROBLEM WITH BEING SELF-FOCUSED

When we are self-focused, it is impossible for us to have an objective view of ourselves or of anybody else. Self-focus translates into us centering our attention on *our own* perceptions and ideas of ourselves; on whether or not *our* needs are being met the way we believe we are entitled to have them met.

When we are self-focused, we either fix our attention on any and all positive things about ourselves that we can find (seeing ourselves as wonderful and magnificent), or we fix our attention on every negative thing that is – or possibly might be – true about us (concluding that we are awful and less than worthless). Everyone either "owes" us or is out to get us.

It really is impossible to be objective when we examine our innermost self using our own perceptions and interpretations of ourselves as the gauge. This is true for two reasons. First, our emotions routinely get in the way of objective reasoning and thought. How we *feel* about ourselves is driven by what we *believe* about ourselves, all based on what we have saturated our minds with about ourselves.

We either magnify the positive, become filled with pride, and exalt ourselves; or we exaggerate the negative, become filled with toxic shame, and decide we are good-for-nothing. Either way, what we "feel" about ourselves too often proceeds from flawed belief, and thus distorts our own self-perception.

The second reason it is impossible for us to be objective is because we are the only one in the universe that sees us the way we see ourselves. Did you know that when you look in the mirror, you are the only person in the universe who sees what you see? What you perceive is a reversed reflection of how you really look.[11]

When it comes to self-focus and self-perception, there can often be a dramatic swing back and forth between two extremes. One moment, we think we are the greatest person who has ever lived and we can conquer the world; the next we are convinced that we are the worst person that has ever lived and the world would be better off without us. We either feel that everything exists to benefit us, or that everything and everyone is against us.

A skewed sense of self also powerfully and dynamically colors our attempts to describe to someone else the kind of person we think we are. Most people will magnify and extol their good qualities while minimizing the bad, or they will magnify the bad while minimizing the good.

They often see themselves as either very good or very bad with no real middle ground. The more shame-filled a person's past the more likely this is. Rarely do we get a clear picture of what someone is *really* like based on their self-report. Rather, most people will describe themselves based on their own inward-focused vision of who they think they are.

Because we are unable to be objective on our own, it is much easier for an emotionally healthy person close to us to truly know us, than it is for us to have a balanced and clear picture of who we really are.

Think about the people in your life that you know well. After a season of

---

[11] Try this: take a small mirror and hold it in your hand so that, when you look in it, you are seeing the other mirror reflected in it. Now try and comb your hair. What happened? This will give you a good idea of just how different reality is from the image in your mind.

getting to know a person – of seeing them in different settings and circumstances over time – don't you find that you have a better idea of what they are really like, sometimes even more than they do themselves? This is why being in a safe, honest, healthy, and caring community – preferably of solid followers of Jesus Christ – is a critical part of our healing journey and our ongoing well-being. As believers, this is why the "one another's" in the Bible are so vital for us.

EXTREMES OF BEING SELF-FOCUSED

THE POSITIVE EMPHASIS (Magnifies the positive)	**THE NEGATIVE EMPHASIS** (Magnifies the negative)
"I got this!"	"Nothing I do is good enough."
"Yes, I AM all that!"	"Never mind me—I don't really matter."
"It's all someone *else's* fault."	"It's all *my* fault."
"I did this; I can do ANYTHING!"	"I knew I would fail at this—I always do."

SURRENDER AND SATURATION ARE (AGAIN) THE KEYS

As long as we hold onto a distorted view of ourselves, we will also have a distorted view of God and of others. If we want to be able to relate to God, others, and ourselves in a healthy way, we can only do so as we deal with the lies we believe about God, ourselves, and others — and especially the ones we believe about ourselves.

Like it or not, we have developed our views about God based on how key people in our lives have influenced us in our opinion about ourselves. The worst thing we can do is to ignore the lies we believe because they are what keep us from being the person God created us to be (see Lesson One). The key is to saturate on the Truth (Christ and His Word), allowing ourselves to see and accept (surrender to) who God says He is and who we are, and then live life accordingly.

There are some who say, "Forget the past; nothing you can do about it.

59

It's time to move on." The problem with this kind of thinking is that it ignores the reality that there are unresolved effects of those past events that truly do affect us today. Unless and until we face that reality and those ill effects are resolved, we will remain in bondage to our past and its negative present-day impact.

When we focus our attention on Christ and what He believes about us, replacing the lies of the past and the present with that truth, then we can more easily begin to see ourselves as Christ sees us. Once we have started to do that, both the sins we have committed and the evils we have suffered become clear — and so does our underlying worthiness in Him. This gives us the ability to be honest with Him about our faults and where we have fallen short, confess and repent of those, and walk forgiven. We also have the ability to let go of what others are responsible for; to let their sins be between them and God.

When we walk forgiven, we experience the reality of being free from condemnation (Romans 8:1), and we can keep in step with His plan for our lives. We no longer have to live bound up in the death and decay of the past.

 Anchor Point: For those who are "in Christ," God's Word and the Truth convince and convict: **they do not condemn** (Romans 8:1). If you are feeling condemned, and yet you have already surrendered your heart and life to Christ (have experienced an authentic conversion), the condemnation you feel comes from someone *other than* God.

THE RESULTS OF BEING SELF-FOCUSED

When we are self-focused, when we are looking "inside ourselves" for truth and using what we see there as our baseline of reality, we will see either a saint or a villain; the wisest person on earth or the stupidest; a great person or a lousy one. Since we never get a clear picture from self-focus of who we really are, the longer we look inside ourselves and not to God, the more confused and irrational we become. And, since our tendency is to continue to do what we've done the way we have been doing it, we become more and more self-focused, which results in us being more confused and less connected to what is real and true.

Soon we become so confused and lost that we give up trying to figure out who we really are, and instead create an "avatar" to project to the world. We dig deep into what we wish we were really like, and then try and pretend to be that kind of person. Some of us have been doing that for a very long time already — which is why we have fewer and fewer authentic and healthy relationships.

This avatar — this false image — quickly becomes an idol. Preserving the image demands and receives more and more of our attention, more and more of our energy, and more and more of our life. We demand that others help preserve the idol, thus making them accomplices in our idolatry. If others do not cooperate, then our internally-focused, self-absorbed sense of entitlement causes us to spiral down even more into bitterness and depression.

Trying to be this make-believe person in this make-believe life only causes us to become phonier, more dishonest, more inauthentic, more selfish, and more demanding. As a result, we become more disillusioned and less personable.

We become embittered as we watch people interact with the avatar (that we are safely hidden behind), all the while knowing in our heart that the people who like and enjoy the avatar don't really like and enjoy *us*.

We maintain this pattern as we strive to preserve a situation *we have created*; one that brings us the *opposite* of what we were after when we started acting like someone we are not. Result? We end up being *less* real, *less* seen, *less* liked, *less* connected, and we finally wind up with even *less* of what we really want and need. Great formula for success, right?

All of this melds together and spirals us ever deeper into a false persona with a false image — to the point that the person we *really* are, and were *really* created to be, is so hidden that we can't locate our true self anywhere. We become more and more afraid that, if people see who we *really* are, they will be even *more* likely to reject us. This adds to our sense of being unknown, disconnected, and feeling "less than" – all of which drives us even further away from God, from others, and from God's best will for our lives.

If you fall into this trap and do not climb out of it, you will *never* become that whole, vibrant, distinctive, and extraordinary person God created you to become.

This does not mean that God intends everyone to be a Mother Teresa or a Martin Luther King Jr. or a LeBron James. What it *does* mean is that God has always intended you to "be," and He has always intended you to "become," the healthiest and most godly version of yourself possible — wherever you are, whatever you're doing, whoever you know, and in whatever circumstances you find yourself.

THE REMEDY FOR BEING SELF-FOCUSED

If we focus our attentions outwardly on Christ and others, instead of inwardly on ourselves, love for Christ and love for others gradually replaces our selfish motivations. This is how we live in harmony with the two things Jesus said are the most important rules in life for everyone (Matthew 22:36-40): Loving God with all that we are and all that we have, and loving others as much (or more) than we love ourselves.

The view that God, and most everyone else, has of us is one that we are unfamiliar with and even uncomfortable with because of our distorted self-focused understanding. But their perspective (that of God and emotionally healthy people close to us), is the *real* image we portray to the world. Few are actually fooled by the avatar we have created for long — except ourselves, maybe.

When we get our perceptions about ourselves from what God says in His Word about us, and from <u>healthy people</u> who live outside of us, we become real, authentic, content, and calmly confident. We no longer live our life disconnected from reality, disconnected from others, and, more importantly, disconnected from God.

Instead, we find ourselves in all of the joyfully messy and exhilaratingly vibrant give-and-receive of a healthy view of life. We also find that the "think-too-highly" and "think-too-lowly" things we have believed about ourselves are lies and that we no longer have to live in bondage to them. We surrender those lies to Christ, replace them with His truth, and live our lives fully in the real world.

Remember this **Anchor Point**? "What we saturate on is what we believe; what we believe is what we live." Now the question is: What truth-claims about you are you saturating on and believing — the ones that are actually true, or the ones that are false?

Grammatical Note: It is important to take note that the saturation verse for this lesson is worded differently than most English translations, and for a very important reason. We usually think that "pursuing His kingdom and righteousness" *results in* Him "providing all these things to you" – as if it reads "and then." The truth is, when you read the full context of the verse, it is BECAUSE He provides all we truly need that we are then free to pursue His kingdom and righteousness. The word "and" couples the two clauses together; the first part does not cause the second part.

80 • 03

Now to Him who is able to do far more abundantly beyond all that we ask or think, according to the power that works within us, to Him be the glory in the church and in Christ Jesus to all generations forever and ever. Amen.

Ephesians 3:20-21

DAILY PRACTICES	DAY 1	DAY 2	DAY 3	DAY 4	DAY 5	DAY 6	"REST" DAY
SATURATION VERSE ___	More ☐ 100 ☐ Less ☐	More ☐ 100 ☐ Less ☐	More ☐ 100 ☐ Less ☐	More ☐ 100 ☐ Less ☐	More ☐ 100 ☐ Less ☐	More ☐ 100 ☐ Less ☐	More ☐ 100 ☐ Less ☐
BIBLE READING	Chapters ___	Chapters ___	Chapters ___	Chapters ___	Chapters ___	Chapters ___	
STUDY MANUAL LESSON # ___	Read Today's Lesson Today Yes ☐ No ☐	Read Today's Lesson Today Yes ☐ No ☐	Read Today's Lesson Today Yes ☐ No ☐	Read Today's Lesson Today Yes ☐ No ☐	Read Today's Lesson Today Yes ☐ No ☐	Read Today's Lesson Today Yes ☐ No ☐	
DAILY REFLECTION	Completed Today's Lesson Today Yes ☐ No ☐	Completed Today's Lesson Today Yes ☐ No ☐	Completed Today's Lesson Today Yes ☐ No ☐	Completed Today's Lesson Today Yes ☐ No ☐	Completed Today's Lesson Today Yes ☐ No ☐	Completed Today's Lesson Today Yes ☐ No ☐	
USED "RESTORE" BOOK	Yes ☐ No ☐	Yes ☐ No ☐	Yes ☐ No ☐	Yes ☐ No ☐	Yes ☐ No ☐	Yes ☐ No ☐	Yes ☐ No ☐
PRE-MEAL SATURATION VERSE	Breakfast ☐ Lunch ☐ Dinner ☐	Breakfast ☐ Lunch ☐ Dinner ☐	Breakfast ☐ Lunch ☐ Dinner ☐	Breakfast ☐ Lunch ☐ Dinner ☐	Breakfast ☐ Lunch ☐ Dinner ☐	Breakfast ☐ Lunch ☐ Dinner ☐	Breakfast ☐ Lunch ☐ Dinner ☐
SPECIAL ITEMS	Yes ☐ No ☐	Yes ☐ No ☐	Yes ☐ No ☐	Yes ☐ No ☐	Yes ☐ No ☐	Yes ☐ No ☐	Yes ☐ No ☐
PRIVATE PRAYER	Time Spent ___	Time Spent ___	Time Spent ___	Time Spent ___	Time Spent ___	Time Spent ___	Time Spent ___
TODAY, I AM THANKFUL FOR....							

Lesson 4 Study Sheet

Each day review the lesson for that week.
Record one thing you are grateful for each day on your Progress Record.

This Lesson's Verse:

"But above all pursue His kingdom and righteousness since all these things will be provided to you as well." Matthew 6:33 (Lamb)

Day 1 Reflection

What kinds of problems has being self-focused created for you? *Additional study passage: Mark 7:21-23*

Day 2 Reflection

What are some of the societal problems in our world today that would fade if people were to focus more outwardly and less on themselves? *Additional study passages: James 3:17-18; 4:1-10*

Day 3 Reflection

Why would being self-focused result in a person feeling that they have to rationalize, justify, and make excuses for their actions? *Additional study passages: Luke 16:15; James 3:14, 16*

Day 4 Reflection

Why would focusing on satisfying one's selfish desires keep a person from actually getting them or, once they've gotten them, wipe out their ability to enjoy them? *Additional study passages: 1 Samuel 18:13-14; Romans 6:7-8*

Day 5 Reflection

What are some of the flawed ideas about yourself that you have accepted and lived with as a result of being self-focused? *Additional study passages: Psalm 6; Isaiah 14:12-14*

Day 6 Reflection

Our relationship with God does not improve by being self-focused; it only gets more difficult and problematic. Why do you think this is? *Additional study passages: Proverbs 8:13; James 4:6*

is NOT a **man**,
that HE should lie;

NOR a **human being**,
that HE should
change HIS mind.

Has HE said,
and will HE not DO it?
Or has HE spoken,
and will HE not
MAKE it happen?"

Numbers 23:19 (NET)

LESSON FIVE
IS GOD FAITHFUL?

Trust is a big issue for many of us and having a hard time trusting others can almost become a "badge of honor" many boldly and confidently wear. "I don't trust *anybody*," we proudly declare, as if that marks us a wise and discerning individual.

What it really means is that we have decided to be protective of ourselves because we have no idea how trust is supposed to work, because it has gone wrong too often, or because it has gone wrong in such hurtful ways. Since we do not really understand legitimate trust and how to arrive at it, we simply opt out. We just won't trust *anyone*.

On the other hand, some people trust just about *anybody* until that person does something severe enough to show that they should *not* be trusted. Of course, by then it's too late.

Many people have come to believe that we are supposed to take everybody at face-value and trust them up front. There are many reasons for this, but the two most common are: 1) The belief that all people are "basically good" (contrary to Scripture, which tells us that "there is no one who is righteous - not a single one!" *Romans 3:10*); and 2) That it isn't fair to distrust people before they have shown themselves undeserving of our trust – and that kind of backward reasoning has led more people into disastrous situations than any other lie.

Legitimate trust has to be based on sound knowledge about a person and their integrity — who they really are, and what they really are about. We come to this knowledge and understanding of a person based on their demonstrated character over time. Until you or I know that person well, or until their reliability is verified by someone that we *can* know and trust, we have no reliable reason to either trust *or* distrust them. And, even then, we may be duped.

If we are wise, we learn to base trust on our history and past experience with someone. If we do not have personal experience with a particular individual, then the experience of someone else we hold in high regard can help. We watch and see if we encounter the same level of integrity and reliability as the person who gave them a good report.

Throughout this program, we teach the need for us to learn and accept things about God's nature and character that are often in conflict with what we *believe* about God at present. This brings an important question to mind: How can we *really know* that what God says about Himself — about His nature, His character, His heart toward us, and what all of this means for our lives — is *true*? How can we *trust* it?

When we look at God's record, when we examine His history, we find that God has proven Himself faithful in *every instance*, with *every person*, in *every circumstance*, throughout *all* time.

We have the Bible as a reliable record, plus we have personal stories of thousands of people throughout the centuries that testify to God's reliability and faithfulness. In a court of law, the amount of testimony in favor of God's unimpeachable character would be overwhelming evidence ("beyond a reasonable doubt") that His trustworthiness is irrefutable.

When we look at all of the promises God makes throughout His Word, we see Him not only keeping each and every one of them, but we also see Him often keeping those promises in spectacular and magnificent ways; in spite of what may have seemed might be likely, or even possible, in the circumstances.

If you are ever going to have the abundant, meaningful life as the person God created and intends for you to be, then you must learn to fully trust God. The terms "faith" and "trust" are interchangeable. His Word says that without faith (trust), it is impossible to please Him and get to know Him (Hebrews 11:6).

Since knowledge of a person is important in developing trust, it seems obvious that the better we know God, our Creator and Heavenly Father, the more we will trust Him. The more we trust Him, the more we will follow Him. The more we follow Him, the more vibrant and abundant the life we can live.

We can intellectually understand and agree with everything the Bible has to say about God—His nature, character, and purpose—yet there can be an enormous gulf between what we "know" and what we "believe."

WORD-PICTURE

The Three "Faith" Sisters is a helpful illustration for understanding how this gap between "know" and "believe" happens. The following is drawn from historical Christian faith and understanding of what faith is as described in the Bible. In Latin the Early Church Fathers called the three aspects of faith notitia [no-TĬ-shuh] (knowledge); assensus [uh-SENSE-us]; and (assent) fiducia [fi'-DOO-she-ah] (trust).

In the picture, you will see Notitia, the sister on the left, leaning in and earnestly sharing information with the other two. "Notitia" is where we take in the information and are able to understand and make sense of it; we "know" it.

You can see that Assensus, the sister in the middle, appears to be seriously contemplating and considering the information she is taking in. This is where we examine and ponder the information, ultimately giving "assent" to its validity. (This is where much of what we say we believe ends up getting stuck: in our intellectual acknowledgment of the truth of something, but it is still a long way from our heart.)

Finally we see Fiducia on the far right. You can see that Fiducia is leaning in, her posture open and trusting. This is where we fully trust in, depend on, and rely upon something as true—to the point that we live our life rooted and grounded on it.

Perhaps you have said, "I know that 'such-and-such' is true about God, but I have a hard time really <u>trusting</u> it." If so, you have expressed perfectly what this picture of the biblical understanding of faith captures.

 Anchor Point: _To know God is to trust Him._ Once we truly know God — know His faithfulness to His own nature and character and know the fullness of His love for us — we will more fully trust Him. Remember: what we saturate on is what we believe; what we believe is what we live.

<u>Some ways for us to get to know God better:</u>

1) Invest time with God in prayer, Bible study, and personal worship —every day, if possible;

2) Pay attention to the promises He made to His children and His faithfulness in keeping those promises;

3) Study the lives of people who have walked faithfully with God and observe how God has shown Himself to be trustworthy in their lives.

1) Invest time with God in prayer, Bible study, and personal worship —every day, if possible.

God created us for loving companionship with Him. He wants us to know Him. One of the most powerful statements God Himself makes about this truth comes in Jeremiah 9:23-24: *"'Wise people ought not boast that they are wise. Powerful people ought not boast that they are powerful. Rich people ought not boast that they are rich. If people want to boast, they should boast about this: They should boast that <u>they understand and know me.</u> They should boast that <u>they know and understand</u> that I, the Lord, act out of faithfulness, fairness, and justice in the earth and that I desire people to do these things,' says the Lord"* (Emphasis added).

Investing time every day in our relationship with God is just as important as investing time getting to know other people in our lives better. Without this kind of investment, any relationship will only be superficial at best. The more "shoulder time" we spend with someone, the better we get to know them and they us. Our relationship with God needs to be of paramount importance, above all others.

As we saw in earlier lessons, we cannot know God apart from Jesus Christ. In John 14:6-7, Jesus made clear to His disciples that, *"I am the way, and the truth, and the life. No one comes to the Father except through me. If you have known me, you will know my Father too. And from now on you do know Him and have seen Him."* Our only approach to God is through our Savior Jesus Christ.

Surrendering to Jesus is simply the beginning. From there, the way to know Christ, our Savior and Lord, is the same way that we know our Heavenly Father: through investing time with Him. We do this by reading His Word and seeing Him shown to us in the Bible's pages; through our time in prayer, authentically sharing our thoughts and our heart with Him, knowing that He has been right where we are (Hebrews 4:15); and through appreciating who Jesus is by celebrating Him in personal worship (John 1:1; Matthew 14:33).

Two questions often arise at this point:

1) How do I pray? and,

2) What is worship?

Unfortunately, you can easily get as many different answers as the number of different people you ask. There are some technical definitions that are not really helpful at this point. For our purposes here, we will use a couple of simple working definitions:

Prayer is expressing to God — earnestly and honestly — what is on our heart and in our mind (Philippians 4:6). It can be adoration, thanksgiving, confession, desperation, gratitude, or even interceding for someone else. The pattern for this is given to us by Jesus in Matthew 6:9-15. The method is not of concern; the intent behind it is. Our prayer simply needs to be authentic and true. The rest is mostly window dressing.

One very effective approach you might try is a "Prayer Journal." Journaling is helpful to us because it helps get spinning thoughts and emotions out of our minds and down onto paper where they will "sit still." By taking those thoughts and emotions and laying them before God as a prayer ("Dear Lord...," "Dear Heavenly Father...," "Lord Jesus...," etc.), we get Him involved on the front-end of every reality in life, and grow in surrendering everything to Him. It is in this surrender that we find God, and that we experience His sufficiency for all our true needs *(Note: There is a paper on page 335 in the*

Supplemental Materials section titled, "A Pattern for Developing Your Prayer-Life," that you might find helpful.)

Worship is showing honor, respect, and reverence for who God *is*. Praise — acknowledging what God has done — may be a component of worship but worship itself is about God's "God-ness," and about His worthiness to be honored. It is celebrating who God is; not what He has done. And, keeping in mind that Jesus is God as much as the Father is God and as much as the Holy Spirit is God, worshiping Jesus is worshiping God (Hebrews 1:8; John 10:30; 1 John 5:20, et al.).

Often in modern Western Christianity, "praise & worship" equals "music and singing." Interestingly enough, if you read through the Psalms (where we find the largest collection of worship for God), while many of them were set to music, many of them were *not*. Worship is an attitude of the heart, not a performance of the body.

2) Pay attention to the promises God made to His children, and to His faithfulness in keeping those promises.

One of the clearest ways to determine a person's trustworthiness is to ask the following: "How consistent are they at keeping their word? How reliable have they been when they have said they would or wouldn't do something? Have they shown up when they said they would, and have they finished what they started?" The best way to see and discern a person's dependability and trustworthiness is to examine how faithful they have been in keeping their word, and how consistent they are at being who they represent themselves to be.

When it comes to trustworthy reliability, God has a flawless record. When people say, "God failed me," or "God promised me and He didn't come through," what actually took place was something else entirely.

Sometimes we expect God to do something He never promised to do. On other occasions, we mistake something in God's Word as a promise when it was either nothing of the sort, or it is a promise made to someone else that we inappropriately take as our own. Ultimately, we can even develop expectations of God that He never gives us the freedom to expect.

An important note about the promises in the Bible: Most of the promises in the Bible were made to a specific person or people group at a specific time in a specific place. Very few are what can be termed "general" promises — promises that are meant for all people, at all times, and in all places. However, even when a promise is specific and not general, it always reveals something of God's character and the way He deals with people — especially *His* people — that we *can* hold on to and trust. God's promises are,

primarily, about the one *making* the promise, not about the contents of the promise itself. In other words, we trust what God says *because of who God is.*

3) Study the lives of people who have walked faithfully with God and observe how God has shown Himself to be trustworthy in their lives.

From the beginning of time, and all throughout history, God has used men and women to accomplish His purposes here on earth. He does the same in, and through, your life today.

The lives of the "great men of God" and "great women of God" are often well-documented in beautiful detail in the Bible, in published biographies, and in autobiographies. They became "great" men and women of God as a result of their faith in Him; their faith in Him being a keeper of His promises, and their willingness to live their lives accordingly.

Studying the lives of these men and women will reveal a common theme among all their stories: As they learned to trust God and to rely on Him, they were able to see more and more His perfect faithfulness. It was their ability to trust God's faithfulness that emboldened them to do what they believed He called them to do, even when it seemed impossible.

The study of God's faithful people who have come before us can be a tremendous faith builder in our own

74

lives, especially when we recognize that we are just as worthy, and are just as much "His," as they were.

Our verse for this week demonstrates that the focus can be, and needs to be, on God's faithfulness that results from His "God-ness."

Right alongside the broad, overarching story of God's redemptive plan throughout human history is the personal aspect of the salvation story; the Gospel applied to us *personally*. As we learn that God is, and always has been trustworthy, and as we see this reality hold true in our own lives, we are able to discover from what God has declared that our own salvation is completely secure in Christ.

There are dozens of Scriptures that proclaim this truth. John 10:27-30 probably speaks the clearest about how God works for us personally and specifically: Jesus declares, *"My sheep listen to my voice, and I know them, and they follow me. I give them everlasting life, and they will never perish; no one will snatch them from my hand. My Father, who has given them to me, is greater than all, and no one can snatch them from my Father's hand. The Father and I are one."*

Indeed, passage after passage resonates with the truth that we are secure in Jesus. Read John 3:16-21, John 6:47, Romans 8:31-39, Romans 10:13, and 1 John 5:13, just to name a few. And as you do, you need to saturate your mind and heart with this powerful truth, especially in times of doubt and uncertainty: ***"God is not a man, that he should lie, nor a human being, that he should change his mind. Has he said, and will he not do it? Or has he spoken, and will he not make it happen?"*** (Numbers 23:19 NET)

It is IMPOSSIBLE for God NOT to do what He says He will do, because it is IMPOSSIBLE for Him to do anything that is contrary to His own nature and character. He just simply would not BE God if He could otherwise violate himself. Here, then, in the "God-ness" of God, stands our sure HOPE!

DAILY PRACTICES	DAY 1	DAY 2	DAY 3	DAY 4	DAY 5	DAY 6	"REST" DAY
SATURATION VERSE ___	More □ 100 □ Less □	More □ 100 □ Less □	More □ 100 □ Less □	More □ 100 □ Less □	More □ 100 □ Less □	More □ 100 □ Less □	More □ 100 □ Less □
BIBLE READING	Chapters ___	Chapters ___	Chapters ___	Chapters ___	Chapters ___	Chapters ___	
STUDY MANUAL LESSON # ___	Read Today's Lesson Today Yes □ No □	Read Today's Lesson Today Yes □ No □	Read Today's Lesson Today Yes □ No □	Read Today's Lesson Today Yes □ No □	Read Today's Lesson Today Yes □ No □	Read Today's Lesson Today Yes □ No □	
DAILY REFLECTION	Completed Today's Lesson Today Yes □ No □	Completed Today's Lesson Today Yes □ No □	Completed Today's Lesson Today Yes □ No □	Completed Today's Lesson Today Yes □ No □	Completed Today's Lesson Today Yes □ No □	Completed Today's Lesson Today Yes □ No □	
USED "RESTORE" BOOK	Yes □ No □	Yes □ No □	Yes □ No □	Yes □ No □	Yes □ No □	Yes □ No □	Yes □ No □
PRE-MEAL SATURATION VERSE	Breakfast □ Lunch □ Dinner □	Breakfast □ Lunch □ Dinner □	Breakfast □ Lunch □ Dinner □	Breakfast □ Lunch □ Dinner □	Breakfast □ Lunch □ Dinner □	Breakfast □ Lunch □ Dinner □	Breakfast □ Lunch □ Dinner □
SPECIAL ITEMS	Yes □ No □	Yes □ No □	Yes □ No □	Yes □ No □	Yes □ No □	Yes □ No □	Yes □ No □
PRIVATE PRAYER	Time Spent ___	Time Spent ___	Time Spent ___	Time Spent ___	Time Spent ___	Time Spent ___	Time Spent ___
TODAY, I AM THANKFUL FOR...							

Lesson 5 Study Sheet

Each day review the lesson for that week.
Record one thing you are grateful for each day on your Progress Record.

This Lesson's Verse:

"God is not a man, that he should lie; nor a human being, that he should change his mind. Has he said, and will he not do it? Or has he spoken, and will he not make it happen?" (Numbers 23:19, NET)

Day 1 Reflection

In your relationships with others in your life, on what have you most often based your trust in them? *Additional study passages: Psalm 40:4; 62:8-9*

Day 2 Reflection

What promise have you discovered in God's Word that is most significant for you - the one you are clinging to and counting on the most? *Additional study passages: Genesis 28:15; Matthew 24:34-35*

Day 3 Reflection

What obstacles do you face in your life that make it difficult for you to believe and trust in God? *Additional study passages: Exodus 3:11; 4:1, 10; 14:10-12*

Day 4 Reflection

What do you think the impact would be in our lives if we did not trust that God kept His promise that our identity and salvation are secure in Christ? *Additional study passage: Galatians 3:1-7*

Day 5 Reflection

What passages of Scripture have you collected in your arsenal to combat the lies that would cause you to not trust God in every situation and circumstance? *Additional study passages: Joshua 1:5-9; Psalm 1*

Day 6 Reflection

What are the possible benefits to us and others, both now and for eternity, of us having and sharing our faith and trust in Christ? *Additional study passage: 1 Thessalonians 5:8-11*

My heart *Rejoices*
and I am *Happy*;
my life is **SAFE**.

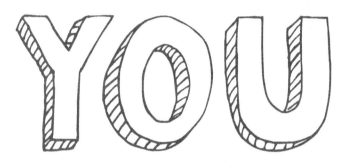

will NOT abandon me
to the place of **Death**;
YOU will NOT allow

your *faithful follower*
to even see the **Pit**."

Psalm 16:9-10 (Lamb, NET)

LESSON SIX
KNOWING GOD — PART 1[12]

Note: The next two lessons are going to provide us with both a "Ladder of Faith" and a "Bridge of Faith" for dealing with the "Pits of Gloom" we face in life. We are going to refer to it as our "Ladder-Bridge of Faith" going forward. The "Ladder" helps us climb out of the "Pits of Gloom" whenever we find ourselves in one. Once we learn to see them coming in advance, the "Bridge" helps us avoid and cross *over* the "Pits" before we end up in the bottom of one. The parts and the sections of the "Ladder" and the "Bridge" are basically the same. It is only *when* and *how* we use them that differ.

God's Word teaches us that mankind is born into a rebellious and troubled world. We are individually given to making rebellious sin-choices, and so is everyone else around us. This means that we can count on trouble happening in this life. We all know that life is never without difficulties, both large and small, and sometimes they can become overwhelming. There are too many things we simply *cannot* control. Life has "Pits of Gloom" with varying degrees of depth and darkness, and we can often find ourselves in the bottom of one with little or no warning.

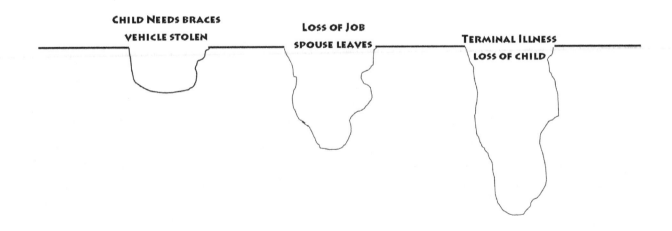

---

[12] Again, special thanks to Pastor Troy Smith for the original "Bridge of Faith" teaching that this and the next lesson grew from.

Thankfully, God has a Bridge that we can build and use to pass over these Pits. We can also stand this same Bridge on end and use it as a Ladder to climb out of the Pits when we have fallen into them.

We use the Bridge to avoid the Pits; we use the Ladder to escape when we have been unable to avoid them. Since we are more accustomed to finding ourselves in the "Pits," we first need to learn to climb out. Once we have that down a bit, then we will turn to working on avoiding them.

If we are unprepared when trouble comes — as we know it will — we can easily end up feeling fearful, anxious, angry, miserable, and we can find ourselves in bleak despair. Hopelessness often follows. If we do not know how to climb out of such Pits of Gloom, we can end up stuck there — for *years* sometimes. As we will learn later in this program, when we are depressed and hopeless our likelihood of making wise decisions is doubtful, at best. Ironically, it is precisely *during* such "Pit" times of trouble and difficulty that we *need* to make the wisest choices. So, we also need something that can get us out of these dark places when we have taken a nose-dive into them.

Unfortunately for many of us, the pattern that we have best perfected is the one of making our most important, life-impacting decisions when we are *in* the Pit of Gloom. Pit-time emotions — like fear, anxiety, and anger — then influence or drive these decisions.

Emotions are not truth, so emotion-driven decisions are often defective and counterproductive. The enemy of our souls (Satan) makes a shovel readily available to us in the form of doubt about God. We grab hold of that shovel with both hands, and we dig the Pit even deeper.

 Anchor Point: When make emotion-driven decisions (versus truth-driven decisions), the underlying problem is that our faith and trust in some aspect of God's nature and character is weak or missing.

We all know that there is no real escape from having to face troubles. Even if we *could* somehow create a trouble-free life, it would not be in our best interest (James 1:2-4). It is vital that we learn to navigate through problems in wise, healthy, and godly ways. It is in the place of struggle that we begin to become mature in dealing with life's troubles; it is here that we begin to grow strong emotionally *and* spiritually.

God knows that our ability to deal well with problems is important in shaping a healthy and abundant life, but He never intended that we deal with these difficulties alone (Matthew 11:28-30).

This leads us to two key questions: 1) How do we climb out of the "Pits of Gloom" we so often find ourselves in?; and, 2) How do we learn to cross over those pits and avoid falling into them in the first place?

We will focus on the first question in this lesson, and the second question in the next one. Before we can tackle either, however, we first need to discuss the raw materials of our "Ladder-Bridge of Faith," and consider how to construct this God-centered apparatus.

ASSEMBLING OUR "LADDER-BRIDGE OF FAITH"

The two main supports (the main "rails") for our Ladder-Bridge of Faith are:

1) *God's Word* — There is nothing in the human experience that God's Word does not address (2 Peter 1:2-4).

2) *Prayer* — Openly and authentically surrendering to God everything that is on our hearts and minds, no matter what it is (Philippians 4:6-7).

Remember our safety deposit box with the two keys (page 9)? We employ those same two "keys" again here. We establish and support our "Ladder-Bridge of Faith" through surrendering everything to Him and by saturating ("abiding," John 8:31-32) in His Word.

Once we have the main supports in place, we begin to lay down the treads that will make up the rungs of the Ladder and the deck of the Bridge. The rungs are what we climb; the deck is where we stand. In both cases, they are where we put one foot after the other as we climb out of, or cross over, the Pits of Gloom. These rungs and planks match up with key attributes and characteristics of God — the particular aspects of His nature and character that specifically connect us to how He interacts with us and intercedes in our life.

If our Ladder-Bridge is to be strong, the rungs and planks must be strong. A rung or plank is strong when we have solid faith and trust in that aspect of God's character. If our faith and trust are weak, then that rung or plank will be weak. Imagine putting your foot on the rung of a ladder or the plank of a bridge that is rotted through. You know exactly what to expect, right? This picture holds true for the strength or weakness of the treads in our "Ladder-Bridge of Faith."

Going forward, then, we need to learn about the identity and make-up of each individual rung or plank in our "Ladder-Bridge of Faith." Then we need to assess which rungs and planks are the strongest, and which are the weakest in our life. Strengthening our "Ladder-Bridge of Faith" will necessitate strengthening our weakest rung or plank first, through the tool of Scripture saturation.

Once you have constructed a strong "Ladder-Bridge of Faith," you will find life begin to rapidly change. Where before you were trapped in a besetting sin-pattern or living as an emotional mess, now your faith in God will be stronger and your life more settled.

As you become increasingly **unbound** from the death and decay you have been in bondage to, the idolatrous heart that previously drove you gets replaced with a clean and right heart. Instead of seeking a substitute for God, you learn to passionately trust in God.

You will probably even find your life more stable than some who have never experienced the kind of bondage you were once in. This is part of the amazing and blessed mystery of the Holy Spirit bearing fruit in our souls.

ABOUT THE RUNGS AND PLANKS FOR OUR LADDER-BRIDGE OF FAITH

Look through your "Ladder-Bridge of Faith" booklet [13] and read the descriptions of the aspects of God's character that constitute our rungs and planks. There is a "Faith

---

[13] There is a full-sized version in the "Supplemental Materials" section; you may also email and request a pocket-size version per the instruction there.

Assessment" on the last page of the booklet that will show you where to begin your saturation work. Below is the list we will be working with (Follow the arrow; read from the <u>bottom to the top</u>. We will focus on the first six in this lesson; the second set of six in the next):

God's **Timing & Trajectory:** *Ecclesiastes 3:11*

God's **Guidance:** *Isaiah 42:16*

God's **Deliverance:** *Isaiah 12:2*

God's **Protection:** *2 Samuel 22:31-32*

God's **Providence:** *1 Chronicles 29:11-13*

God's **Presence:** *Psalm 46:7, 11*

God's **Mercy:** *Psalm 103:3-5*

God's **Grace:** *Ephesians 2:4-9*

God's **Love:** *Romans 5:6, 8, 10*

God's **Omnipotence:** *Revelation 1:8*

God's **Omniscience:** *Psalm 139:1-16*

God's **Goodness:** *Psalm 106:1*

How do we get out when we find ourselves in a Pit of Gloom?

We begin our journey out of the Pit of Gloom with the first attribute of God on our list as the <u>first tread</u> of the Ladder-Bridge of Faith: **God's Goodness.** By understanding what "God's Goodness" means and saturating on the truth of it, we take our first step out of whatever Pit of Gloom we find ourselves in.

God is not only the Greatest of all beings, but the Good-est. When you think of someone who is a "good person," what kinds of things do you think are true about them? Probably that they are kind; that they are considerate of others; that they are humble; that they are joyful; that they are never mean or petty; that they think of others first; that they are never shady or dishonest in any way; that they are

85

dependable and trustworthy; that they have integrity; that they do all they can to stay away from evil. Someone who is "good" is decent, ethical, upright, blameless, safe, benevolent, reliable, well-mannered, righteous, pleasant, able, competent, just, and helpful.

Would you say the above description is a pretty fair summary of "good?" It is at least a suitable place to start thinking about God's Goodness, but, in reality, His goodness goes beyond that! Apart from Him, nothing would be good; nothing *could* be good. The core quality of all of God's character and love is totally, completely, and fully *good*! In fact, if God is not good, then many of His other characteristics would be terrifying!

Starting from God's Goodness, we next place our foot firmly on the second tread, which is **God's Omniscience.** Being "omniscient" means that He has always known only and everything that is true — including all true potentialities. By this it is meant that, even if something did not *actually* take place, God has always known the truth of whether or not it *could* take place, and what the result *would* have been had it actually happened. Why does this matter? Simply because, instead of us

having to be anxious about potentialities (those pesky non-realities), we can fully surrender them to God because He knows (and has always known) whether or not they can or will take place, and He is fully prepared for whichever of those is true, for whether or not they will or will not happen.

We can always trust and depend on the fact that there is nothing in our heart, mind, or life — or in the heart, mind, and life of anyone else — that God does not know, has not always known, as is not totally prepared to address.

God's Omnipotence is the third tread of our Ladder-Bridge of Faith. God is able in every respect for every action that is possible for Him. He has unlimited ability to be, and to do, all that He has said He is and will do. He is all-powerful, almighty. There is nothing God cannot do that is in keeping with His own nature and character. For example, God *cannot* lie. He is Himself the Truth, so lying is not in His character or ability. If God could do anything contrary to His nature or character, He would cease to be God at that point, and He can never *not* be God!

God's omnipotence matters to us because it means, among many things, that we can count on there being nothing in our lives that is impossible for Him. There is nothing He has said He will do for us that He cannot and will not do. There is no promise He cannot and will not keep, and there is no one and nothing stronger or mightier than He.

Of course, all of this is in perfect balance with **God's Love**, our <u>fourth tread</u>. In a later study, we will delve into love more deeply, but for now, understand that love — biblically speaking — as it flows from God's nature and character, is "a passionate desire for God's best for someone else, even at great cost to oneself;" and that "love gives without expectation of return."

The Apostle Paul, in Philippians 2:5-8, spells out for us the greatest example of God's love. Here we see that Jesus, who is God just as much as God the Father is, loved us so deeply that He willingly laid aside everything He was entitled to *as* God. He did so in order to take on human form and obey the Father's will, even to the point that He bore God's wrath on the cross for human sin so that humankind would not have to (Lesson 2)

God desires His best will for us and for everyone else. But He never forces us to accept His best. Rather, He always leaves it up to us to decide to accept or reject His love. And this too, is love. God is not some cosmic stalker, chasing us around, forcing us to "love" Him, because that isn't love at all, is it? In His Goodness, He cannot and will not do that.

Our consideration of God's love leads quite naturally to the <u>fifth tread</u> of the Ladder-Bridge: **God's Grace**. Grace is the undeserved kindness, support, and help that God extends to all — especially His Children. Apart from God's grace, no one would stand a chance. But, as it applies to those who are His by surrender to Christ, God's Grace is an active and powerful force in our lives. Whenever we receive what we do not deserve, that is grace. And whenever we *do not* receive the punishment that we deserve for our willfulness and sin, that is "merciful grace."

There is an old acronym that can be helpful to keep in mind when thinking about grace: **G**od's **R**iches **A**t **C**hrist's **E**xpense. It is because of God's grace that the Father asked Jesus to die in our place. It is because of His grace that Christ said, "Yes," to bearing God's wrath for our sin in our place. And it is because of His grace that we have any hope at all, let alone a *great* hope.

We need to think of Grace as a two-sided coin, the reverse of which is **God's Mercy**, our <u>sixth tread</u> in the Ladder-Bridge of Faith. Mercy means that God, in His Grace, instead of giving us what we *do* deserve — an immediate and everlasting outpouring of His wrath on each and every sinner for each and every sin — is patient and long-suffering, not wanting anyone to perish, but wanting instead for all to come to repentance (2 Peter 3:9). Again, God will not force us, but He delays His punishment for our sins, giving us every possible opportunity to willingly turn in repentance toward Him. If we do, then Christ has taken our punishment in our place, and we will never have to bear it (1 Thessalonians 5:9-10).

It is in **God's Mercy** that His <u>forgiveness is found</u>. While we are undeserving of any good thing, God nonetheless created us worthy of His Love, His Grace, and His Mercy (Lesson One). It is through His Son, Jesus, that these have been bought for and made available to us (Lesson Two). It is in Christ, therefore, that we find forgiveness and restoration to God's Original Intent for us in relation to Him.

Here in *Unbound*, through God's Word, there is a great deal we can and will learn about forgiveness (Lesson 14, especially). All of it springs from the Original Source of forgiveness, namely God Himself. We need to know that God has established a very specific pattern and flow for forgiveness, one that is rooted and grounded in His nature and character, and in His sense of righteousness, justice, and love. There are two brief points for you to consider about forgiveness even now, before we press on.

First, know that God's forgiveness is the outcome of the substitutionary work of Christ on the Cross.

Second, know that forgiveness is His response to our repentance. God extends but does not grant forgiveness to those who are unrepentant. Yet, for those who are *truly* repentant, He is quick to "forgive and cleanse us of all unrighteousness" (1 John 1:9).

We will end here for this lesson and pick up next time with our study of the other six attributes of God that comprise our "Ladder-Bridge of Faith." As you go forward, consider this: The only differences between the "Ladder" and the "Bridge" of Faith are perspective and timing. The Ladder helps us escape the Pit of Gloom — that place where we feel abandoned, hopeless, fearful, and alone. The Bridge — once we are healthier, stronger, and better able to see ahead — helps us to avoid and cross over those Pits of Gloom before we ever fall (or dive) into them.

Peter showed us the avenue of escape from life's Pits when he found himself sinking beneath the waves during his walk on the water. Having taken his eyes off Jesus to pay attention to the storm (Matthew 14:22-33), Peter began to sink. He knew (and trusted) that Jesus was his only hope. "Lord, save me!" he cried. Jesus *immediately* reached out and rescued His disciple and friend. Christ has the answer to all life's problems. No problem will ever exist that He is not more than sufficient for! **HE IS GOD, OUR SAVIOR.**

଼ • ଷ

Be sure to go through your "Ladder-Bridge of Faith" booklet and keep it handy. Do the self-assessment in the back every six or seven weeks or so to see how strong your "treads" are. Saturate on the corresponding verses for the weaker one(s) often. Doing so will change what you believe, which will change how you live. It is when our ability to believe in some aspect of God's nature and character is weak or gone that we fall back into the death and decay of our old idolatries.

↓ ATTRIBUTE | DATE →	8/17	10/05	11/23
GOD'S GOODNESS	1	2	4
GOD'S OMNISCIENCE	2	2	3
GOD'S OMNIPOTENCE	4	4	4
GOD'S LOVE	1	3	4 ½
GOD'S GRACE	2	3	4
GOD'S MERCY	2	4	4
GOD'S PRESENCE	1	3	3
GOD'S PROVIDENCE	2	3	3
GOD'S PROTECTION	½	2	3
GOD'S DELIVERANCE	½	1	2
GOD'S GUIDANCE	1	3 ½	5
GOD'S TIMING & TRAJECTORY	0	3	4

DAILY PRACTICES	DAY 1	DAY 2	DAY 3	DAY 4	DAY 5	DAY 6	"REST" DAY
SATURATION VERSE ___	More □ / 100 □ / Less □	More □ / 100 □ / Less □	More □ / 100 □ / Less □	More □ / 100 □ / Less □	More □ / 100 □ / Less □	More □ / 100 □ / Less □	More □ / 100 □ / Less □
BIBLE READING	Chapters ___	Chapters ___	Chapters ___	Chapters ___	Chapters ___	Chapters ___	
STUDY MANUAL LESSON # ___	Read Today's Lesson Today Yes □ No □	Read Today's Lesson Today Yes □ No □	Read Today's Lesson Today Yes □ No □	Read Today's Lesson Today Yes □ No □	Read Today's Lesson Today Yes □ No □	Read Today's Lesson Today Yes □ No □	
DAILY REFLECTION	Completed Today's Lesson Today Yes □ No □	Completed Today's Lesson Today Yes □ No □	Completed Today's Lesson Today Yes □ No □	Completed Today's Lesson Today Yes □ No □	Completed Today's Lesson Today Yes □ No □	Completed Today's Lesson Today Yes □ No □	
USED "RESTORE" BOOK	Yes □ No □	Yes □ No □	Yes □ No □	Yes □ No □	Yes □ No □	Yes □ No □	Yes □ No □
PRE-MEAL SATURATION VERSE	Breakfast □ Lunch □ Dinner □	Breakfast □ Lunch □ Dinner □	Breakfast □ Lunch □ Dinner □	Breakfast □ Lunch □ Dinner □	Breakfast □ Lunch □ Dinner □	Breakfast □ Lunch □ Dinner □	Breakfast □ Lunch □ Dinner □
SPECIAL ITEMS	Yes □ No □	Yes □ No □	Yes □ No □	Yes □ No □	Yes □ No □	Yes □ No □	Yes □ No □
PRIVATE PRAYER	Time Spent ___	Time Spent ___	Time Spent ___	Time Spent ___	Time Spent ___	Time Spent ___	Time Spent ___
TODAY, I AM THANKFUL FOR...							

Lesson 6 Study Sheet

Each day review the lesson for that week.

Record one thing you are grateful for each day on your Progress Record.

This Lesson's Verse:

"My heart rejoices and I am happy; my life is safe. You will not abandon me to the place of Death; You will not allow your faithful follower to even see the Pit." Psalm 16:9-10 (Lamb)

Day 1 Reflection

Which of the two essential disciplines for constructing and maintaining your **Ladder-Bridge of Faith** do you think is going to be your greatest challenge? Why? *Additional study passage: Isaiah 40:28-29*

Day 2 Reflection

When considering the first six of the twelve rungs and planks in your Ladder-Bridge of Faith, which do you believe to be your strongest, and which your weakest? Please explain. *Additional study passages: 1 Thessalonians 5:16-24*

Day 3 Reflection

What is your action plan (so far) for strengthening your weakest tread? *Additional study passage: Psalm 119:9-16*

Day 4 Reflection

Why is it important when we are involved in this type of a program that we choose our companions, our activities, and even the conversations we take part in, with great care? *Additional study passages: Matthew 16:11; 1 Corinthians 15:33; Galatians 5:7-9*

Day 5 Reflection

What are some of the attitudes and influences in the world around you that seem to undermine your faith in God? *Additional study passage: Galatians 5:19-21*

Day 6 Reflection

As you have progressed through the lesson this week, what have you discovered about God and about yourself? *Additional study passages: Lamentations 3:40; Isaiah 55:7; 2 Corinthians 3:18*

The Lord says,

"Because he is *devoted* to Me,
I will DELIVER him;
I will PROTECT him
because he is *loyal* to Me.
When he *calls out* to Me,
I will ANSWER him.
I will be WITH him
when he is in trouble;
I will RESCUE him
and bring him *honor*."

Psalm 91:14-15 (NET)

LESSON SEVEN
KNOWING GOD — PART 2

In the last lesson we discovered that the two supports for our "Ladder-Bridge of Faith" are **God's Word** and **Prayer**. We focused last time on the first six treads (starting from the bottom). This session, we will focus on treads seven through twelve. Here is our diagram as a reminder:

- God's **Timing & Trajectory:** *Ecclesiastes 3:11*
- God's **Guidance:** *Isaiah 42:16*
- God's **Deliverance:** *Isaiah 12:2*
- God's **Protection:** *2 Samuel 22:31-32*
- God's **Providence:** *1 Chronicles 29:11-13*
- God's **Presence:** *Psalm 46:7, 11*
- God's **Mercy:** *Psalm 103:3-5*
- God's **Grace:** *Ephesians 2:4-9*
- God's **Love:** *Romans 5:6, 8, 10*
- God's **Omnipotence:** *Revelation 1:8*
- God's **Omniscience:** *Psalm 139:1-16*
- God's **Goodness:** *Psalm 106:1*

In this lesson we want to complete our list of the twelve <u>Attributes of God</u> that constitute the treads for our "Ladder-Bridge of Faith." We also want to turn our attention toward learning how to lay the "Ladder of Faith" down in order to use it as a "Bridge of Faith." With the "Bridge of Faith," we can avoid and crossover the Pits of Gloom *before* we wind up in the bottom of them.

Treads seven through twelve are (in order from the bottom to the top of the list above):

- God's Presence
- God's Providence
- God's Protection
- God's Deliverance
- God's Guidance
- God's Timing & Trajectory

God's Presence, our <u>seventh tread</u>, can be a difficult one for us to have faith and confidence in for many reasons. There is so much that happens in life that we do not understand, do not want to have to face, that we think is unfair, or that seems too difficult and overwhelming. In order to strengthen our grasp on the reality of God's Presence, we first need to understand a principle known as *God's Omnipresence*.

"Omnipresence" literally means "everywhere present." The literal meaning, however, does not really capture what the doctrine of God's Omnipresence entails. A better definition is this: "Everywhere is in God's presence."

We define God's Omnipresence as "Everywhere is in God's presence" simply because God is not in someone's cupboard, or inside someone's pocket, or in the back of a pickup truck. In Psalm 139:7, David put it this way: "Where can I go to escape Your Spirit? Where can I flee to escape Your presence?"

Throughout this Psalm, David uses several word pictures to express the idea that, no matter where he (or anyone else) goes, he will always be in God's Presence.

Now, if God is present, we wonder, "Why does He let so many horrible things happen?" This is, of course, the wrong question to be asking. "Why" questions are "sovereignty" questions. God is sovereign: He is the Creator, Sustainer, and Master over all of Creation; even over time itself. His thoughts and ways are beyond our comprehension (Isaiah 55:8-9).

Still, for many reasons, when God does not fit what *we think* He should be like, we ask, "Why?" Interestingly enough, our brains do not have the capacity to understand the answer to this why question, even if God decided to give us the full answer. They would literally disintegrate from overload.

Rather than ask "why" about difficult times and circumstances — the answer to which we couldn't understand, even if God chose to give it — we are far better off approaching life's issues with this sort of question (building on the first six treads from the last lesson) instead: "Since God is Good, All-Knowing, All-Powerful, Faithfully Loving, Gracious, and Merciful, what does that tell me about where He was when I faced the situation that put me at the edge (or bottom) of this Pit of Gloom?" We can count on all of these things being true about God, all at the same time. And, as you see how these attributes of God and the rest relate to us and our lives, hopefully you begin to get a clearer picture about the construction of your Ladder-Bridge of Faith and how to use it.

From God's Presence we move on to the eighth tread: **God's Providence**. This word, derived from the word "provision" (which means "to see ahead"), refers to God's sovereign oversight of not only each one of our lives, but over all of time and creation as well. Think of settlers getting ready to head West in the wagon trains of long ago. They had to "see ahead," and make plans and "provision" for what they would need throughout the journey. In a far greater sense, God "sees ahead" because of His Omniscience.

Since He has always known everything that is or could possibly be true (Psalm 33:13-15), He has also always known everything you or I could ever need; every situation any and all of us would ever face; each and every choice every one of us would make; and He has always known both His best plan for "providing" for every need, and what His best remedies are for every situation (Psalm 139:4, 16). Even seemingly chance events are known by and involve God (Proverbs 16:33).

We should note, God's Providence also refers to His guiding hand being always involved in the affairs of His creation. He is not a God who sees ahead, makes provision, and then steps back. Rather, He remains intimately present with His creation, even with respect to those things that are evil (Jeremiah 18:1-6). This is not to say that God creates or causes evil. It simply means that *in spite of* evil, God's best will is going to be accomplished and He is always going to supply for our every *true* need, no matter what (God knows you need shelter. Guess what...you may *want* a 2500 square-feet home, but you do not *need* a 2500 square-feet home!).

In His Providence, God also protects. Hence, our <u>ninth tread</u> is **God's Protection**. This is so closely related to the previous two treads that they are best understood together. Psalm 91 is perhaps one of the clearest expressions in all of Scripture about God's Protection, written by someone who knows and understands that protection in the direst of circumstances.

God's Protection is not always a protection *from*; it is often a protection *through*. While God may not protect us *from* difficulty (indeed, as Job's story teaches, He often ordains difficulty for our good) or even horrible circumstances, He will *always* protect us *through* each and every moment of life.

Consider Noah: During the Flood that destroyed almost all of life on earth and completely transformed the globe, Noah and his family were protected *through* the Flood, not *from* the Flood (see Genesis 7-9). In spite of the deep lack of understanding they had about what was happening and what the outcome was going to be, they knew that God would protect and preserve them, and that He would fulfill His promise to them. This is, in fact, what God did and always *will* do. We, too, can count on His faithfulness to protect!

From God's Protection, we quite naturally arrive at our tenth tread: **God's Deliverance**. God delivered Noah and His family *through* the Flood, not *from* the Flood. Also, the version of Earth that He delivered them to would never be the same as the one they left behind, except for one thing: God would still always be who He is; would always be with them; always provide for and protect them; always love and guide them. And, since we know that God does not and cannot change (Numbers 23:19), we can also know and trust that

He is the same now as He was then. God is our Deliverer! (2 Samuel 22:2)

God's Guidance, our eleventh tread, can be another of God's attributes that is difficult to understand and recognize regularly. And yet, it is one that we cannot get through life without.

Often, when we are wondering about God's guidance, we look through the lens of, "How can God help manage the details of my life so that I always choose the things that will make me happiest?" God's Guidance — while He will help us discern His best choice for us when we truly seek His best — is mostly in the realm of the spiritual. He guides us to walk in ways that are consistent with being His child, and that are in accord with His desire for us to live righteously.

When it comes to discerning God's guidance, we must ground ourselves in God's Word. It is God's Word that provides us with all we need regarding all matters of faith and practice (2 Timothy 3:16-17; 2 Peter 1:3-4). When we purpose to know His will and live accordingly, God shows His faithful followers the way they ought to live (Psalm 25:12). So, no matter where we are or what we are doing, our focus needs to be living in a way that is pleasing to Him (2 Corinthians 5:9).

When we understand that God wants us to promote justice, live faithfully, and be obedient to His Word (Micah 6:8), we can count on Him making clear to us what His will is. In fact, one of the key passages of Scripture that drives this curriculum is Romans 12:2: "*Do not be conformed to this present world, but be transformed by the renewing of your mind, **so that you may test and approve what is the will of God – what is good and well-pleasing and perfect*** (emphasis added)."

Ultimately, knowing God's will depends on knowing *Him*. Jeremiah 9:23-24 tells us not to boast or brag about anything we have, know, or can do other than, "'*If people want to boast, they should boast about this: They should boast that they understand and know me. They should boast that they know and understand that I, the Lord, act out of faithfulness, fairness, and justice in the earth and that I desire people to do these things,' says the Lord.*" As we know our God, we will know His will!

This brings us, finally, to the <u>twelfth tread</u>, **God's Timing & Trajectory**. These two concepts — "Timing," and "Trajectory" — go together; they are "two sides to the same coin," as it were. One of the best examples of God's Timing & Trajectory appears in the story of Jonah, with all its intricate details of time and place. For instance, in the first half of Jonah 2:1 (Lamb) we read: "*The Lord had arranged for a huge fish to swallow Jonah...*" God protected and dealt with his prophet by arranging for a great fish to be in exactly the right place, at exactly the right moment.

We see this same pattern again, in Jonah 4:6-8, where God also "arranged for" a little plant to grow up and shade Jonah, then sent a worm to attack the plant so that it dried up, then ensured that Jonah experienced a hot east wind and scorching sun – all to get through to Jonah in the one way God knew would work.

While God's dealings with Jonah might sound harsh, especially at the tail-end of the story, the point is that God's Timing and Trajectory are perfect, flawless. He has so ordered the universe as to make provision for every choice every human being will ever undertake, such that His best will is ultimately going to be accomplished (Job 42:2; Isaiah 46:10). His Timing & Trajectory that cause all things to flow together are *flawless*.

Consider the storm-tossed sea that Jonah and his traveling companions faced; a storm so violent that the highly experienced sailors on the ship were *terrified*. For *that kind* of fish to be in *that exact place*, at *that exact time*, so that Jonah would *not* die but be preserved, so that he could and would carry out God's will, is a phenomenal orchestration of people, events, creatures, and even weather.

Flawless!

For as amazing as the Jonah story is, God topped Himself some 800 years after this prophet and his intriguing tale. With the coming of Jesus Christ, God put his Timing and Trajectory on magnificent display. Galatians 4:4 (Lamb) points to this magnificence when Paul writes: *"But when the ideal moment in time had come, God sent his Son here..."* Jesus came at *precisely* the right moment. At no other time in history were the political, sociological, economic, spiritual, and linguistic conditions so prepared for the Christ to come into the world, be crucified, and for the Gospel to then be spread following His Resurrection and Ascension.

In fact, the Romans who ruled the Mediterranean region and beyond at that time had constructed a sophisticated and complete system of roads throughout their empire. These roads allowed followers of Christ to access much of the "known" world more easily than at any other time in history.

This same Good, Omniscient, Omnipotent, Loving, Gracious, Merciful, Ever-Present, Providentially Sovereign, Protecting, Delivering, Guiding God whose Timing & Trajectory are flawless, is the *same* God who created you in His image. He created you for the purpose of loving you and one day inviting you to share in His glory. He has invited you to be adopted as His child, and so desires His absolute best will for your life that He sacrificed Himself to make it all possible.

~ ✝ ~

Remember that Jesus said, *"The thief comes only to steal and kill and destroy; I have come so that they may have life and may have it abundantly"* (John 10:10). That abundant life is rooted in our ability to know and understand Him (John 15:5), so that we may know and understand His will (Jeremiah 9:23-24). We do this by knowing

100

and understanding His Word (John 8:31-32; Romans 12:2). It is here that we find ourselves unbound, set free, and walking free in Christ.

৪০ ● ୦3

Be sure to read the short paper "A Word on Abiding" that comes right after the Study Sheet for this lesson.

DAILY PRACTICES	DAY 1	DAY 2	DAY 3	DAY 4	DAY 5	DAY 6	"REST" DAY
SATURATION VERSE ___	More ☐ 100 ☐ Less ☐	More ☐ 100 ☐ Less ☐	More ☐ 100 ☐ Less ☐	More ☐ 100 ☐ Less ☐	More ☐ 100 ☐ Less ☐	More ☐ 100 ☐ Less ☐	More ☐ 100 ☐ Less ☐
BIBLE READING	Chapters ___	Chapters ___	Chapters ___	Chapters ___	Chapters ___	Chapters ___	
STUDY MANUAL LESSON # ___	Read Today's Lesson Today Yes ☐ No ☐	Read Today's Lesson Today Yes ☐ No ☐	Read Today's Lesson Today Yes ☐ No ☐	Read Today's Lesson Today Yes ☐ No ☐	Read Today's Lesson Today Yes ☐ No ☐	Read Today's Lesson Today Yes ☐ No ☐	
DAILY REFLECTION	Completed Today's Lesson Today Yes ☐ No ☐	Completed Today's Lesson Today Yes ☐ No ☐	Completed Today's Lesson Today Yes ☐ No ☐	Completed Today's Lesson Today Yes ☐ No ☐	Completed Today's Lesson Today Yes ☐ No ☐	Completed Today's Lesson Today Yes ☐ No ☐	
USED "RESTORE" BOOK	Yes ☐ No ☐	Yes ☐ No ☐	Yes ☐ No ☐	Yes ☐ No ☐	Yes ☐ No ☐	Yes ☐ No ☐	Yes ☐ No ☐
PRE-MEAL SATURATION VERSE	Breakfast ☐ Lunch ☐ Dinner ☐	Breakfast ☐ Lunch ☐ Dinner ☐	Breakfast ☐ Lunch ☐ Dinner ☐	Breakfast ☐ Lunch ☐ Dinner ☐	Breakfast ☐ Lunch ☐ Dinner ☐	Breakfast ☐ Lunch ☐ Dinner ☐	Breakfast ☐ Lunch ☐ Dinner ☐
SPECIAL ITEMS	Yes ☐ No ☐	Yes ☐ No ☐	Yes ☐ No ☐	Yes ☐ No ☐	Yes ☐ No ☐	Yes ☐ No ☐	Yes ☐ No ☐
PRIVATE PRAYER	Time Spent ___	Time Spent ___	Time Spent ___	Time Spent ___	Time Spent ___	Time Spent ___	Time Spent ___
TODAY, I AM THANKFUL FOR...							

Lesson 7 Study Sheet

Each day review the lesson for that week.
Record one thing you are grateful for each day on your Progress Record.

This Lesson's Verse:

"The Lord says, 'Because he is devoted to Me, I will deliver him; I will protect him because he is loyal to Me. When he calls out to Me, I will answer him. I will be with him when he is in trouble; I will rescue him and bring him honor."
Psalm 91:14-15

Day 1 Reflection

When considering the last six of the twelve treads in your Ladder-Bridge of Faith, which do you believe to be your weakest? What makes you believe this? *Additional study passages: Psalm 119:73, 133*

Day 2 Reflection

As you have been saturating on Scripture to strengthen whichever was weakest for you of the first six treads (last lesson), what have you experienced and what are your thoughts so far? *Additional study passage: 1 Thessalonians 5:16-24*

Day 3 Reflection

What do you think will be the outcome of making strong the treads that are weak now? *Additional study passages: Proverbs 2:6-9; Luke 16:10*

Day 4 Reflection

How are you doing with being more selective of the conversations, situations, and relationships you are investing and involving yourself in? *Additional study passage: 2 Corinthians 6:14*

Day 5 Reflection

What are the most difficult mental "but's" for you to overcome in this portion of your journey to freedom? *Additional study passage: James 1:5-6*

Day 6 Reflection

As you have progressed through the lesson, what more have you discovered about God and about yourself? *Additional study passage: Isaiah 55:6-9*

"My sheep hear My voice, and I know them, and they follow Me; and I give eternal life to them, and they will never perish; and no one will snatch them out of My hand."

John 10:27-28

A WORD ON "ABIDING"

As you have progressed through this curriculum to this point, we trust that you have grown in your relationship with God through Jesus Christ. This being so, there is a key concept that we all need to keep in mind: Abiding in Christ.

As we have seen throughout *Unbound*, abiding in Christ is a daily and ongoing practice. To abide in Him is to abide in His love and to abide in His Word. 1 John 4:16b helps us obtain a clearer idea of what it means to "abide," and how abiding in Christ ties to our understanding of God's love: "God is love, and the one who *resides [menō]* in love *resides [menō]* in God, and God *resides [menō]* in him."

The word *menō* means "to stay, remain, live, dwell, abide; to be in a state that begins and continues, yet may or may not end or stop." *To abide in Christ* is to follow his example of a life obedient to the will of God. We see this idea in several other places as well:

- John 5:37b-38: "You people have never heard his voice nor seen his form at any time, nor do you have his word **residing** in you, because you do not believe the one whom he sent."

- John 8:31-32: "If you **continue** [abide] in my Word, you are truly my disciples and you will know the truth, and the truth will set you free."

- And the clearest of all, John 15:4-11: "**Abide** in Me, and I in you. As the branch cannot bear fruit of itself unless it abides in the vine, so neither can you unless you **abide** in Me. I am the vine, you are the branches; he who **abides** in Me and I in him, he bears much fruit, for apart from Me you can do nothing. If anyone does not **abide** in Me, he is thrown away as a branch and dries up; and they gather them, and cast them into the fire and they are burned. If you **abide** in Me, and My words **abide** in you, ask whatever you wish, and it will be done for you. My Father is glorified by this, that you bear much fruit, and so prove to be My disciples. Just as the Father has loved Me, I have also loved you; **abide** in My love. If you keep My commandments, you will **abide** in My love; just as I have kept My

Father's commandments and **abide** in His love. These things I have spoken to you so that My joy may be in you, and that your joy may be made full."

To abide in Christ is to be obedient to His Word. To abide in Christ is to have Him abide in us by the power of the Holy Spirit and by the truth of His Word. To abide in Christ is to seek to grow in our understanding of God's nature and character, and to live out that truth in love. To abide in Christ is to practice the "one anothering" mentioned throughout the New Testament. And to abide in Christ is to be invested in pouring into the lives of others that with which He has so richly blessed us. In so doing, although we may grow tired, we will never grow weary of doing what is "good" ("Let us not grow tired of doing good, for in due time we shall reap our harvest, if we do not give up." Galatians 6:9).

℘ • ℭ

Therefore, since we are surrounded by such a great cloud of witnesses, we must get rid of every weight and the sin that clings so closely, and run with endurance the race set out for us, keeping our eyes fixed on Jesus, the pioneer and perfecter of our faith.

For the joy set out for Him He endured the cross, disregarding its shame, and has taken His seat at the right hand of the throne of God. Think of Him who endured such opposition against Himself by sinners, so that you may not grow weary in your souls and give up.

Hebrews 12:1-3 (NET)

GOAL

DEVELOP A SOUND MIND

DEVELOP A SOUND MIND

Usually the most consistently miserable people of all are those who live their lives driven by their emotions. Making decisions based on our emotions is like allowing a drunk to get behind the wheel of a school bus - it's going to be all over the road, and it isn't going to turn out well for anyone.

A healthy, abundant, fulfilling life is only possible if we have a healthy mind and heart that know and believe the truth as God has declared it to be. Uncontrolled emotions are the greatest deterrent to a healthy mind and heart. Our objective now is to bring our thoughts and emotions into agreement and alignment with the reality of God and the truth that is in Him. We do this by learning to delay decision-making until our mental, emotional, and spiritual states are in a position of balance. We will also learn to identify our destructive patterns and replace them with healthy, righteous, God-honoring ones.

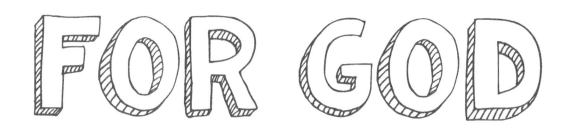

has not given us a spirit of

fearfulness,

but a spirit

of *power,*

of *love,*

and of a *sound mind.*"

2 Timothy 1:7 (Lamb)

LESSON EIGHT
EVICTING ANXIETY

As we delve into "Goal 3: Develop A Sound Mind," it is important to remember that our emotions often have more of a driving effect in our lives than logic and reason because we *feel* them, but we don't feel *truth*.

One of the most intense and debilitating emotional combinations a person can experience is what we commonly called "Anxiety." So, building on what we have learned already, and making sure to carry our Ladder-Bridge of Faith with us, now is the perfect time for us to attack and "evict" Anxiety.

"Anxiety is where I *LIVE!*" Ever thought that; felt that; *said* that? For a great many people, anxiety is a regular companion. As we press forward on this path of being "Unbound," we can often find ourselves more anxious and more doubtful than when we started. Our hearts and faith can feel very weak, like they could give out at any moment, and quitting seems like the best plan. This is when pursuing the truth is actually our *best* option, not our worst.

Some folks wake up in the morning so anxious that they start hyperventilating before they even get out of bed. Others seem to do okay for a time, and then are suddenly overwhelmed by an anxiety that grows into a full-fledged "panic attack." Still others fall somewhere along a broad spectrum that we can simply call "anxiousness." Anxiety is something we do not understand well, and so it seems hard to "beat." But, when we see it for what it is, from a Biblical and balanced perspective, we can understand both what causes anxiety, and what keeps it going. This, in turn, makes anxiety a whole lot easier to defeat and become unbound and free from.

Here are **three Anchor Points** to keep in mind about anxiety (we will add another in a moment):

1. **Anxiety is unfocused fearfulness based on an unreal, imaginary, and/or intangible threat.**

2. **Anxiety is fearfulness over potentialities, not realities.**

3. **Anxiety prophecies a future *that never happens!***

Consider this scenario: Imagine you are walking down the street and a fast-moving car coming toward you, jumps the curb, and starts rushing straight at you. <u>The fear you feel is authentic and is based on a real and tangible threat</u>. Your fight-or-flight mechanisms fire up and, hopefully, you get out of the way and are safe.

Now imagine the same scenario, only, this time, the fast-moving car does *not* jump the curb, does *not* come speeding toward you, and puts you in *no danger*. If you start to feel fearful that it *might*, that it *could*, and fantasize about all the danger such a situation would put you in, <u>this is unfounded fear without a tangible threat, which quickly becomes fearfulness and results in anxiety</u>.

The result is that, not only are you believing and trusting a lie (maybe even petitioning God to help you in a situation that is unreal and that does not exist), you also rob yourself of the mental and emotional ability to solve the *real* problems you face.

THE BRAIN AND THE BODY AS "CO-CONSPIRATORS"

When confronted by danger, there are survival mechanisms God has hard-wired into our brains that kick into action. When a person faces a threat, real or perceived, a signal is sent to the *amygdala* (pronounced, *"uh-**mig**-duh-luh"*). The amygdala then communicates with the adrenal gland, which in turn releases epinephrine (also known as adrenaline) and *cortisol*. This starts an avalanche of processes that *rapidly* merge into a symphony of chemical, neurological, mental, and physical responses and additional processes, all of which focus our *entire being* on fighting the foe or fleeing the danger.

There are several effects of epinephrine in the body, and they all combine to provide intense and potent energy, so that our major muscles can respond to the perceived threat. Muscles, skin, lungs, internal organs — everything collaborates to ensure the body can quickly and effectively do whatever it needs to do to survive.

On the emotional side of things, the *fear* that we feel provides the *emotional will* for us to live. When the threat is tangible and real, our physical and emotional processes enable us to survive the very real threat we face. When the threat is *intangible* and *not real*, that energy and emotion need an

114

outlet. Since an *anticipated* problem causes all of the same brain responses, physical reactions, and emotional distress experienced when a *real* problem exists – with one *anticipated/potential* problem piling on top of other *anticipated/potential* problems is a superhighway to an ever-increasing, ever-growing fearfulness — and can even lead to the dreaded "anxiety attack."

INTERRUPTING THE PHYSICAL REACTIONS

A long, slow intake of breath through the nose will immediately start to interrupt the physical reactions that accompany anxiety. Slowly letting that air out through the mouth causes the lungs (inflated by the epinephrine/adrenaline) to empty, which allows them to relax.

(A useful physical prompt to remind yourself to inhale through your nose is to place your finger vertically under your nose and lightly press the skin with the tip of your finger. This closes the mouth and forces you to breathe through your nose.)

First, this will inhibit the production of *cortisol* — the hormone the amygdala tells the adrenal system to release in order to, among other things, conserve the high-potency energy in the epinephrine (which the adrenal gland has also released into the body). Second, with the energy conserving hormone inhibited, the epinephrine can then be used by the body right away, allowing for the fight-or-flight mechanisms to begin to relax.

TAKING THOUGHTS (AND EMOTIONS) CAPTIVE

In 2 Corinthians 10:3-5, Paul provides great encouragement to everyone who feels they face enormous battles too big to win. One of the encouragements he provides is that we (the redeemed) do not engage in battle the way the world (the unredeemed) does battle, and the weapons we have available are not weapons of this earth. In fact, when we add a Scripture, or the Scriptural principle of saturation, onto the physical interruption techniques above, we rapidly get back to reality and back in control. If we do not do this, our imaginations can easily concoct multiple and varied *potential* scenarios, all of which are as unreal as the one that triggered the initial reaction.

The emotional distress related to worry piled upon worry, and anxiety piled upon anxiety, renders us mentally and emotionally *incapable* of effectively dealing with the legitimate problems that we face daily. Our entire *focus* becomes the anxiety we feel and how to get relief from it, even if only for a moment. This pattern is *not* how God intended for us to live. In fact, there is an enormous promise for us in 2 Timothy 1:7: *"For God has not given us a spirit of fearfulness, but a spirit of power and of love, and of a sound mind."*

In order to understand and apply the truth of 2 Timothy 1:7, we need to begin with the "not" statement the verse opens with: "God has <u>not</u> given us a spirit of fearfulness." To be "fearful" means to be "full of fear," which means to be driven by, gripped with, and focused on indefinable imagined dangers.

 <u>Your fourth **Anchor Point** for this lesson</u>: Think of having a "spirit of **fearfulness**" as being like someone running frantically around, looking for water to put out fires that are not burning.

You end up pouring enormous amounts of emotional, mental, physical, and even spiritual energy into things that are imagined and not real. Exhausting, right? Seen that way, it sounds silly, doesn't it?

Though seemingly silly, our tendency toward fearfulness demonstrates an even deeper dynamic that we need to grasp. In the midst of all our anxiety, we try to be our own savior, our own sovereign, the one who manages and directs all of our affairs and all of our outcomes. In short, we want to be God! This shows that one or more of the treads in our "Ladder-Bridge of Faith" is either defective or missing.

What is the answer to all of this? Put off that anxiety! Evict it! Purge it; reject it; eject it! God has not given you a spirit of fearfulness, "but of power, love, and a sound mind." Trust Him; saturate on who He is and what that means in relation to your fears. That's right...instead of the driving force in your life being fearfulness, as an adopted child of the Most High, your driving force is actually the Holy Spirit.

In Him there is no fear, no doubt, no uncertainty, no powerlessness, and no confusion. He is *in* you (Ephesians 1:13-14). He knows your every thought *and* your every need. Even when you do not know how or what to pray, He intercedes between you and your Heavenly Father (Romans 8:26-27).

Scripture, in several places, tells us, "Do not be anxious." Thankfully though, the Bible does not leave us with only a "don't" that we need to put off. God also makes sure we have the "put on" that is its holy replacement. No matter what the cause, our "put on" response to anxiety begins with God himself (back to the Ladder-Bridge of Faith).

God is the same, whether in the Old Testament or the New Testament. There are several key verses that tell us about His unchangeableness, and also explain why we have no cause for fearfulness or anxiety. We have looked at some of them from the perspective of our worth. Now we want to see them from the perspective of there being no cause for us to be anxious.

Let us start with a profoundly significant section that we have already looked at: Matthew 6:25-35. In this portion of the Sermon on the Mount, Jesus begins with this statement: *"Therefore I tell you, do not worry about your life, what you will eat or drink, or about your body, what you will wear."* Throughout the rest of this part of Christ's discourse, He fleshes out why being anxious is unnecessary.

One of the verses we often suggest for saturation when people face difficult situations is Deuteronomy 31:8: *"The Lord is indeed going before you — He will be with you; He will not fail you or abandon you. Do not be afraid or discouraged!"*

Here is an interesting note on this verse: While Deuteronomy 31:8 appears in the 3rd person ("He"), the writer of Hebrews quotes the same passage as God's own words, put in the 1st person ("I"). In doing so, the author of Hebrews shows that the promise is more about God than about the person receiving the promise: *"Your conduct must be free from the love of money and you must be content with what you have, for He has said, 'I will never leave you and I will never abandon you.' So we can say with confidence, 'The Lord is my helper, and I will not be afraid. What can man do to me?'"* (Hebrews 13:4-6).

He ends this admonition with a quote from Psalm 118:6, another reminder that we are not in this alone and that God is "in our corner" (See also Psalm 56:8-9).

Another place where we find encouragement against fear and anxiety comes in Isaiah 41:10, in the heart of a section where God encourages His people as they look at impending disaster. He says, *"Don't be afraid, for I am with you! Don't be frightened, for I am your God! I strengthen you — yes, I help you — yes, I uphold you with my saving right hand!"*

Later on, the Apostle Peter also takes up the theme against fear and anxiety when he gives us another clear "put off/put on" statement in 1 Peter 5:6-7: *"And God will exalt you in due time, if you humble yourselves under His mighty hand by casting all your anxieties on Him because He cares for you."* Peter points to one of the reasons we hold on to our anxiety, namely because we doubt God, thinking we have to handle it all ourselves.

Finally, Paul does an excellent job of giving us perhaps the most succinct "put off/put on" prescription in Philippians 4:6-7: *"Do not be anxious about anything.* **Instead***, in every situation, through prayer and petition with thanksgiving, tell your requests to God. And the peace of God that surpasses all understanding will guard your hearts and minds in Christ Jesus."* (Emphasis added.)

Anxiousness can and needs to be evicted from our lives. There is no real merit to it. It does us no good, and it is rooted in our belief in things that are not real. It is also rooted in our distrust if God, placing greater trust in ourselves (which we already realize is pointless).

God has promised throughout His Word that He knows and will supply for our every need (that is *need*, not desire). Even when times are dark, He has gone before us, prepared the way, and is with us every step. That is true, despite anxiety's attempt to convince us otherwise.

"For God has not given us a spirit of fearfulness, but a spirit of power, of love, and of a sound mind."

— 2 Timothy 1:7, Lamb —

mariah hatfield
2020

DAILY PRACTICES	DAY 1	DAY 2	DAY 3	DAY 4	DAY 5	DAY 6	"REST" DAY
SATURATION VERSE ___	More □ / 100 □ / Less □	More □ / 100 □ / Less □	More □ / 100 □ / Less □	More □ / 100 □ / Less □	More □ / 100 □ / Less □	More □ / 100 □ / Less □	More □ / 100 □ / Less □
BIBLE READING	Chapters ___	Chapters ___	Chapters ___	Chapters ___	Chapters ___	Chapters ___	
STUDY MANUAL LESSON # ___	Read Today's Lesson Today Yes □ No □	Read Today's Lesson Today Yes □ No □	Read Today's Lesson Today Yes □ No □	Read Today's Lesson Today Yes □ No □	Read Today's Lesson Today Yes □ No □	Read Today's Lesson Today Yes □ No □	
DAILY REFLECTION	Completed Today's Lesson Today Yes □ No □	Completed Today's Lesson Today Yes □ No □	Completed Today's Lesson Today Yes □ No □	Completed Today's Lesson Today Yes □ No □	Completed Today's Lesson Today Yes □ No □	Completed Today's Lesson Today Yes □ No □	
USED "RESTORE" BOOK	Yes □ No □	Yes □ No □	Yes □ No □	Yes □ No □	Yes □ No □	Yes □ No □	Yes □ No □
PRE-MEAL SATURATION VERSE	Breakfast □ Lunch □ Dinner □	Breakfast □ Lunch □ Dinner □	Breakfast □ Lunch □ Dinner □	Breakfast □ Lunch □ Dinner □	Breakfast □ Lunch □ Dinner □	Breakfast □ Lunch □ Dinner □	Breakfast □ Lunch □ Dinner □
SPECIAL ITEMS	Yes □ No □	Yes □ No □	Yes □ No □	Yes □ No □	Yes □ No □	Yes □ No □	Yes □ No □
PRIVATE PRAYER	Time Spent ___	Time Spent ___	Time Spent ___	Time Spent ___	Time Spent ___	Time Spent ___	Time Spent ___
TODAY, I AM THANKFUL FOR...							

Lesson 8 Study Sheet

Each day review the lesson for that week.
Record one thing you are grateful for each day on your Progress Record.

This Lesson's Verse:

For God has not given us a spirit of fearfulness, but a spirit of power, of love, and of a sound mind." (2 Timothy 1:7, Lamb)

Day 1 Reflection

What have you learned from this lesson about your own tendency toward anxiety and where it comes from? What thoughts and emotions did you experience as you read the lesson? *Additional study passage: Matthew 6:25-35*

Day 2 Reflection

Explain why anxiety can so quickly and easily overtake a person's life. *Additional study passage: James 1:5-7*

Day 3 reflection

When anxiety rises up and begins to dominate a person's life, what is going on in their heart? What is the solution? *Additional study passages: Matthew 14:22-33; Philippians 4:6-7*

Day 4 Reflection

What is it that causes *you* to be anxious? What are you committed to doing in order to get free of it? *Additional study passage: 1 Peter 5:5-7*

Day 5 Reflection

Why is real and permanent change in this area of our lives not likely to happen without employing the "Two Keys" (see Goal 1) that unlock God's solutions for anxiety and doubt? *Additional study passages: Psalm 119:105-107; John 15:5*

Day 6 Reflection

Which passages from this lesson did you find the most challenging? Which did you find to be the most encouraging? How can these help you going forward? *Additional study passages: Psalm 51:1-2; Psalm 119:137-144*

For the **mind** SATURATED
with the things of the **flesh**
results in
condemnation
and death,

but the *mind* SATURATED
with the things of the
Spirit
results in
Life and Peace.

Romans 8:6 (Lamb)

LESSON NINE
WHO'S DRIVING? [14]
PART 1

We live in an emotionally-charged and emotion-driven world. Most of what we classify as "mental illness" today are actually emotional and spiritual problems. Granted, some are very severe; but the severity of a problem does not make reclassifying it valid. Despite many contributing factors to our mental or emotional distress, often the real issue is that we are trying to manage and deal with problems and emotions God never intended for us to deal with, or we attempt to deal with legitimate problems in ways that God never prescribed for us.

Given a world infected by sin, we face many things in life that God never intended for mankind to deal with when He created us. Consider the following examples:

- When God created mankind, he did not design us to have to deal with **guilt** and **shame**. Those weren't part of mankind's relationships on any level. However, once "The Rebellion" (Genesis 3) happened, guilt and shame immediately flooded the scene. That is part of why God sent Jesus Christ: to lift our guilt and shame from us and restore us to God's original intention for human life.

- God also never intended for us to carry or "manage" **anger**. That is why He warns us not to let the sun go down on the cause of our anger (Ephesians 4:26).

  (Note: This is a personal admonition for us to take our anger and work it out with God. It has nothing to do with married people staying up all night talking things through.)

- We are not designed to live in **fearfulness** or **anxiety**.

- **Lust** is another fast-burning and corrupt emotion that can become all-consuming as well. Lust is not really about sexuality, although it

---

[14] The concept for the emotional tracking graphs included with the lessons involving the "Safe Zone," as well as the "Safe Zone" idea itself, are originally found in the "SAFE Manual," by Pastor Troy Smith.

can be. Lust is "the passionate desire to fill a God-given need in an ungodly manner and/or to an ungodly degree" (our working definition). We need to learn to trust that God knows and supplies all of our needs (Matthew 6:25-34) and does so in the quantity and timing that we actually need.

These and other emotions can quickly destroy our emotional health and our spiritual balance. They spiral up into either pride and self-absorption or nose-dive us into depression and despair.

As we saw in Lesson 8 ("Evicting Anxiety"), this causes our body to try and bring us "out on top" by releasing epinephrine and other chemicals into our bloodstream. However, because the real problems and troubles are not dealt with by following God's prescription, the distorted emotions that started the process grow stronger and deepen. We find ourselves driven further down and away from the place of balance and peace with God.

The world often deals with these "Pits of Gloom" through the use of medicating chemicals and medicating behaviors to numb, mask, and escape the emotions attached to them. Things like alcohol, drugs, prescription medications, food, work, video gaming, social media, extreme sports, illicit sex, and a host of other shoddy substitutes are offered (and too often gleefully employed) to help us rise out of the "Pits of Gloom" where depression and despair lurk waiting for us.

Before long, our emotions swing between high and low like a roller-coaster. We spend most of our time either depressed, on an artificially-induced high, or oscillating up and down from one to the other. Our emotional situation can even change (and often does) many times throughout any given day.

This sort of ongoing (and increasing) emotional instability makes it harder and harder for us to live a healthy, abundant life, and our relationships deteriorate—especially our relationship with God. The most miserable people in the world are the ones who live life based on their emotions.

Anchor Point: The key to gaining and maintaining emotional stability is the understanding that, <u>although real</u>, emotions simply are <u>not the truth</u>.

Even though our emotions may be *based* on the truth, they themselves are *not* the truth. Feelings change — facts do not. The Truth plays no favorites and it picks on no one; it simply "shows up" and is *true*.

Emotions are not bad or wrong in and of themselves. Rather, it is what we *do* with our emotions that will be either right or wrong, good or bad. Since the truth has no emotional content to it, we do not "feel" the truth, but we do feel our emotions. That is why we usually pay far more attention to what we "feel" than to what is true.

We have to choose: either our emotions will control us and determine the path of our lives, or we will get our emotions under control and allow reason, based on the Truth, to guide and direct us (remember the word-picture of the drunk behind the wheel of the school bus?).

God and His Word have the only viable plan for overcoming the tyranny of unruly emotions. We must surrender ourselves to Christ and saturate our minds with the truths in God's Word. We must bring our thoughts into submission to those truths. Then, we must put off the old wrong beliefs and behaviors and put on the new right beliefs and behaviors. In doing so, we experience further freedom (further "unbinding") from the death and decay of the past.

Now, before we can address our emotions through surrender and saturation, we need to understand the differences between being emotionally balanced and emotionally volatile; between being of a "sound" mind and heart, and being of an "unsound" mind and heart:

Features of Emotional Volatility

1) Not allowing reason and rationality to drive, but instead being controlled by our emotions. We may *know* what is best, but we find ourselves surrendering to our emotions in the moment and doing what is foolish and destructive instead;

2) Much of our time is spent in those Pits of Gloom. We persistently and relentlessly seek a way to lift ourselves out of those Pits. We focus much of our thoughts and energy on producing the high times;

3) We relegate decision-making and important conversations to those

times when we are either emotionally high or low. We don't seem to make a decision unless we are emboldened by self-exaltation or driven by low desperation. We base our decisions on how we feel instead of what is truly wise.

The diagram below can help us see the relationship between what our emotions are doing and the state of our mind.[15]

Emotionally high and based on ultra-optimism.

Proud, arrogant, grandiose beliefs and boastfulness.

EMOTIONALLY HIGH

Thinking, feeling, believing all in balance.

SAFE ZONE
Faith & Trust in God and His Truth-Claims

Calm, confident peace.

EMOTIONALLY LOW

Emotionally low and based on ultra-pessimism.

Depressed, bitter, often self-loathing. Feeling rejectable and worthy of the worst.

When our emotions are in the driver's seat, we spend most of our lives in the upper or lower zones of our emotional range. When we are too high or too low, rationality and reason are absent. Our decisions are poor and ineffective.

On the high side, the higher we go, the greater our expectations. We can easily become puffed-up and prideful. Everything revolves around us. Others are simply visitors in our universe.

On the low side, we can rapidly sink into the "Pits of Gloom," resulting in depression and bitterness. We see few or no solutions. We have little if any hope. We feel helpless. We feel

---

[15] Credit again goes to Pastor Troy Smith for the basic framework for the diagraming in this lesson.

abandoned and alone. Too long here, and we can become convinced that we are totally worthless and useless. Here is where people often get to the point where they believe that the best solution is to "end it all."

We can only make the best decisions when we are emotionally stable and in our "Safe Zone"; that place where our thoughts, emotions, and spiritual connection to God are balanced and steady. It is that stability, founded on the truth as God has proclaimed it to be, that we need to set as our daily objective. This is what the Bible means by "contentment."

Features of Emotional Stability:

1) **It is where our decision-making is best and most in keeping with God's truth and His will.** This is one reason why Moses conveyed God's promise to Joshua that, in spite of the 5½ years of warfare he faced, Joshua had no reason to fear or to become discouraged (Deuteronomy 31:8). It is why Jesus promised that, yoked together with Him, the burden would be light and the load easier to bear (Matthew 11:28-30). It is also why Jesus told His disciples that, even though He would leave and they were to carry on without Him, He nonetheless promised a peace that was unusual and exceptional compared to the world's idea of peace (John 14:27).

2) **When we are emotionally stable, we can think things through and *respond* instead of *reacting*.** Too many times people let their emotions control them. God loves giving us wisdom (read that: a sound mind), but it does not come unless we are emotionally stable. Read carefully James 1:5-8. The promise here for wisdom from God only comes when we are single-minded (sound-minded) and emotionally stable.

3) **It is the quality God is looking for in His leaders.** In fact, it is a quality any person must have to be a good leader. We find the character qualities God mandates for those who lead others in His body in 1 Timothy 3:1-13. It seems evident that what is described here is the fruit of life for a person who is content and emotionally stable.

Keys to Being Stable:

1) **Commit to never making ANY major decision or having any important conversation when you are not in your "Safe Zone."**

 THIS IS A CRITICAL RULE AND AN ANCHOR POINT TO KEEP HANDY AND COMMIT TO FOLLOWING!

In other words, be quiet and sit still when you are not in your Safe Zone. Learn to recognize your own patterns and warning signs that you are either about to go, or are already, out of your "Safe Zone." Be aware of and alert to the actions and attitudes that show you are in "un-safe" territory.

2) **Desire and pursue God's peace that comes from having a sound mind instead of the selfish and artificial offerings of the world's solutions.** This starts with us choosing to make this a daily focus. Once we have done that, we need to make it a key value of our life. (Remember that key values are the things about which we say, "Nothing is more important to me than...".)

3) **Do what you must to get surrendered to God and His truth as soon as you recognize that you are out of your Safe Zone.** Get and stay surrendered and saturating. He will bring you back to the place of safety, peace, and a sound mind (1 Peter 5:10).

PROUD. ARROGANT. I'M INDESTRUCTIBLE. I'M UNDEFEATABLE. WISDOM NOT NEEDED.

BALANCE

PEACE

SAFE ZONE

WISDOM

HOPE

Faith & Trust in God and His Truth-Claims

LOVE

SELF-LOATHING. I'M WORTHLESS. I'M AS BAD AS BAD CAN BE. I'M UNNECESSARY.

The "Safe Zone" is the place where we are mentally, emotionally, and spiritually balanced; where we have a sense of God's peace and presence. It is not a flat and rigid place, but there is a calm and confident sense of balance no

130

matter the circumstances. That is not to say that we do not feel the stresses and strains of life's difficulties, nor that we can't be proud of a job well done. It simply means that we find we are in our Safe Zone when, driven by God's truth, we arrive at "all things in balance."

The more we live in the "Safe Zone" (or return to it once we have moved out of it), the more others learn they can trust us. When people learn they can trust us, our relationships become healthier for all involved, and our life is much more God-honoring.

Using the Tracking Graphs

There is a "Daily Emotions Tracking Graph" for you to make copies of and use every day for however long you work through this lesson. In the next lesson, there is a "Weekly Emotions Tracking Graph." It will help you gain a broader picture of your patterns over the course of the entire week. If your pattern this week is marked by frequent and dramatic changes you will want to use a "Daily Graph" for each day of next Lesson as well.

You will find a *SAMPLE* on the next page to give you an idea of how to use the graph. Following the *SAMPLE* page, you will find an actual graph for you to copy and use.

80 • 03

DAILY EMOTIONS TRACKING GRAPH

Morning		Mid-Day		Evening		Late

GOT READY ON TIME

LOTTERY TICKET WORTH $1000

Above this   line we are   prideful

FIRST PART OF DAY, ALL WENT WELL.

SAFE ZONE

NEEDS ARE MET—I'M OKAY.

WOKE UP RESTED

Below this   line is a   sense of   hopeless ness

CAR WOULDN'T START FOR A WHILE.

2-YEAR PROJECT DROPPED BY BOSS.

LOST THE TICKET!

DAILY EMOTIONS TRACKING GRAPH

Morning		Mid-Day		Evening		Late

Above this line we are prideful

- -

S   A   F   E

- -

Below this line, we battle worthlessness

MAKE AS MANY COPIES AS YOU NEED

DAILY PRACTICES	DAY 1	DAY 2	DAY 3	DAY 4	DAY 5	DAY 6	"REST" DAY
SATURATION VERSE ____	More □ 100 □ Less □	More □ 100 □ Less □	More □ 100 □ Less □	More □ 100 □ Less □	More □ 100 □ Less □	More □ 100 □ Less □	More □ 100 □ Less □
BIBLE READING	Chapters ____	Chapters ____	Chapters ____	Chapters ____	Chapters ____	Chapters ____	
STUDY MANUAL LESSON # ____	Read Today's Lesson Today Yes □ No □	Read Today's Lesson Today Yes □ No □	Read Today's Lesson Today Yes □ No □	Read Today's Lesson Today Yes □ No □	Read Today's Lesson Today Yes □ No □	Read Today's Lesson Today Yes □ No □	
DAILY REFLECTION	Completed Today's Lesson Today Yes □ No □	Completed Today's Lesson Today Yes □ No □	Completed Today's Lesson Today Yes □ No □	Completed Today's Lesson Today Yes □ No □	Completed Today's Lesson Today Yes □ No □	Completed Today's Lesson Today Yes □ No □	
USED "RESTORE" BOOK	Yes □ No □	Yes □ No □	Yes □ No □	Yes □ No □	Yes □ No □	Yes □ No □	Yes □ No □
PRE-MEAL SATURATION VERSE	Breakfast □ Lunch □ Dinner □	Breakfast □ Lunch □ Dinner □	Breakfast □ Lunch □ Dinner □	Breakfast □ Lunch □ Dinner □	Breakfast □ Lunch □ Dinner □	Breakfast □ Lunch □ Dinner □	Breakfast □ Lunch □ Dinner □
SPECIAL ITEMS	Yes □ No □	Yes □ No □	Yes □ No □	Yes □ No □	Yes □ No □	Yes □ No □	Yes □ No □
PRIVATE PRAYER	Time Spent ____	Time Spent ____	Time Spent ____	Time Spent ____	Time Spent ____	Time Spent ____	Time Spent ____
TODAY, I AM THANKFUL FOR...							

Lesson 9 Study Sheet

Each day review the lesson for that week.
Record one thing you are grateful for each day on your Progress Record.

This Lesson's Verse:

"For the mind saturated with the things of the flesh results in condemnation and death, but the mind saturated with the things of the Spirit results in life and peace." (Romans 8:6, Lamb)

Day 1 Reflection

When do you find yourself normally making decisions: When you are emotionally frazzled, when you are emotionally elated, or when you are balanced and calm? *Additional study passage: James 3:13-18*

Day 2 Reflection

Can you remember making a *wise* decision while you were excessively emotionally high or while you were emotionally depressed? Can you remember making an *unwise* decision under either of those conditions? Explain. *Additional study passage: 1 Samuel 12:21*

Day 3 Reflection

Why would it be foolish to make important decisions or have important conversations when we are emotionally too high or too low? *Additional study passage: Psalm 25*

Day 4 Reflection

What are some of the conditions in life and society that can easily create unstable emotions for you? *Additional study passages: Romans 1:18-32; Galatians 5:19-21*

Day 5 Reflection

Considering what you know about the nature of God so far, why would stable emotions and a sound mind be important for having a close relationship with Him? *Additional study passage: Job 28:12-28*

Day 6 Reflection

Share your thoughts on why a "Safe Zone" life would be a benefit in improving your relationships with the people in *your* life. *Additional study passage: Romans 12:9-21*

YOU

will keep in

perfect peace

and safety,

those who maintain their *faith*,
because they *trust* in

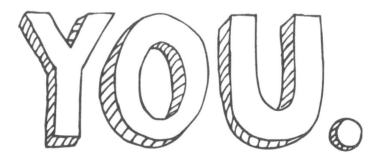

YOU.

Isaiah 26:3 (Lamb)

LESSON TEN
WHO'S DRIVING?
PART 2

As we have seen, there are any number of situations and circumstances that can "trigger" an emotional reaction from us. Hopefully, by going through the last lesson's exercise you discovered some of what tends to "trigger" you.

Our purpose now is to learn how to make our emotions take a backseat instead of being in the driver's seat. Identifying the things that puncture our emotional stability and set it off balance is the first step to identifying the things that trigger our self-destructive patterns (Lesson 11). Replacing the self-destructive patterns with wise and healthy ones will be our next undertaking (Lesson 12).

For Lesson 10, we are going to revisit much of the last lesson. The more we saturate with truth, the more we understand and believe it, and the more we live our lives based on what is true. This second look at our "Safe Zone" concept will allow you the chance to observe yourself not only hour-by-hour, but also daily, across the scope of a whole week.

Given a world infected by sin, we face many things in life that God never intended for mankind to deal with when He created us. Consider the following examples:

- When God created mankind, he did not design us to have to deal with **guilt** and **shame**. Those were not part of mankind's relationships on any level. However, once "The Rebellion" (Genesis 3) happened, guilt and shame immediately flooded the scene. That is part of why God sent Jesus Christ: to lift our guilt and shame from us and restore us to God's original intention for human life.

- God also never intended for us to carry or "manage" **anger**. That is why He warns us not to let the sun go down on the cause of our anger (Ephesians 4:26).

(Note: This is a personal admonition for us to take our anger and work it out with God. It has nothing to do with married people staying up all night talking things through.)

- We are not designed to live in **fearfulness** or **anxiety**.

- **Lust** is another fast-burning and corrupt emotion that can become all-consuming as well. Lust isn't really about sexuality, although it can be. Lust is "the passionate desire to fill a God-given need in an ungodly manner and/or to an ungodly degree" (our working definition). We need to learn to trust that God knows and supplies all of our needs (Matthew 6:25-34) and does so in the quantity and timing that we actually need.

These and other emotions can quickly destroy our emotional health and our spiritual balance. They spiral up into either pride and self-absorption or nose-dive us into depression and despair.

As we saw in Lesson 8 ("Evicting Anxiety"), this causes our body to try and bring us "out on top" by releasing epinephrine and other chemicals into our bloodstream. However, because the real problems and troubles are not dealt with by following God's prescription, the distorted emotions that started the process grow stronger and deepen. We find ourselves driven further down and away from the place of balance and peace with God.

The world deals with these "Pits of Gloom" through the use of medicating chemicals and medicating behaviors to numb, mask, and escape the emotions attached to them. Things like alcohol, drugs, prescription medications, food, work, video gaming, social media, extreme sports, illicit sex, and a host of other shoddy substitutes are offered (and too often gleefully employed) to help us rise out of the "Pits of Gloom" where depression and despair lurk waiting for us. Before long, our emotions swing between high and low like a roller coaster. We spend most of our time either depressed, on an artificially-induced high, or oscillating up and down from one to the other. Our emotional situation can even change (and often does) many times throughout any given day.

This sort of ongoing (and increasing) emotional instability makes it harder and harder for us to live a healthy, abundant life, and our relationships deteriorate—especially our relationship with God. The most miserable people in the world are the ones who live life based on their emotions.

> **Anchor Point:** Key to gaining and maintaining emotional stability is the understanding that, <u>although real</u>, emotions simply are <u>not the truth</u>.

Even though our emotions may be *based* on the truth, they themselves are *not* the truth. Feelings change — facts do not. The Truth plays no favorites and it picks on no one; it simply "shows up" and is *true*.

Emotions are not bad or wrong in and of themselves. Rather, it is what we *do* with our emotions that will be either right or wrong, good or bad. We don't "feel" the truth, but we do feel our emotions. That is why we usually pay far more attention to what we "feel" than to what is true. We have to choose: either our emotions will control us and determine the path of our lives, or we will get our emotions under control and allow reason, based on the Truth, to guide and direct us (remember the word-picture of the drunk behind the wheel of the school bus?).

God and His Word have the only viable plan for overcoming the tyranny of unruly emotions. We must surrender ourselves to Christ and saturate our minds with the truths in God's Word. We must bring our thoughts into submission to those truths. Then, we must put off the old wrong beliefs and behaviors and put on the new right beliefs and behaviors. In doing so, we experience further freedom (further "unbinding") from the death and decay of the past.

COMMIT TO NEVER MAKING ANY MAJOR DECISION OR HAVING ANY IMPORTANT CONVERSATION WHEN YOU ARE NOT IN YOUR "SAFE ZONE."

<u>THIS IS A CRITICAL RULE AND AN **ANCHOR POINT** TO KEEP HANDY AND COMMIT TO FOLLOWING!</u>

In other words, <u>be quiet and sit still</u> when you are not in your Safe Zone! Learn to recognize your own patterns and warning signs that you are either about to go, or are already, out of your "Safe Zone." Be aware of and alert to the actions and attitudes that show you that you are in "un-safe" territory.

The more we live in the "Safe Zone" (or return to it once we've moved out of it), the more others learn they can trust us. When people learn they can trust us, our relationships become healthier for all involved, and our life is much more God-honoring.

For this lesson, unless your Daily Emotional Tracking Graphs from Lesson 9 look like a major earthquake on a seismic graph (rapid oscillations between high and low with little or no time in the Safe Zone), track your entire week on a single graph page (see next two pages). If your graphs from Lesson 9 show a great deal of emotional activity, then continue using the Daily Graph, along with the Weekly Emotions Tracking Graph (see below), for this for this lesson as well.

80 • 03

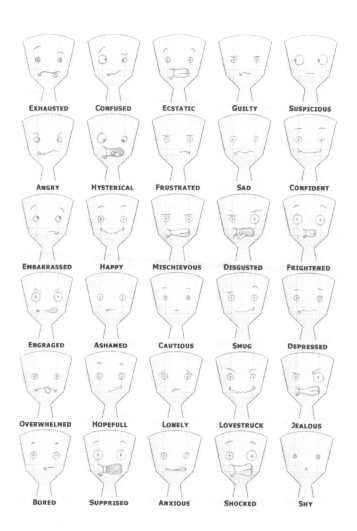

NOTES

WEEKLY EMOTIONS TRACKING GRAPH

Sunday	Monday	Tuesday	Wednesday	Thursday	Friday	Saturday
	BEAT JOE TO WORK				**PAY RAISE !!**	
		Above this	line we are	prideful		
				ALMOST AS GOOD A DAY		
GREAT DAY WITH THE FAMILY			**SATURATED ALL DAY**			**SLEPT IN, FELT RESTED ALL DAY**
	Below this	line is a	sense of	hopeless ness		
	FLAT TIRE: LATE GETTING HOME	**LOUSY DAY**				

SAFE ZONE

WEEKLY EMOTIONS TRACKING GRAPH

Sunday	Monday	Tuesday	Wed.	Thursday	Friday	Saturday

Above this line we are prideful

S A F E

Below this line, we battle worthlessness

DAILY PRACTICES	DAY 1	DAY 2	DAY 3	DAY 4	DAY 5	DAY 6	"REST" DAY
SATURATION VERSE	More ☐ 100 ☐ Less ☐ ___	More ☐ 100 ☐ Less ☐	More ☐ 100 ☐ Less ☐	More ☐ 100 ☐ Less ☐	More ☐ 100 ☐ Less ☐	More ☐ 100 ☐ Less ☐	More ☐ 100 ☐ Less ☐
BIBLE READING	Chapters ___ ___	Chapters ___ ___	Chapters ___ ___	Chapters ___ ___	Chapters ___ ___	Chapters ___ ___	
STUDY MANUAL LESSON # ___	Read Today's Lesson Today Yes ☐ No ☐	Read Today's Lesson Today Yes ☐ No ☐	Read Today's Lesson Today Yes ☐ No ☐	Read Today's Lesson Today Yes ☐ No ☐	Read Today's Lesson Today Yes ☐ No ☐	Read Today's Lesson Today Yes ☐ No ☐	
DAILY REFLECTION	Completed Today's Lesson Today Yes ☐ No ☐	Completed Today's Lesson Today Yes ☐ No ☐	Completed Today's Lesson Today Yes ☐ No ☐	Completed Today's Lesson Today Yes ☐ No ☐	Completed Today's Lesson Today Yes ☐ No ☐	Completed Today's Lesson Today Yes ☐ No ☐	
USED "RESTORE" BOOK	Yes ☐ No ☐	Yes ☐ No ☐	Yes ☐ No ☐	Yes ☐ No ☐	Yes ☐ No ☐	Yes ☐ No ☐	Yes ☐ No ☐
PRE-MEAL SATURATION VERSE	Breakfast ☐ Lunch ☐ Dinner ☐	Breakfast ☐ Lunch ☐ Dinner ☐	Breakfast ☐ Lunch ☐ Dinner ☐	Breakfast ☐ Lunch ☐ Dinner ☐	Breakfast ☐ Lunch ☐ Dinner ☐	Breakfast ☐ Lunch ☐ Dinner ☐	Breakfast ☐ Lunch ☐ Dinner ☐
SPECIAL ITEMS	Yes ☐ No ☐	Yes ☐ No ☐	Yes ☐ No ☐	Yes ☐ No ☐	Yes ☐ No ☐	Yes ☐ No ☐	Yes ☐ No ☐
PRIVATE PRAYER	Time Spent ___	Time Spent	Time Spent	Time Spent	Time Spent	Time Spent	Time Spent ___
TODAY, I AM THANKFUL FOR...							

This Lesson's Verse:

"You will keep in perfect peace and safety those who maintain their faith, because they trust in You." (Isaiah 26:3, Lamb)

Day 1 Reflection

What, if any, common thread have you found running through the things that drive you out of the "Safe Zone" - either up or down? What are your thoughts on that? *Additional study passages: James 1:5-6; Jeremiah 17:7-9*

Day 2 Reflection

What passages of Scripture did you find (both in the last lesson and this one) that helped you get back into your Safe Zone; that place where you are mentally, emotionally, and spiritually balanced? *Additional study passages: Psalm 9:10; 28:7*

Day 3 Reflection

When making important decisions or having important conversations, why do you think it is best to do so only when you are in your Safe Zone? *Additional study passage: Psalm 131:1-2*

Day 4 Reflection

What are some of the things you struggle with the most and that drive you most easily out of your Safe Zone? *Additional study passages: Psalm 30:1-5; Isaiah 30:15*

Day 5 Reflection

Considering what you know about the nature of God, why would it be so easy sometimes to forget what you know and surrender to the emotional triggers? *Additional study passage: Job 8:11-14*

Day 6 Reflection

Share about the benefits you hope to find as a result of mastering living in the Safe Zone as much as possible. *Additional study passages: Psalm 37:37; 2 Corinthians 13:11*

For those who live according to **the flesh** have their OUTLOOK shaped **by the things of the flesh,** but those who live according to *the Spirit* have their OUTLOOK shaped *by the things of the Spirit.*

Romans 8:5 (NASB)

LESSON ELEVEN
RENEWING THE MIND
PART 1 - PUT OFF

Imagine that your mind and heart are like one of those orange buckets from Home Depot.

Next picture that bucket full of the thickest, gooiest, stinkiest black sludge you can imagine. This sludge is the lies you have saturated on throughout your life and have come to believe are true. It is the evil you have suffered because of the sin choices of others. It is the guilt and shame you still carry from sins you have committed and have not been able to get straightened out between you and God somehow. It is the false guilt and toxic shame that come from thinking it is your fault someone did evil things to you.

Now, picture taking a garden hose and sticking the open end into that bucket and then turning the spigot on part way. What do you think is going to happen to the guck in the bucket? *Exactly!* The water is going to start working on that sludge, at first making it bubble over (probably making a mess for a while), and then starting to thin it out more and more as the water keeps running into the bucket.

See it? Crystal-clear running water...sludge getting thinner, and thinner, and thinner, until — eventually — the cool, clean water replaces all of the sludge. The bucket may be stained, but the sludge is *gone!*

The water coming out of the hose is the Word of God. As we saturate on God's Word, we are "washing with the water of the Word," as described in John 15:3 and Ephesians 5:26. As we saturate our minds with the truth as God has defined it, the lies are replaced, our minds are renewed, and we experience transformation. Our part is the renewing-the-mind part. God's part is the transforming part. This is the PERFECT partnership — and an excellent example of what it means to be yoked together with Christ (Matthew 11:28-30).

God has long taught His people that one of the most important roles parents play in the lives of children, from the moment of their birth, is to saturate their days with His truth (Deuteronomy 6:4-9; Ephesians 6:4). This is the best way for an understanding of, belief in, and love for

151

God and His truth to be experienced — the younger, the better. For those who did not have this experience, or who instead experienced lies packaged as truth-claims poured into their hearts and minds, it is still never too late.

As Jesus taught us in John 8:31-32, as we saturate with and abide in His Word, we will truly be His followers. We will know the truth, and the truth will set us free. And, if He sets us free, we are absolutely free (John 8:36)!

Remember these **Anchor Points**:
- What we focus on is what we hit;
- What we focus on is what we are saturating on;
- What we saturate on is what we believe;
- What we believe is what we live.

In order to understand how we can renew our minds, we need to keep in mind how our minds function. We learned in earlier lessons that only about 10% or less of our decision-making is "conscious" (intentionally thinking things through), while 90% or more is unconscious or subconscious (remember that we use this term in a general, not a psychoanalytical way).

Information passes through our senses, gets processed by our mind, and then is stored in other parts of our mind that are not always "ready-recall." Some of it is engrafted into our hearts and our souls and becomes our belief system. This occurs, often without our realizing it, because saturation bypasses the logical, thinking part of our minds and

goes right to the core of our being (Note: This is also why saturation works faster and more effectively than memorization does).

As an example, picture a sponge and a bucket of red paint. If you want to saturate the sponge with red paint, do you scoop red paint out of the bucket and pour it onto the sponge, or do you plunge the sponge down into the paint and start squeezing out the air in every little pocket?

Of course, to saturate the sponge you want to plunge it deep into the paint and completely soak paint into every pore and crevice. When you've done that, what happens to anything that you set the sponge on? It gets red paint on it, right? And what happens if you bump or squeeze (put the pressure on) the sponge? Red paint comes out of it — because it is FULL of it, SATURATED with it!

This is the effect that saturating with Scripture has on your life. What we are fullest of is what comes out of us (see Mark 7:20-23 — and keep in mind that the way we use "subconscious" is what the Bible means by "heart"). When the pressure is on (when we are squeezed), what our hearts hold dearest is what flows from us.

We remember best what has happened most recently, those things we are emotionally invested in, and those things we think about most often. If our thoughts are unhealthy or shameful, our minds and hearts become saturated with trash and garbage.

This saturation in turn affects everything we do, flavoring every relationship — including our relationship with ourselves. If our thoughts are on how wonderful and flawless we are, our hearts are filled with pride and we are unteachable, unapproachable, and of little use to anyone — especially God. The same will be true from a different angle if our heart and mind are filled with fearfulness, unforgiveness, anxiety, and doubt. But what if instead of such thoughts, our minds and hearts are filled with love, trust, truth, and confidence in God? Then, our whole life becomes filled with these things instead (what we focus on is what we hit).

Once our heart and mind have become saturated with unhealthy thoughts, we form self-destructive patterns of dealing with the emotions that arise from this thinking. These cycles we refer to as **SDBC's** (Self-Destructive Bondage Cycles[16]).

Once these cycles are firmly in place in our mind and heart, they are very difficult to break because they are emotion-driven (Lesson 3). And, since we remember best what we are most emotionally invested in, these patterns become second-nature to us. Once your SDBC gets started, your emotions will kick in, compelling you to follow through to your usual end — that place where you say, "Here I am again...why do I always end up here?"

Keep in mind that when working to break free of these destructive cycles, the earlier we recognize the pattern, the

---

16 Modified from the "Subconscious Self-Destruct Cycle" (Week 7: Renewing the Mind), S.A.F.E. Program (Pastor Troy Smith, 1990)

earlier we put-off the pattern, putting on instead a healthy pattern in its place (which we will discuss further in Lesson 12). This practice of "pattern replacement" means that we steadily move toward operating in the realm of truth and freedom.

The Emotional Tracking Graphs from previous lessons are where you want to look for your "triggers." These are most often the kinds of incidents and conversations that consistently get our SDBC started.

In this Lesson we are concentrating on the "Put Off" aspect of Renewing the Mind. Next Lesson we will concentrate on the "Put On" aspect of Renewing the Mind. We call these **RMC's** (Renewed Mind Cycles). Good news: eventually, with repetition and practice, the SDBC's will be completely bypassed and we end up in the RMC almost right away...the unbinding and setting free is so close we can taste it!

At the end of this lesson there are two examples of these destructive cycles. You ought to be able to map out your own SDBC's using these as a guide. Your cycles will probably look different, so do not expect yours to be identical to the examples shown. Following the examples page, you will find a blank version for you to copy and use.

Start with one or two of the most common SDBC's you currently find yourself falling into. These are the root of your "besetting sin" patterns and what brought you here in the first place.

☜ • ☞

NOTES

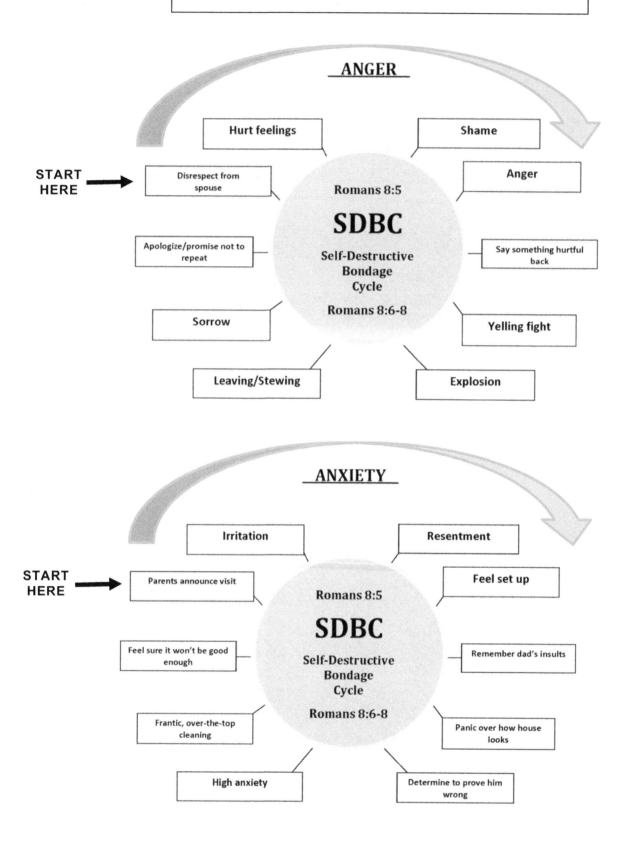

Here are some samples to work from. These are only examples. Your patterns will look different.

ANGER

Hurt feelings

Shame

START HERE →

Disrespect from spouse

Anger

Romans 8:5

SDBC

Self-Destructive Bondage Cycle

Romans 8:6-8

Say something hurtful back

Apologize/promise not to repeat

Sorrow

Yelling fight

Leaving/Stewing

Explosion

ANXIETY

Irritation

Resentment

START HERE →

Parents announce visit

Feel set up

Romans 8:5

SDBC

Self-Destructive Bondage Cycle

Romans 8:6-8

Remember dad's insults

Feel sure it won't be good enough

Panic over how house looks

Frantic, over-the-top cleaning

High anxiety

Determine to prove him wrong

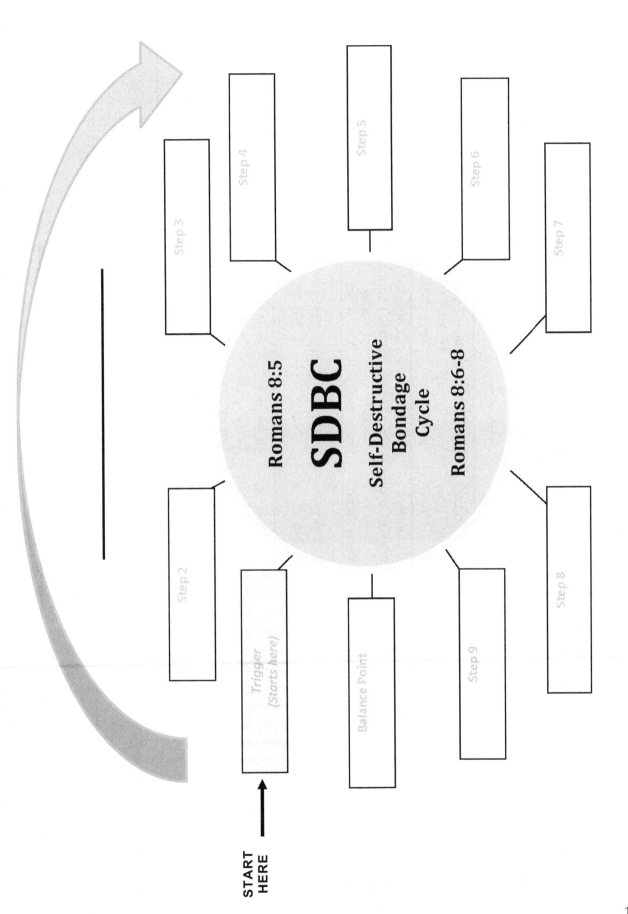

START
HERE

157

DAILY PRACTICES	DAY 1	DAY 2	DAY 3	DAY 4	DAY 5	DAY 6	"REST" DAY
SATURATION VERSE ___	More ☐ 100 ☐ Less ☐	More ☐ 100 ☐ Less ☐	More ☐ 100 ☐ Less ☐	More ☐ 100 ☐ Less ☐	More ☐ 100 ☐ Less ☐	More ☐ 100 ☐ Less ☐	More ☐ 100 ☐ Less ☐
BIBLE READING	Chapters ___ ___	Chapters ___ ___	Chapters ___ ___	Chapters ___ ___	Chapters ___ ___	Chapters ___ ___	
STUDY MANUAL LESSON # ___	Read Today's Lesson Today Yes ☐ No ☐	Read Today's Lesson Today Yes ☐ No ☐	Read Today's Lesson Today Yes ☐ No ☐	Read Today's Lesson Today Yes ☐ No ☐	Read Today's Lesson Today Yes ☐ No ☐	Read Today's Lesson Today Yes ☐ No ☐	
DAILY REFLECTION	Completed Today's Lesson Today Yes ☐ No ☐	Completed Today's Lesson Today Yes ☐ No ☐	Completed Today's Lesson Today Yes ☐ No ☐	Completed Today's Lesson Today Yes ☐ No ☐	Completed Today's Lesson Today Yes ☐ No ☐	Completed Today's Lesson Today Yes ☐ No ☐	
USED "RESTORE" BOOK	Yes ☐ No ☐	Yes ☐ No ☐	Yes ☐ No ☐	Yes ☐ No ☐	Yes ☐ No ☐	Yes ☐ No ☐	Yes ☐ No ☐
PRE-MEAL SATURATION VERSE	Breakfast ☐ Lunch ☐ Dinner ☐	Breakfast ☐ Lunch ☐ Dinner ☐	Breakfast ☐ Lunch ☐ Dinner ☐	Breakfast ☐ Lunch ☐ Dinner ☐	Breakfast ☐ Lunch ☐ Dinner ☐	Breakfast ☐ Lunch ☐ Dinner ☐	Breakfast ☐ Lunch ☐ Dinner ☐
SPECIAL ITEMS	Yes ☐ No ☐	Yes ☐ No ☐	Yes ☐ No ☐	Yes ☐ No ☐	Yes ☐ No ☐	Yes ☐ No ☐	Yes ☐ No ☐
PRIVATE PRAYER	Time Spent ___	Time Spent ___	Time Spent ___	Time Spent ___	Time Spent ___	Time Spent ___	Time Spent ___
TODAY, I AM THANKFUL FOR...							

This Lesson's Verse:

"For those who live according to the flesh have their outlook shaped by the things of the flesh, but those who live according to the Spirit have their outlook shaped by the things of the Spirit. (Romans 8:5)

Day 1 Reflection

When you consider your "mental diet," what are the good and bad effects of what you are putting into your mind? What do you think the long-term effects are going to be on your life? *Additional study passage: Matthew 15:18-20*

Day 2 Reflection

What are some positive decisions and steps you can make to improve your "mental diet?" *Additional study passages: Philippians 4:8; Colossians 3:1-2*

159

Day 3 Reflection

At the end of the day, how much do you tend to dwell on reviewing the wrongs others have committed against you? How much do you dwell on your own "failings" of the day? *Additional study passage: Psalm 4:8*

Day 4 Reflection

When you think of your earliest childhood memory, what do you experience? What impact has it had on you over the years, and what impact does it have in your life now? *Additional study passage: Deuteronomy 5:9-10; 29*

Day 5 Reflection

As you learn to identify and surrender (put off) the old ways of thinking and behaving, what do you think you need to have and do that will help you to replace (put on) those with what God's best is for your life? *Additional study passage: 2 Peter 1:2-8*

Day 6 Reflection

How do you think you are doing at gaining control of your thinking and your emotions? What tools are helping the most? What are the strongest skills you find yourself developing? *Additional study passage: Psalm 1*

OUR BATTLE IS TO

bring down EVERY
deceptive imagining
and EVERY prideful argument
erected against

THE TRUE KNOWLEDGE OF GOD.

WE FIGHT TO

trap EVERY thought
and cause it to SURRENDER

TO THE AUTHORITY OF CHRIST.

2 Corinthians 10:4b-5 (Lamb)

LESSON TWELVE
RENEWING THE MIND
PART 2 — PUT ON

Now that we have mapped out the "here-I-am-again" negative patterns of thinking/believing/feeling/behaving, it is time to put those OFF and put ON the healthy/godly/righteous patterns. This is where **The RMC** (Renewed Mind Cycle) comes into play. We want to put ON God's truth, in God's Word, with the help of a Renewed Mind Cycle.

As soon as you recognize that you are in one of your SDBC's, use that recognition to immediately "trigger" a jump; a jump from the SDBC to an RMC.

What we find is that, over time, as a person begins to recognize their SDBC earlier and earlier, and trigger the RMC earlier and earlier, eventually, what would normally trigger the SDBC becomes the trigger for the RMC!

THE ANSWER TO BREAKING THE PATTERNS IS TO "PUT OFF/PUT ON"

We need to employ the Biblical principle of "put off/put on" (Ephesians 4:22-24)

1. We do this first by <u>taking our thoughts captive</u> and bringing them into surrender to the truth;
2. Then we break the old patterns and replace them with new ones by using <u>the RMC</u>: "put off/put on."

I.   TAKING OUR THOUGHTS CAPTIVE

We have talked several times already about how easy it is for things to become buried in our heart and mind, and for us to become entombed in the wreckage of our past. We remember best things, people, or events to which we are most emotionally connected. Sometimes that connection depends on time. Our memory is often clearer on what happened yesterday than what happened last year. For instance, while we may well remember a conversation with our boss from a month ago, we may remember very little of what happened in our early childhood. In this sense, time and distance are the "Great Eroders."

But it is not always true that we remember best that which is closest to the present. Consider how, on occasion, we may have pretty clear recollections about a significant event in our past but can't remember the conversation we had with our spouse twenty minutes ago. The point is simply this: Memory often ties with emotion. We remember best that to which we are most emotionally connected.

Knowing that we remember best things, people, and events we are most emotionally connected to will help us when old and hurtful memories surface. There are those who teach that some memories need to be buried and left behind; that we can bury memories simply by refusing to think about or dwell on them. This is not really true. Why? Because you cannot bury a live snake. There is legitimate emotional content to the things we have experienced. To deny the truth of what happened and the effect on us is to live a lie — and living a lie is never welcome in God's kingdom, nor is it part of His prescription for our life.

Instead, when a hurtful memory surfaces, we face it full on, take it before the Lord, and pour out our heart to Him in full emotional authenticity (Philippians 4:6-7). We walk *through* the pain, knowing we are not alone and that we are walking right beside Him (See Psalm 23:6; Isaiah 9:2; Matthew 11:28-30).

As we do this, we remind ourselves, "That was then; this is now. 'Then' is gone, and I do not have to go through or 'relive' that anymore." We take our thoughts captive, bring them into submission to the Truth (2 Corinthians 10:5), and focus on renewing our minds by resting in the list of "have's" in Philippians 4:8.

If we are to be successful in changing our life, we must change what we think about, how we think about it, and who we choose to believe.

IN ORDER TO RENEW OUR MIND, THERE ARE TWO THINGS WE MUST DO:

A. _We must deal with destructive thoughts and emotions as soon as we become aware of them._ These often have become buried deep within our heart and mind so that their effect is both unpredictable and difficult to control. We need to learn to take these thoughts captive, replacing the thoughts with God's truth about them and about ourselves. We must also train our minds to refuse to dwell on unhealthy thoughts and memories.

B. _We must fill our mind with those things taught to us in God's Word._ We must replace unwanted thoughts with God's Word and the values and principles we find there. The Unbound Program has been designed and crafted to help with this quite specifically.

II. BREAKING DESTRUCTIVE PATTERNS AND DEVELOPING NEW — THE "RMC"

A. _We must break old cycles at the earliest possible point._ The best and easiest time to transpose an old pattern of behavior into a new one is before we become very emotionally engaged. We can't really control the things that trigger an SDBC, but we can control the way we deal with one.

We must learn to immediately take our thoughts captive, surrender them to the truth, refocus our attention on the Lord, and set out on a new pattern of thinking and behaving. Jesus is the Truth in the flesh, and He is the source of true peace and of a sound mind. Once we get our emotions under control, we can then start to use the principles that apply to wise and effective problem-solving (Lesson 16).

B. _We do this by shifting our thoughts and emotions to an "RMC," a "Renewed Mind Cycle."_

The RMC follows this path:

1. Take my thoughts captive and bring them into submission to what the Word of God says about them (2 Corinthians 10:5);

2. Agree with God as to my sinful thinking and believing, and as to any resulting behavior (1 John 1:9);

3. Agree with God that I am no longer a slave to sin and do not have to follow the path of sin (Romans 6:17-18). I no longer have to live in bondage to the old patterns;

4. Honestly and transparently lay all of my thoughts and emotions before God, and gratefully trust Him to be true to His Word (Philippians 4:6-7);

5. Saturate my mind with the eternal goodness and promises of God, getting my eyes off of myself and my circumstances (Colossians 3:1-3);

6. Find a "put off" passage of Scripture that specifically speaks to whatever SDBC I have found myself in;

7. Find a "put on" passage of Scripture that addresses the same matter from a little different perspective and tells me what to do INSTEAD;

8. Humble myself before God and willingly submit to whatever He asks of me, even if it is to trust Him and walk through the situation in faith without complaint (1 Peter 5:6);

9. Commit myself to being graciously obedient to what I believe God is asking of me (John 14:23);

10. Saturate with the verses God has taught me that transform my heart and mind; verses that help me think what God thinks, and believe what God believes, about my circumstances and about me.

C. _We then develop a new lifestyle and new habits, new beliefs, new desires, new interests, new friends, new priorities, new goals, and new attitudes_. We continue to work on creating new patterns of living. Once we've done so, they will be as hard to break as the old ones are now. We must also remain committed to making no important decisions or choices when we are NOT in our Safe Zone.

D. _We continue to saturate on the truth about God's nature and character._ As we connect more and more with who God is, what He has done, why He has done it, what His heart is toward us, and what He intends for us to do in response to all of this, our lives are truly and magnificently transformed into the living Masterpiece He designed them to be.

A very effective way to use the different steps (or "legs") of the RMC wheel is to personalize them after we have saturated several times on the passage itself. This helps us connect our hearts with the truth.

Example: "Taking Thoughts Captive" (Leg 1), can be personalized with, "I am taking hold of these thoughts and wrestling them into submission to the truth by reminding myself that these _are_ lies, and I do not have to believe them anymore"

Anchor Point: Emotions have a seat on the bus, just not the driver's seat. And when our emotions are allowed to be involved in a healthy way, that means our heart is involved — which really is the point, isn't it?

Following are three examples of RMC's for your reference. You ought to be able to map out your own RMC's with these as a guide. Following the examples page, you will find a blank version for you to copy and use.

ANXIETY

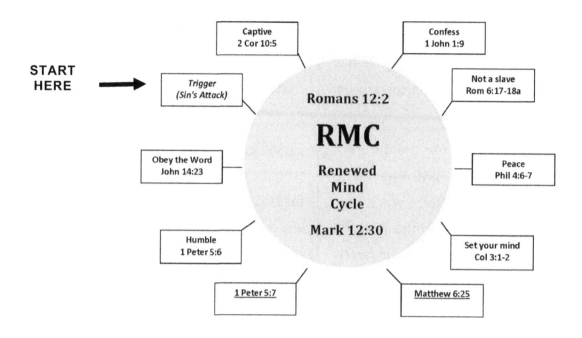

WORRY

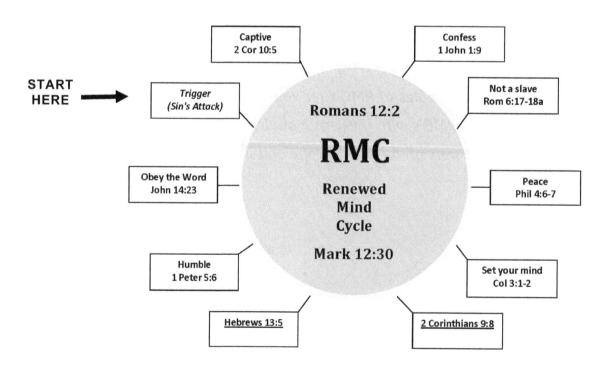

RESENTFUL

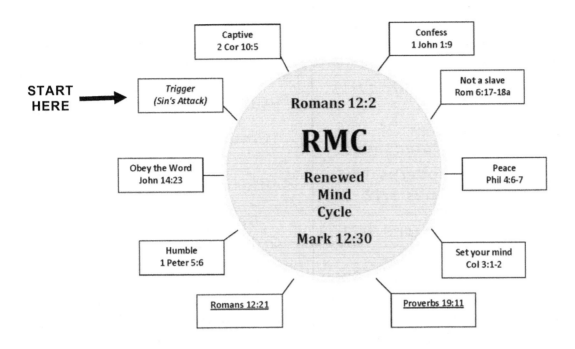

START HERE →

Trigger
(Sin's Attack)

Captive
2 Cor 10:5

Confess
1 John 1:9

Not a slave
Rom 6:17-18a

Romans 12:2

RMC

Renewed
Mind
Cycle

Mark 12:30

Obey the Word
John 14:23

Peace
Phil 4:6-7

Humble
1 Peter 5:6

Set your mind
Col 3:1-2

Romans 12:21

Proverbs 19:11

Sample "Put-off/Put-on" Passages of Scripture
Ephesians 4:22-24
(You can add your own and keep this handy)

PUT OFF	VERSE	PUT ON	VERSE
Bitterness	Hebrews 12:15	Tenderhearted Forgiveness	Ephesians 4:32
Pride	Proverbs 16:5 James 4:6	Humility	Romans 12:3 1 Peter 5:6
Selfishness	Proverbs 18:1 James 3:13-14	Selflessness	Luke 9:23 Philippians 2:2-4
Ingratitude	Romans 1:21	Deep Gratitude	1 Thess. 5:16-18 Ephesians 5:20
Laziness	Proverbs 18:9	Diligence	Colossians 3:23
Anxiety	Matt. 6:25-32 1 Peter 5:7a	Faith	2 Timothy 1:7 1 Peter 5:7b
Wrathfulness	James 1:19-20		Proverbs 16:32
Lust	1 Peter 2:11	Pure Desires	Titus 2:12
Critical Spirit	Galatians 5:15	Love	John 13:34-35
Vengefulness	Romans 12:19	Mercy	Col. 3:12-13 Romans 12:20

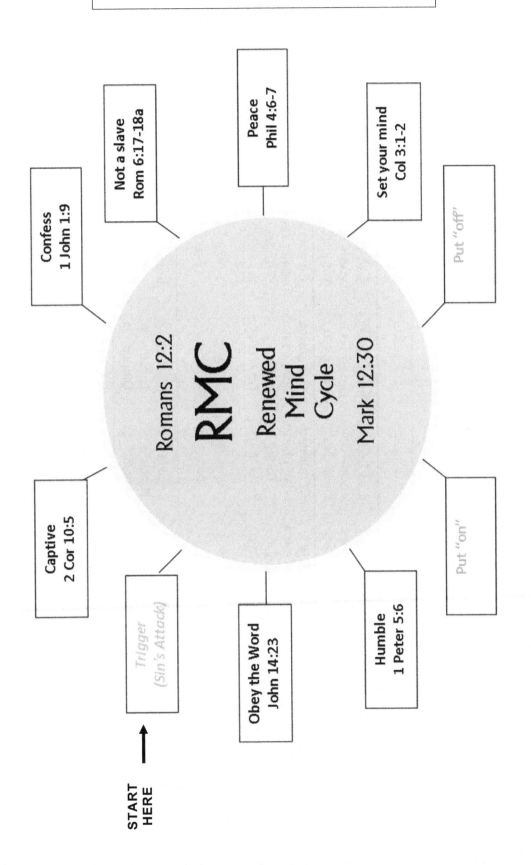

Confess
1 John 1:9

Not a slave
Rom 6:17-18a

Peace
Phil 4:6-7

Set your mind
Col 3:1-2

Put "off"

Romans 12:2
RMC
Renewed
Mind
Cycle
Mark 12:30

Captive
2 Cor 10:5

Trigger
(Sin's Attack)

Obey the Word
John 14:23

Humble
1 Peter 5:6

Put "on"

START
HERE

DAILY PRACTICES	DAY 1	DAY 2	DAY 3	DAY 4	DAY 5	DAY 6	"REST" DAY
SATURATION VERSE ____	More ☐ 100 ☐ Less ☐	More ☐ 100 ☐ Less ☐	More ☐ 100 ☐ Less ☐	More ☐ 100 ☐ Less ☐	More ☐ 100 ☐ Less ☐	More ☐ 100 ☐ Less ☐	More ☐ 100 ☐ Less ☐
BIBLE READING	Chapters ____	Chapters ____	Chapters ____	Chapters ____	Chapters ____	Chapters ____	
STUDY MANUAL LESSON # ____	Read Today's Lesson Today Yes ☐ No ☐	Read Today's Lesson Today Yes ☐ No ☐	Read Today's Lesson Today Yes ☐ No ☐	Read Today's Lesson Today Yes ☐ No ☐	Read Today's Lesson Today Yes ☐ No ☐	Read Today's Lesson Today Yes ☐ No ☐	
DAILY REFLECTION	Completed Today's Lesson Today Yes ☐ No ☐	Completed Today's Lesson Today Yes ☐ No ☐	Completed Today's Lesson Today Yes ☐ No ☐	Completed Today's Lesson Today Yes ☐ No ☐	Completed Today's Lesson Today Yes ☐ No ☐	Completed Today's Lesson Today Yes ☐ No ☐	
USED "RESTORE" BOOK	Yes ☐ No ☐	Yes ☐ No ☐	Yes ☐ No ☐	Yes ☐ No ☐	Yes ☐ No ☐	Yes ☐ No ☐	Yes ☐ No ☐
PRE-MEAL SATURATION VERSE	Breakfast ☐ Lunch ☐ Dinner ☐	Breakfast ☐ Lunch ☐ Dinner ☐	Breakfast ☐ Lunch ☐ Dinner ☐	Breakfast ☐ Lunch ☐ Dinner ☐	Breakfast ☐ Lunch ☐ Dinner ☐	Breakfast ☐ Lunch ☐ Dinner ☐	Breakfast ☐ Lunch ☐ Dinner ☐
SPECIAL ITEMS	Yes ☐ No ☐	Yes ☐ No ☐	Yes ☐ No ☐	Yes ☐ No ☐	Yes ☐ No ☐	Yes ☐ No ☐	Yes ☐ No ☐
PRIVATE PRAYER	Time Spent ____	Time Spent ____	Time Spent ____	Time Spent ____	Time Spent ____	Time Spent ____	Time Spent ____
TODAY, I AM THANKFUL FOR...							

Lesson 12 Study Sheet
Each day review the lesson for that week.
Record one thing you are grateful for each day on your Progress Record.

This Lesson's Verse:

"Our battle is to bring down every deceptive imagining and every prideful argument erected against the true knowledge of God. We fight to trap every thought and cause it to surrender to the authority of Christ. (2 Corinthians 10:4b-5, Lamb)

Day 1 Reflection

When you consider your "mental diet" for this week, what have you changed since beginning this journey? What effects in your life have you observed as a result of this change? *Additional study passages: Romans 6:6, 12-15*

Day 2 Reflection

What are some additional positive decisions and steps you can make to improve your "mental diet?" *Additional study passages: Philippians 4:8; Colossians 3:1-2*

Day 3 Reflection

As you look to incorporate the RMC more consistently in dealing with the destructive patterns of your life, what thoughts and emotions do you experience? Please discuss. *Additional study passages: Psalm 119:81; 114; Isaiah 30:19*

Day 4 Reflection

What do you see as your greatest challenge(s) in breaking free from the destructive patterns of your life? What is your greatest victory so far? *Additional study passage: Romans 8:31-39*

Day 5 Reflection

As you increasingly learn to identify the lies you have believed and surrender to the truth, what are some of the ways you think you can share these blessings with others in your life? *Additional study passage: Galatians 6:1-2*

Day 6 Reflection

Now that you have reached the end of the core lessons in this material, what other things do you feel a need to better understand from God's perspective? *Additional study passages: Isaiah 55:8-9; Jeremiah 9:23-24*

GOAL

CULTIVATE RESPONSIBILITY

CULTIVATE RESPONSIBILITY

My Commitment: "'Being responsible' means accepting responsibility for my own decisions and actions, and not accepting responsibility that is not mine to carry. Being responsible is an essential quality for any mature person, especially one who is maturing as a believer. Being responsible is a necessary character trait for me to develop if I am to have the life God intends for me to have. **Therefore**, I hereby purpose to develop the practices of being responsible and being accountable for my own actions in every area of my life. Christ is the greatest example of what it means to be responsible, so I will endeavor daily to learn from His Word the keys to successfully living as a responsible person."

There is therefore now **NO CONDEMNATION** for those who are *in Christ Jesus.*

For the law of the *life-giving Spirit in* Christ Jesus has set you **FREE** from the law of **sin** and **death.**

Romans 8:1-2 (NET)

LESSON THIRTEEN
STOP "SHOULDING" YOURSELF

"Words matter. And usually, small words matter most." This quote, from a professor and professional Biblical counselor, has already been shown to be profoundly true thus far in our journey. This lesson fleshes that out in some very significant ways.

We have already seen the importance of understanding the difference between "worthy" and "deserving." We have discovered how powerful saturating with Scripture is in contrast to memorizing. We have developed a deep understanding of the distinction between "real" and "true" when it comes to emotions.

The next key area for taking back ground that we've surrendered because of the disparity between the words we use and what they actually signify is in the area of "should."

Simply put: **Should = Shame!** When we go around "Shoulding" ourselves (or others), we are laying on a burden of performance based on expectation; and expectations are usually rooted in a sense of entitlement.

As we will see in a later lesson, expectations are like the ceiling: People can jump up and touch it, but they cannot live there. When we "should" ourselves, we have an intrinsic sense of expectation for performing — usually flawlessly, and nothing else will suffice — that then becomes our gauge for worth and value.

Example: "I *should* be over this by now." Really? You *should* be over this by now because why? Because, if you aren't, then there is something wrong with you, something defective about you, something lacking in you? You aren't living up to some expectation that you've been unable to live up to, so that means what?

Do you see the danger in this kind of thinking?

Interestingly enough, God never tells us we "should" *anything*. He says, "My people *shall*; My people *shall not*." (think of "shall" and "shall not" as "ought" and "ought not.")

When we are "shall-notting" the "shall's" and "shalling" the "shall-not's," we are out of step with God and *need* (key word) to get back *in* step with Him.

There are "ought's" in the Bible, but those are the transcendent ethic that is rooted in the nature and character of God. We "ought not (shall not) steal," because stealing denies the providence, love, and goodness of God which results from our not believing what God has said about Himself. We take matters into our own hands, thinking that God has made a mistake, or that He is failing to do what He said He would do, we have to handle it ourselves.

The Law (think "The 10 Commandments") is there for us to use as a gauge: It brings no salvation, it offers no sacrifice for sin, and it provides no forgiveness. It simply shows us where we are in correlation to God and His character. (For a deeper study and better understanding of this, read carefully Romans 2:11-23.)

Jesus had the strongest language and used the most terrifying of words when He addressed the "Should-ers" in the Gospels. He told the Scribes and Pharisees (the professionals in the Law, the professional "Should-ers") that they were hypocrites, that they created rituals that superseded and replaced God's Law, and that they were so busy "Shoulding" others that the people couldn't bear up under the burden placed on them by those "shoulds."

The most terrifying word in *all* of Scripture is the word, "Woe!" To the Should-ers, Jesus says over a *dozen times*, "Woe to you, Scribes and Pharisees; hypocrites!"

That word, "Woe," means, "Prepare for agonizing torment and doom!" It is a word reserved for God—and His prophets when they spoke to God's people for Him—in warning about the punishment that was going to come upon them for their serial, unrepentant rebellion against Him and His Law. It was also used to express deep sadness over significant loss.

When we are Shoulding ourselves, we are setting a standard for ourselves that is even more stringent that what God sets for us. He never expects us to be flawless. Even in the often-quoted verse where Jesus says, "Be perfect, even as your Father in Heaven is perfect," the original word used there for perfect is not "flawless," but "complete." The sense there is that we are to fulfill God's intent for our lives, just as God Himself fulfills His own intent for Himself.

So, what do we do instead of Shoulding ourselves (or others)? We trade out the word "should" for "*need*."

- "I *need* to take better care of myself."

180

- "I _needed_ to have paid more attention to what I was doing. Because I didn't, _x_ happened."

- "I _need_ to surrender these old memories to God and allow Him to bring me to a place of healing instead of rehashing them over and over in my mind."

- "I _need_ to get refocused on my saturation work if I'm going to replace the lies I believe with the truth."

You get the idea, of course. When we switch from "should" to "need," the emotional content and effect of what we are saying changes dramatically.

Think about how filled your self-talk is with "shoulds." Think about how shamed and shameful you feel whenever you talk to yourself that way. Does it produce motivation to change? Usually it does the opposite, producing a sense of toxic shame that quickly deteriorates into hopelessness and the rest of the dark emotions waiting for you in the "Pit of Gloom".

A WORD ABOUT SHAME

There are two kinds of shame we experience in this life. First, there is righteous shame. This is the shame we feel when we have done something bad. This is the shame that causes us to blush; to be remorseful over the wrong we have done and the harm we have caused; and it brings us to the place of confession, repentance, and restoration. Righteous shame is the right shame for us to feel when we are guilty of wrong.

The second kind of shame we experience is toxic shame. This is the shame that says, "I am bad" instead of "I did badly" or "I am wrong" instead of "I did wrong." Toxic shame results from us taking the guilt that is someone else's to carry.

We believe we are guilty, so we beg and plead for forgiveness, but it never comes – because we cannot be forgiven for something that we are not guilty of! We feel unforgiven and unforgivable because, technically, we are – God does not provide forgiveness for sins we are not guilty of.

In addition, toxic shame hijacks every other emotion, thought, and

181

perception, attaching itself to those things like the HIV virus attaches itself to healthy cells and camouflages itself, wreaking havoc throughout the immune system and eventually destroying the one infected.

Toxic shame operates that same way on a person's emotions, thought processes, sense of worth, and their perceptions about God, others, and even themselves.

Anchor Point: <u>There are two types of sorrow and shame for sin</u> (2 Corinthians 7:10): One is from God; the other is from man.

The shame that comes from God results in repentance without regret (an ongoing sense of the heaviness of guilt) because we have received the forgiveness that God promises (1 John 1:9) as a result of our true repentance for a wrong we have done (true repentance comes simply because it is wrong and others have been wronged as a result).

The second is the type, the one that comes from you or from someone else, is either self-focused (I feel regret over what this cost me) or it results from feeling shame for something we are not guilty of.

When we go to God and ask to be forgiven for a sin we have committed, the guilt we carry to Him is ours to carry. Jesus already paid the price for that, so forgiveness and restoration are now available to us.

But, when we go to God and ask to be forgiven for something we are *not guilty of*, He says, "No," because *we cannot be forgiven for a sin we are not guilty of.* We walk around feeling unforgiven and unforgivable because — technically — we are: there is no forgiveness for us for sins committed by someone else!

There is more to this, but this is enough for now. This is where we need to start in order to understand how important it is to know the truth, and speak the truth, and live the truth. Remember, part of God's economy is that we will "know the truth, and the truth will set you free" (John 8:32).

There is nothing God asks of us or requires of us that He has not provided what we need in order to accomplish it. While Jesus clearly states in John 15:5, *"Apart from Me, you can accomplish nothing,"* Paul assures us of something we all need to keep in mind whenever we think that what we are facing is *too* much: *"I am able to do all [that God asks of me] through the one who strengthens me"* (Philippians 4:13; clarification added).

And as a final reminder of what we have already learned from our work with the "Ladder-Bridge of Faith," Paul also tells us, *"No trial has overtaken you that is not faced by others. And God is faithful: He will not let you be tried beyond what you are able to bear, but with the trial will also provide a way out so that you may be able to endure it"* (1 Corinthians 10:13).

This means that, since we are free in Christ (Galatians 5:1-2), and since we are no longer slaves to sin (Romans 6:6-7), as we surrender more and more to the indwelling Christ (Galatians 2:20), our lives will more and more bear the fruit of a truly surrendered life (John 15:5; Galatians 5:22-23; Romans 8:29).

So, our point is: ***Stop Shoulding Yourself: Exchange "Should" For "Need."*** The toxic shame of not living up to man-made expectations will be steadily replaced by a heart that is devoted to fulfilling God's will more and more each day.

૪ • ୧

DAILY PRACTICES	DAY 1	DAY 2	DAY 3	DAY 4	DAY 5	DAY 6	"REST" DAY
SATURATION VERSE ___	More ☐ 100 ☐ Less ☐	More ☐ 100 ☐ Less ☐	More ☐ 100 ☐ Less ☐	More ☐ 100 ☐ Less ☐	More ☐ 100 ☐ Less ☐	More ☐ 100 ☐ Less ☐	More ☐ 100 ☐ Less ☐
BIBLE READING	Chapters ___	Chapters ___	Chapters ___	Chapters ___	Chapters ___	Chapters ___ ___	
STUDY MANUAL LESSON # ___	Read Today's Lesson Today Yes ☐ No ☐	Read Today's Lesson Today Yes ☐ No ☐	Read Today's Lesson Today Yes ☐ No ☐	Read Today's Lesson Today Yes ☐ No ☐	Read Today's Lesson Today Yes ☐ No ☐	Read Today's Lesson Today Yes ☐ No ☐	
DAILY REFLECTION	Completed Today's Lesson Today Yes ☐ No ☐	Completed Today's Lesson Today Yes ☐ No ☐	Completed Today's Lesson Today Yes ☐ No ☐	Completed Today's Lesson Today Yes ☐ No ☐	Completed Today's Lesson Today Yes ☐ No ☐	Completed Today's Lesson Today Yes ☐ No ☐	
USED "RESTORE" BOOK	Yes ☐ No ☐	Yes ☐ No ☐	Yes ☐ No ☐	Yes ☐ No ☐	Yes ☐ No ☐	Yes ☐ No ☐	
PRE-MEAL SATURATION VERSE	Breakfast ☐ Lunch ☐ Dinner ☐	Breakfast ☐ Lunch ☐ Dinner ☐	Breakfast ☐ Lunch ☐ Dinner ☐	Breakfast ☐ Lunch ☐ Dinner ☐	Breakfast ☐ Lunch ☐ Dinner ☐	Breakfast ☐ Lunch ☐ Dinner ☐	
SPECIAL ITEMS	Yes ☐ No ☐	Yes ☐ No ☐	Yes ☐ No ☐	Yes ☐ No ☐	Yes ☐ No ☐	Yes ☐ No ☐	
PRIVATE PRAYER	Time Spent ___	Time Spent ___	Time Spent ___	Time Spent ___	Time Spent ___	Time Spent ___	
TODAY, I AM THANKFUL FOR...							

Lesson 13 Study Sheet

Each day review the lesson for that week.
Record one thing you are grateful for each day on your Progress Record.

This Lesson's Verse:

"There is therefore now no condemnation for those who are in Christ Jesus. For the law of the life-giving Spirit in Christ Jesus has set you free from the law of sin and death. Romans 8:1-2 (NET)

Day 1 Reflection

Share what you experienced as you read through this lesson. *Additional study passages: 2 Corinthians 7:10; 1 Peter 2:5*

Day 2 Reflection

What are some of the most frequent "shoulds" that you saturate with? How valid do you still think those are? What effect do you see this having on your sense of God and of yourself? *Additional study passage: Psalm 19:14*

Day 3 Reflection

On a scale of 0 to 5, with 5 being the heaviest, how heavy a burden do you see "Shoulding" and toxic shame being in your life? What, if any, plan do you have to change that? *Additional study passages: Psalm 19:14; 119:17-24*

Day 4 Reflection

When you think of the sins you have committed and the evils you have suffered, how clear are you on who is responsible for what? Explain. *Additional study passages: Romans 8:1-2; 14:12; 2 Corinthians 5:10*

Day 5 Reflection

As you learn to identify and surrender the toxic shame and "Shoulding" that you've lived with for so long, what do you believe the results might look like? *Additional study passage: John 8:36*

Day 6 Reflection

What do you believe is your best course of action for you (or anyone) if you find yourself falling into the trap of Shoulding yourself and resurrecting toxic shame? *Additional study passages: Psalm 139:23-24; 1 Corinthians 4:3-5*

"Be kind
to one another,
tender-hearted,
forgiving one
another, just as
God in Christ also
has forgiven you."

Ephesians 4:32
NASB

mariah Hatfield 2020

LESSON FOURTEEN
FORGIVENESS: WHAT IT IS, WHAT IT'S NOT

Forgiveness is poorly understood and even more poorly taught in many Christian circles today. A combination of defective hermeneutics (the rules of proper Bible interpretation), bad logic, weaving together incompatible ideas, added to a certain level of emotionalism, and all blended together with one person after another repeating the same misinformation, has created an unbiblical and unhealthy view of forgiveness. This lesson is intended to help you understand forgiveness from God's perspective. We trust it will be a help.

The Defective-Hermeneutics (hur-muh-NOO-tiks)[17] **Spiral**

In Psalm 103:12 we read: *"As far as the east is from the west, so far has He removed our transgressions from us."*

In Isaiah 43:25 the Lord is quoted as saying, *"I, even I, am the one who wipes out your transgressions for My own sake, and I will not remember your sins."*

Then, in Hebrews 8:12 (quoting Isaiah 43:25; Jeremiah 31:34; Jeremiah 50:20; and Micah 7:18-19) we read, *"For I will be merciful to their iniquities, and I will remember their sins no more."*

These passages are often conflated and over-extrapolated and the result is the false doctrine of "Forgive, Forget, and Move On." Because of a misunderstanding of the biblical languages and a weak approach to hermeneutics, we are often taught that the phrases "remember no more," and "will not remember," mean that God develops the equivalent of "Divine Amnesia."

In reality, this is not at all the case. Both the Hebrew and the Greek words used in these and comparable passages where the idea of remembering/not remembering is present refer to a "being mindful of," or "mentioning" (and similar concepts).

---

[17] Hermeneutics is the art and science of Biblical interpretation. There are specific "do's" and "don'ts" that must be followed if we are going to understand the true meaning and significance of God's Word.

189

When this misunderstanding is combined with Philippians 3:13 (where Paul speaks of "forgetting what is behind" — referring to his pedigree and accomplishments, as well as to what others have done to him), taken out of context and misapplied, they arrive at the defective idea that, as Christians, we are to, "Forgive, forget, and move on." As regards forgiveness, nothing could be more unbiblical.

In fact, this false teaching regularly re-traumatizes people and, very often, becomes a stranglehold on a person's ability to escape false guilt and the associated toxic shame (See Lesson 13).

It is important that we take hold of God's view of forgiveness and adhere to it if we are to live healthy and free, and become able to walk in authentic, godly forgiveness.

Despite a great deal of misunderstanding and inaccurate teaching in the church regarding forgiveness, we want to leave this session with a clearer understanding of this crucial truth. We need to base our understanding not only on what the Word truly says, but also on what God has Himself demonstrated.

THREE KINDS OF FORGIVENESS

There are three kinds of forgiveness described in the Bible. One is completely up to God; one is up to us; and one cannot and ought not to happen without a certain amount of work on the part of the offending party.

1. **Judicial Forgiveness:** This is the complete pardon of all sin granted by God that only He can provide to someone when someone personally goes to Him in confession and repentance of their sin — and no one else's. Through such repentance and our faith in Christ's atoning sacrifice, God (as the Supreme and Righteous Judge) grants "Judicial Forgiveness."

Everyone has to go to God on their own to receive this type of forgiveness. We will never be able to be forgiven for the sins of other people. Thinking that we need to be is part of what causes false guilt, toxic shame, and destructive idolatries in our lives.

Judicial Forgiveness precedes our **Relational Forgiveness** with

God and, as we've already said, requires two things on our part: Confession and true repentance (1 John 1:9).

"WORDS MATTER"

Confess: The word translated "confess" in 1 John 1:9 is a judicial term which means "to be in verbal agreement on the exact nature and character of our wrong." In our judicial system today, there is a similar term used: "allocute," which means "to speak out formally." In practice when 1 John was written, and in American jurisprudence today, this means, "To verbally agree on the exact nature and character of the wrong [crime] without rationalizing, justifying, minimizing, or blameshifting."

Repent: Repentance is more than a "change of mind;" it is a change of heart and of direction. Ephesians 4:28 gives us one of the best examples in Scripture of the "put off/put on" characteristics of authentic repentance:

"The one who steals must steal no longer; rather he must labor, doing good with his own hands, so that he may have something to share with the one who has need."

Not only does the offender cease from doing bad, he replaces the unrighteous behavior with the opposite righteous behavior – and continues doing so *over time* – and does so for the good of another (heart change).

Contrite Heart: Apart from a contrite heart, true confession and authentic repentance cannot exist. A contrite heart means the guilty party has a wide-open acceptance of their responsibility — without minimizing, without blame-shifting, and without excuse — for the evil someone else has suffered as a result of their sin choice.

Now, we need to note that there are many instances in the Bible where, even though God forgave the sins of a person or of the people, He did not remove the consequences of their sin (David, 2 Samuel 12:7-13; Children of Israel, Numbers 14:20-23). This means that while forgiveness is available, forgiveness does not mean "absence of consequences."

We also need to keep in mind the **Anchor Point** from Lesson 13: <u>There are two types of sorrow and shame for sin</u> (2 Corinthians 7:10); one is remorse, the other is regret.

2. **Internal Forgiveness:** This is where we extend mercy to the person who has wronged us, such that we completely forsake retaliation and revenge, leaving that person in the hands of God. Our best plans for revenge will fall far short of what God has planned because He seeks His righteous justice, not revenge. He *does* have a plan and we can trust Him in that (See Genesis 50:20).

Forsaking revenge does *not* mean, however, that the person who has wronged us is not held accountable for their actions, nor does it mean that we stuff our emotions about what happened and ignore them. That will set us on a downward spiral into the same destructive lies we have been working to become free from.

This level of forgiveness is almost impossible unless we have already gone to God and received His Judicial Forgiveness for ourselves. Experiencing Judicial Forgiveness ourselves provides the seed-bed for us to forgive others. Consider this: If God's forgiveness of us is not the foundation of our forgiveness of others, then we are, in actuality, establishing our own standards and patterns for forgiveness.

In such a scenario we expect other people to live up to a standard for forgiveness that we have set in our own heart. The sin issue at stake then becomes a matter between them and us, and not, as it ought to be, an issue between them and God. We have to be able to say, "This matter of sin stands between them (the other person) and God, based on His standards, and not between them and me, based on my standards.

When we live in unforgiveness, it is like carrying a backpack full of sharp, jagged rocks. We tote them around constantly. While we may learn to live with the pain and discomfort, our lives lack joy and God's peace. By contrast, when we forgive, we remove those jagged rocks and hand them over to God.

We walk away from them and leave them where they belong. Walking in unforgiveness means trying to bear something that is not ours to bear. Let that person be God's business, not yours. Romans 12:19: Leave room for the wrath of God ("Leave it to Me," says God).

3. **Relational Forgiveness:** God does not forgive relationally – we are not reconciled to or united with God – without confession and repentance on our part. Similarly, He does not require or even allow us to forgive others relationally without confession and repentance by the offending party (1 John 1:9; Luke 3:8).

This means that our ability to extend relational forgiveness to another person depends on their complete agreement as to the exact nature and character of their wrong (the meaning of the Biblical word "confess"). It also means that such forgiveness depends on those who have wronged us investing much energy and effort to "bear fruit in keeping with repentance" (Matthew 3:8; Ephesians 4:22, 24, 28).

When we speak here of another person confessing and repenting, we do not mean a mere change of behavior. Rather, confession and repentance that allows relational forgiveness flows from a change of heart. *The heart attitude is the key. It is the necessary ingredient underlying real change* – change in which fruitful behavior replaces old toxic and sinful behavior. Such change takes time to prove itself genuine (Note: By way illustration, imagine a newly planted apple tree. We have to wait from 3 to 5 years for it to produce fruit – and the first crop is usually bitter).

Someone saying, "I'm sorry," is not confession, neither is it repentance, nor has there been any time for fruit to develop. Someone saying, "I'm really, *really* sorry," is neither confession nor repentance either.

A helpful parallelism for understanding the contrast between the prerequisites for forgiveness and the prerequisites for reunion (Relational Forgiveness) can be found in Lewis Smedes', *The Art of Forgiving*: [18]

> *It takes one person to forgive.*
> *It takes two to be reunited.*
>
> *Forgiving happens inside the wounded person.*
> *Reunion happens in a relationship between people.*
>
> *We can forgive a person who never says he is sorry. We cannot be truly reunited unless he is honestly sorry.*
>
> *We can forgive even if we do not trust the person who wronged us once not to wrong us again. Reunion can happen only if we can trust the person who wronged us once not to wrong us again.*
>
> *Forgiving has no strings attached.*
> *Reunion has several strings attached.*

---

[18] Lewis Smedes, *The Art of Forgiving: When You Need to Forgive and Don't Know How* (Nashville, TN: Moorings, 1996), 27.

194

TRUE REPENTANCE IS:

- A GRIEVING OVER THE SINS ONE HAS COMMITTED;

- A FULL AND OPEN ACCEPTANCE OF THE RESPONSIBILITY FOR THE EVIL SUFFERED BY THOSE WE HAVE WRONGED;

- A COMPREHENSIVE FORSAKING OF THOSE SINS AND ANYTHING THAT MAKES THAT SIN EASY TO RECOMMIT;

- AND A REPLACING OF THE SINFUL ATTITUDE AND BEHAVIOR WITH THE OPPOSITE RIGHTEOUS ATTITUDE AND BEHAVIOR, ALL *FOR THE SAKE OF GOD AND OTHERS* (SEE EPHESIANS 4:28).

The Bible teaches us that knowing the truth will set us free. It is hard for us to practice good until we know what *is* good. Once we have recognized and accepted the truth, then we are free to practice it.

A person who does not know the truth is like someone blind in a strange place. That person stumbles around, never sure of themselves, and is always lost. Confession and repentance depend on truth, because they require a conviction that what we have done has violated *God's* moral code. Authentic confession and repentance do not come simply because we wish to avoid consequences.

For most of us, the first step to God's forgiveness has to be a willingness to internally forgive those who have wronged us. We must not continue in unforgiveness, knowing that this is a path to self-destruction.

WHAT ABOUT FORGIVING MYSELF?

Some object to the idea of a person "forgiving themselves." The most common argument against this idea is that the Bible never mentions anyone forgiving themselves. It only speaks of God forgiving people and people forgiving each other. While this is

195

technically correct, it is not entirely correct.

The assumption that we should not forgive ourselves is based on *technical theology*, not *practical theology*. *Technical theology* is a theology that can be supported with specific words and phrases in passages of Scripture. *Practical theology* is how we live out our understanding of God and His Word. *Practical theology* is often a "real-life" application of *technical theology*, based on wisdom.

We could point to multiple examples of beliefs and convictions held true by Christians throughout history that derive not so much from an explicit statement of Scripture as from a wise application of the Bible to life. In other cases, the descriptive portions of Scripture help us to understand God's ways apart from direct commands. In either case, that which we wisely discern from God's Word in partnership with the Holy Spirit we understand to be true and binding on our lives.

When it comes to "self-forgiveness," *practical theology* matters. To forgive ourselves is a matter of practicing for ourselves what we discern in the Bible about forgiveness. We need to apply the same principles we have been discussing in this lesson: Are you holding yourself responsible and accountable for something that you are not responsible for, something for which God has already forgiven you in His Judicial Forgiveness? If so, then you need to apply the principles of Internal Forgiveness to yourself.

To internally forgive someone who has harmed you in their sin means to surrender that person and their sin to God, since He is the only true and rightful Judge. When we feel like we cannot forgive ourselves, we must do the same. We must surrender any judgment, condemnation, and expectation of vengeance against ourselves to God.

To refuse internal forgiveness to ourselves is, essentially, to declare that our moral standard is the ultimate moral standard of righteousness. This puts us in opposition to God. It puts us in the position where (in our minds and hearts) we take God's place as Judge and Savior. This prevents us from receiving and walking in God's forgiveness on every level.

So, if someone says you have no business talking about forgiving yourself, it may be simply because they do not understand the practical theology of forgiveness.

ANCHOR POINTS

- God is the Author and Source of all forgiveness. Forgiveness is a matter of the heart and the will.

- In God's economy, consequences are often a part of the transaction, even when confession, repentance, and forgiveness take place. Forgiveness does not equal no consequences.

- Believers are to have hearts that tend toward forgiveness, but it is a forgiveness that needs to be Biblical in its formulation and execution.

- There are three types of forgiveness, the responsibility for which is mostly mine in only one instance.

- Internal and Relational Forgiveness are *not* synonymous. One does not necessarily lead to the other.

- God does not require or allow for Relational Forgiveness without specific prerequisites first being met.

- God does not expect us to forgive relationally until the offending party has done their part. The restoration of relationship is not a simple affair and must be done in accordance with God's directives.

- Inappropriate forgiveness puts us at odds with God. Appropriate forgiveness puts us in partnership with God.

- Apology-making is NOT forgiveness-seeking.

ᙍ • ᙓ

DAILY PRACTICES	DAY 1	DAY 2	DAY 3	DAY 4	DAY 5	DAY 6	"REST" DAY
SATURATION VERSE ___	More ☐ 100 ☐ Less ☐	More ☐ 100 ☐ Less ☐	More ☐ 100 ☐ Less ☐	More ☐ 100 ☐ Less ☐	More ☐ 100 ☐ Less ☐	More ☐ 100 ☐ Less ☐	More ☐ 100 ☐ Less ☐
BIBLE READING	Chapters ___	Chapters ___	Chapters ___	Chapters ___	Chapters ___	Chapters ___	
STUDY MANUAL LESSON # ___	Read Today's Lesson Today Yes ☐ No ☐	Read Today's Lesson Today Yes ☐ No ☐	Read Today's Lesson Today Yes ☐ No ☐	Read Today's Lesson Today Yes ☐ No ☐	Read Today's Lesson Today Yes ☐ No ☐	Read Today's Lesson Today Yes ☐ No ☐	
DAILY REFLECTION	Completed Today's Lesson Today Yes ☐ No ☐	Completed Today's Lesson Today Yes ☐ No ☐	Completed Today's Lesson Today Yes ☐ No ☐	Completed Today's Lesson Today Yes ☐ No ☐	Completed Today's Lesson Today Yes ☐ No ☐	Completed Today's Lesson Today Yes ☐ No ☐	
USED "RESTORE" BOOK	Yes ☐ No ☐	Yes ☐ No ☐	Yes ☐ No ☐	Yes ☐ No ☐	Yes ☐ No ☐	Yes ☐ No ☐	Yes ☐ No ☐
PRE-MEAL SATURATION VERSE	Breakfast ☐ Lunch ☐ Dinner ☐	Breakfast ☐ Lunch ☐ Dinner ☐	Breakfast ☐ Lunch ☐ Dinner ☐	Breakfast ☐ Lunch ☐ Dinner ☐	Breakfast ☐ Lunch ☐ Dinner ☐	Breakfast ☐ Lunch ☐ Dinner ☐	Breakfast ☐ Lunch ☐ Dinner ☐
SPECIAL ITEMS	Yes ☐ No ☐	Yes ☐ No ☐	Yes ☐ No ☐	Yes ☐ No ☐	Yes ☐ No ☐	Yes ☐ No ☐	Yes ☐ No ☐
PRIVATE PRAYER	Time Spent ___	Time Spent ___	Time Spent ___	Time Spent ___	Time Spent ___	Time Spent ___	Time Spent ___
TODAY, I AM THANKFUL FOR...							

Lesson 14 Study Sheet

Each day review the lesson for that week.
Record one thing you are grateful for each day on your Progress Record.

This Lesson's Verse:

"Be kind to one another, tender-hearted, forgiving one another, just as God in Christ also has forgiven you." Ephesians 4:32

Day 1 Reflection

Share what you learned about forgiveness in this lesson. *Additional study passages: 2 Timothy 2:13; 1 Peter 3:18a; 1 John 1:9*

Day 2 Reflection

Can you clearly see that you have experienced "Judicial" forgiveness from God? *Additional study passages: Psalm 103:12; Jeremiah 15:19a*

Day 3 Reflection

What are your thoughts about the differences made in the lesson between "Internal" and "Relational" forgiveness? *Additional study passages: Isaiah 59:1-2; Matthew 6:14-15*

Day 4 Reflection

What are some of the most difficult "Internal Forgiveness" challenges that you face right now? Explain. *Additional study passages: Exodus 10:16; Psalm 51:3-4; Romans 3:23*

Day 5 Reflection

Have you pushed yourself or been pushed by others to Relationally Forgive in inappropriate ways? Explain. *Additional study passage: John 8:36*

Day 6 Reflection

If you have surrendered your heart and life to Christ, and He is both Lord and Savior to you, what do you do with the old feelings of guilt when they come up? *Additional study passages: Romans 6:23; Ephesians 2:1-10; Colossians 1:21-23a*

Do NOT be **deceived**.
GOD will NOT be made a fool.
For a person WILL
REAP what he sows,

because the person who
sows to his own **flesh**
will reap **corruption**
from the **flesh**,

but the one who
sows to the *Spirit*
will reap *everlasting life*
from the
Spirit.

Galatians 6:7-8 (NET)

LESSON FIFTEEN
WHO'S TO BLAME?

It can be easy to believe that we are not accomplishing much of anything worthwhile with our lives. When things go wrong, it can feel like nothing seems to ever go right. Because our lives are not what we want them to be or think they *should* be, the obvious question is: *Who's to blame for all of this?*

Our first tendency is to look around for someone or something *else* to blame; some person or circumstance outside of ourselves that is responsible for our misfortune. All too often we can easily find co-conspirators who will support us in this desire to fix the blame and pin the responsibility elsewhere — anywhere — but on ourselves.

There are a great many people — even some who call themselves "Christian counselors" — who make their living helping us find someone else to blame for our troubles. Certainly, our fathers, our mothers, our brothers, our sisters, our teachers, our coaches, our employers, our friends, general society, and even God are all very handy when we need a villain for our story.

While there may be bad things in our life brought on by the actions of some such people, they will not be held liable by God for the decisions that *we* have made.

The fact of the matter is that blame-shifting may make us feel better temporarily, but it does nothing to solve our problems or to transform our lives.

All we have managed to do is try to make someone else look like the bad guy so that we can look like the good guy; someone else is responsible so that we are not; someone else is the "loser" so we can be the "winner."

Anchor Point: <u>The only way we can walk in the light of truth and improve the state of our life </u>is to fully accept responsibility for our own lives and move forward from there.

203

Is it better to convince ourselves that we are not responsible for a mistake or a transgression, or to take responsibility and allow God to completely cleanse us and bring His healing into that area of our life?

The obvious answer is the second option. The benefits are great when we do not turn to excuses, but instead, honestly accept full responsibility for our decisions and our actions. This is easy to see, simple to say, and anything but easy to do. Our pride gets in the way, such that image and self-protection become more important than the truth and righteousness.

It is pointless to try to rationalize and justify the wreckage we have caused. It is fruitless to blame-shift for sins we have committed. The potential and responsibility for being fruitful in life lies within us as we speak the truth and walk it out. Regardless of their nature, what we do in and with the circumstances we experience will either push us toward, or push us away from, the life God means for us to live. Our willingness to take complete responsibility for our own actions —

coupled with strong faith in God — assures us of real fruitfulness. **Fruitfulness has less to do with our situation or circumstances than it does with how we face them.**

The Bible is *full* of stories of those who faced difficult, even impossible situations, only to rise to greatness:

Joseph went from being a teenaged captive and slave to being a mighty ruler in Egypt.

Gideon was a weak, timid, and gutless young man who God turned into one of the mightiest warriors in the ancient world.

Daniel, who was also a teenaged captive and slave like Joseph, was made a chief adviser to the king of Babylon. After the Medio-Persian Empire conquered Babylon, Daniel became that king's chief advisor as well.

David was a shepherd boy who became the second king of Israel and the founder of a great dynasty. God delights most in using those whose success shocks and confounds the world. Look at those He chose as His disciples. Not a "most-likely-to-succeed" among them!

If we are to be fruitful and flourish in life, there are three attitudes that are "musts." <u>Each day we need to say</u>, **"I will**:

1) Accept full responsibility for my actions and the results of my decisions.

2) Glance at, but not focus on, the past to learn from it, surrendering the good and the bad to God.

3) View difficulties, deficiencies, and even the abuses of others as opportunities for growth, knowing that my hope and strength are in Christ."

1) *Accept full responsibility for my actions and the results of my decisions.*

We eagerly accept credit when we have made good and wise choices. However, if we are going to be honest and authentic and be successful at life, we must also accept responsibility when we have made wrong or unwise choices.

When we refuse to accept responsibility, we continue to repeat those same wrong and unwise choices. Through such refusal, we doom ourselves to repeated disappointment - even disaster. In addition to this, others lose confidence in us and eventually become repelled by our unwillingness to be responsible.

Although we may convince ourselves that we are not to blame for our sins and shortcomings, rarely is anyone else fooled. We would be much better-off accepting the blame for something for which we are not responsible than blaming someone else when things go wrong.

We need to remember that **we must accept responsibility for our own wrong actions if we are to be forgiven**.

Jesus said, *"It is not those who are healthy who need a physician, but those who are sick"* (Matthew 9:12). As long as we proclaim our innocence when we are guilty, we will never see a need to ask Christ to forgive and cleanse us.

Confession (being in agreement with God on the exact nature and character of our wrong) is the first step to forgiveness. Read 1 John 1:9 again and you will see that our confession unlocks the forgiveness Christ died to provide us.

When the prophet Nathan confronted King David with his multi-layered, multi-victim sin, David humbly stated with a contrite heart, *"I have sinned,"* and the prophet immediately answered that God had forgiven him! (Note from Lesson 13: A contrite heart is one that has a wide-open, honest acceptance — without excuse — for the evil another has suffered as a result of our sin).

Once we admit our sin and turn to Christ, He stands ready to forgive. Is it better to acknowledge our sin and receive God's forgiveness, or to make excuses and hold on to our guilt?

As we think about accepting responsibility, let's be very clear: It is essential that we do **not accept any responsibility that is someone else's to carry.** While we can experience forgiveness for our own confessed and repented of sins, God *cannot* and *will not* forgive *us* for someone *else's* sin!

This is important because feeling guilt and shame for the sin choices of others places a burden on us that is not ours to carry (Toxic shame). We need to leave such burdens between God and others to work out.

2) *Glance at but not focus on the past to learn from it, surrendering the good and the bad to God.*

As you will remember from our "Renewing the Mind" lessons, one of the keys to having a sound mind lies in what we saturate on. If we consistently dwell on the wrongs of the past (ours and others'), we set our sail for the "Sea of Lack" and the "Isle of Hopelessness." Our "mental diet" *matters!*

When we saturate on *"whatever is true, whatever is worthy of respect, whatever is just...,* (Philippians 4:8)" we set our course toward recognizing and being grateful for the "have" (instead of the "lack") and we find hope. We acknowledge the negatives of the past, but we do not focus on them.

Alternatively, when we go over and over the wrongs of the past, when we see our many "failures," we become saturated with a sense of despondency and gloom. From there we can quickly begin looking for somebody (else) to blame.

Once we have received God's forgiveness for our wrongs (and hopefully learned what we needed to learn), we must "forgive ourselves" and allow God to be our Judge.

(NOTE: As we mentioned in Lesson 14, a great deal of debate goes on about this idea "forgive yourself." For our purposes in this curriculum, we recognize that many people carry a grudge against themselves and have become embittered against themselves, sitting as their own Judge (Lesson 20). This is what unforgiveness-of-self is.)

Sometimes we ask God for forgiveness but then continue to condemn ourselves. When we continue to condemn ourselves after we have truly confessed and asked God for forgiveness, it is as if we are saying that the cross was not enough, and that Christ's sacrifice was inadequate for *our* sins. God tells us that when HE forgives sin, He never accuses us of it again.

What good could possibly come from dwelling on our forgiven sin?

---

3) View difficulties, deficiencies, and even the abuses of others as opportunities for growth, knowing that my hope and strength are in Christ.

The stories we often like to hear told again and again are the stories about people who have overcome insurmountable odds, enormous difficulties, severe handicaps, or the vilest of conditions, and have come out on top.

Our personal heroes often are ones who have faced and won in the severest, most dangerous, and seemingly most impossible of situations. We *love* the underdog that beats the odds and triumphs over disaster!

The heroes of the greatest stories of all are men and women who, by faith, faced trouble and difficulties as the conquerors God proclaims all of His children to be (Romans 8:37, [31-39]). Trials and difficulties are opportunities for us to grow in our faith (James 1:2-4). In fact, facing these hardships is a cause for rejoicing, not despairing (John 16:33; Romans 5:3).

We need to learn to face hard times with the faith and assurance that God will turn that difficulty into the greatest good by using it to make us more Christ-like in the end. (Read Romans 8:28-29)

DAILY PRACTICES	DAY 1	DAY 2	DAY 3	DAY 4	DAY 5	DAY 6	"REST" DAY
SATURATION VERSE ___	More ☐ 100 ☐ Less ☐	More ☐ 100 ☐ Less ☐	More ☐ 100 ☐ Less ☐	More ☐ 100 ☐ Less ☐	More ☐ 100 ☐ Less ☐	More ☐ 100 ☐ Less ☐	More ☐ 100 ☐ Less ☐
BIBLE READING	Chapters ___	Chapters ___	Chapters ___	Chapters ___	Chapters ___	Chapters ___	
STUDY MANUAL LESSON # ___	Read Today's Lesson Today Yes ☐ No ☐	Read Today's Lesson Today Yes ☐ No ☐	Read Today's Lesson Today Yes ☐ No ☐	Read Today's Lesson Today Yes ☐ No ☐	Read Today's Lesson Today Yes ☐ No ☐	Read Today's Lesson Today Yes ☐ No ☐	
DAILY REFLECTION	Completed Today's Lesson Today Yes ☐ No ☐	Completed Today's Lesson Today Yes ☐ No ☐	Completed Today's Lesson Today Yes ☐ No ☐	Completed Today's Lesson Today Yes ☐ No ☐	Completed Today's Lesson Today Yes ☐ No ☐	Completed Today's Lesson Today Yes ☐ No ☐	
USED "RESTORE" BOOK	Yes ☐ No ☐	Yes ☐ No ☐	Yes ☐ No ☐	Yes ☐ No ☐	Yes ☐ No ☐	Yes ☐ No ☐	Yes ☐ No ☐
PRE-MEAL SATURATION VERSE	Breakfast ☐ Lunch ☐ Dinner ☐	Breakfast ☐ Lunch ☐ Dinner ☐	Breakfast ☐ Lunch ☐ Dinner ☐	Breakfast ☐ Lunch ☐ Dinner ☐	Breakfast ☐ Lunch ☐ Dinner ☐	Breakfast ☐ Lunch ☐ Dinner ☐	Breakfast ☐ Lunch ☐ Dinner ☐
SPECIAL ITEMS	Yes ☐ No ☐	Yes ☐ No ☐	Yes ☐ No ☐	Yes ☐ No ☐	Yes ☐ No ☐	Yes ☐ No ☐	Yes ☐ No ☐
PRIVATE PRAYER	Time Spent ___	Time Spent ___	Time Spent ___	Time Spent ___	Time Spent ___	Time Spent ___	Time Spent ___
TODAY, I AM THANKFUL FOR...							

Lesson 15 Study Sheet

Each day review the lesson for that week.
Record one thing you are grateful for each day on your Progress Record.

This Lesson's Verse:

"Do not be deceived. God will not be made a fool. For a person will reap what he sows, because the person who sows to his own flesh will reap corruption from the flesh, but the one who sows to the Spirit will reap everlasting life from the Spirit." Galatians 6:7-8 (NET)

Day 1 Reflection

When you are faced with guilt and shame for something you have done, what is your normal way of dealing with that? *Additional study passages: Ezekiel 18:30-32; 2 Peter 3:9*

Day 2 Reflection

This lesson deals with taking responsibility for our own choices and actions. What is God's view on us following through on our commitments if we decide later that it is too inconvenient or difficult to do so?" *Additional study passages: Numbers 30:1-2; Matthew 5:37*

Day 3 Reflection

Explain why shifting blame to others does not relieve you of the responsibility for your own actions. *Additional study passage: Genesis 3:1-9*

Day 4 Reflection

Tell how we can turn our blunders and our wrong choices into benefits in our lives and in the lives of others. *Additional study passage: Luke 19:2-10*

Day 5 Reflection

When we refuse to accept responsibility for our actions, when we go against what God has said His will is, we sacrifice many blessings God has promised to those who live in loving obedience. Describe what this has looked like in your own life. *Additional study passage: Psalm 10*

Day 6 Reflection

What is one key responsibility God has charged you with that, in accepting it, will make the greatest difference in your life? What are you doing about that? *Additional study passages: Matthew 7:24-27; Ephesians 4:25-32*

"*So then...*

DO NOT WORRY
about TOMORROW,

for TOMORROW
WILL WORRY
about itself.

TODAY
has ENOUGH
trouble
of its OWN."

Matthew 6:34 (NET)

LESSON SIXTEEN
STARTING FRESH

As we become more spiritually mature, it shows in our calm confidence and peace when we face difficult situations. It reflects in our level-headed problem-solving abilities, and in our capacity for establishing and maintaining healthy relationships.

We need to learn how to neutralize the harmful emotions and destructive ways of thinking that rob us of our ability to be realistic and logical when trying to problem-solve.

Our world is crying out for men and women who can face trouble and difficulties with a clear, cool head, and provide the best solutions.

I.   START FRESH

It is impossible for us to be good problem-solvers if we attempt to deal with too many problems at the same time. In order to sort through and know what has to be dealt with and when, we need to learn how to prioritize what we are facing.

If we are distracted from a problem that needs our attention by a secondary problem that seems more urgent in the moment, we will be easily consumed by the less important — or the unimportant — and do a poor job of solving problems altogether. Our first priority must be clearing away anything but the most important problem facing us.

A.   We set aside problems that are imagined, future, or potential. God is a God of truth and deals in reality. He cannot help us with problems that are not current and real. While God is intimately involved in every aspect of our lives, He cannot help us solve problems that do not exist or that we do not yet face. Fantasies and fears may *seem* real, but God is a God of truth, and not a God of untruths or fantasies. If it is real, God is there. If it is not, then there is no place for God to "be," right?

Ironically, it is usually not the real problems that cause greatest concern in people's lives; it is those pesky *anticipated* problems. Real or not, if the things we face are not actual, current, or active, there is nothing for God to help us with, at least not yet. And it seems that for every in-the-moment problem we face, there are dozens and dozens of potential problems waiting just over the horizon.

Focusing on those not only robs us of our peace of mind, it also robs us of our ability to deal well with what we actually face. Focusing on potential problems — no matter how likely they are — robs us of the emotional and mental energy to address and deal with the real problems that face us.

(*Revisited from Lesson 8*)

Consider this scenario: Imagine you are walking down the street and a car driving toward you on the road jumps the curb and starts coming straight at you. The fear you feel is authentic and is based on a real and tangible threat. Your fight-or-flight mechanisms fire up and – hopefully – you get out of the way and are safe.

Now imagine the same scenario, only this time the car does *not* jump the curb, does not come speeding toward you, and puts you in no danger. If you start to get worried that it *might*, that it *could*, and fantasize about all the danger that would create, you enter into unfounded and unwarranted fear. This results in anxiety. **Anxiety is unfocused fearfulness based on an unreal, imaginary, or intangible threat.**

When you give yourself over to anxiety, not only are you believing and trusting a lie (maybe even petitioning God to help you in a situation that is unreal and that does not exist), you are also robbing yourself of the mental and emotional ability to solve *real* problems.

Since an *anticipated* problem causes all the emotional distress of a *real* problem, piling one *anticipated* problem onto another is an expressway to an ever-increasing fearfulness, and can even lead to an "anxiety attack."

The emotional distress related to worry piled upon worry, and anxiety piled upon anxiety, renders us mentally and emotionally incapable of effectively dealing with the legitimate problems that we face daily.

B. We surrender the problems we have no control over. God does not expect us to have the solution to every problem in our lives, and He *really* does not expect us to solve everybody else's problems, either — only He can do that. As a matter of fact, when we look in His Word to find out what God *does* require of us, here is what we read: *"He has told you, O man, what is good, and what the*

Lord really wants from you: He wants you to promote justice, to be faithful, and to live obediently before your God" (Micah 6:8).

As we each, in our own lives, prioritize our walk with Christ, He directs us to fulfill whatever part He has for us to play in God's unfolding work. Since we only play a part in each circumstance, and He takes care of the whole, the outcomes are not ours; they are His. He will often use us to be *part* of His solution to a problem, but when we try to fix everything in sight we can actually get in God's way. In any situation, we can become an obstacle and not a help to God in His purpose of working something good in the lives of those involved. God very often uses problems to bring us closer to Him and to build spiritual maturity in our lives (Romans 8:28-29; James 1:2-4).

The key to knowing what role (if any) we are to play in solving any problem lies in a healthy relationship with, and a life surrendered to, Jesus Christ (remember Goal 1?).

By being in and living out His Word, by being connected with Him through prayer and personal worship, and by being connected to Him through healthy Christian relationships, we are able to be in tune with His voice and His will.

From this point, we then lay down those things that are of concern to us, those things that are troubling us, and thank Him for already having the answers we need. Not only will we experience the immense peace that He alone can bring, but He also jettisons the confusion and wasted effort that is often so much a part of how we manage our lives.

C. We shelve those problems that are better dealt with later. When solving problems, God's timing is crucial. God will only help and guide us with the problems he means for us to deal with when it is time to deal with them. If we want God's help with our problems, we must yield to His timing and His trajectory.

So, how do we know when and how to tackle a problem? Answer: Only when our hearts are soft toward God. It is impossible to determine something as profound as God's timing if there is any rebelliousness or unconfessed sin in our lives.

Our timing is not God's timing. Very often, God's answer when we ask Him what we should do is, "Wait." Yet we also need to be prepared to move when God says, "Go!", and do so knowing that He has gone before us, prepared the way for us, and will be with us every step of the way (Deuteronomy 31:8).

II. LAUNCH OUT ONLY FROM THE "SAFE ZONE"

Along with "Starting Fresh," we need to make sure we are in our "Safe Zone" before we will be able to problem-solve effectively (Lessons 9 & 10).

A. Focus on Christ: Jesus is and has the answer to all of our problems, and He is also the source of any real peace in our lives. His unequaled wisdom, His ability to bring peace in the midst of any storm, and His more than adequate power for any situation, makes Him the logical first choice when we are in need. His promise that He will never leave us is priceless when we are in distress. God has infinite answers for any, and every, real problem we face. While there may be many *good* answers to a dilemma, He has only one *best* answer.

B. Saturate with Scripture: The best tool for calming the spirit and gaining God's mind about something is God's Word. You will be amazed at how quickly that one well-chosen verse can calm troubled or tender emotions. While reading one or more of the Psalms is an immense help when we are in distress, it is Scripture saturation that both calms our emotions and prepares our heart (subconscious mind) against future turmoil. Both reading a Psalm (like Psalm 91) when we feel overwhelmed and anxious, and saturating on one of the verses *in* that Psalm, combine to become a powerful antidote to anxiety and distress.

C. Pray: James tells us that we do not have because we do not ask, or because we ask with wrong (selfish) motives (James 4:2c). Solomon admonishes us to not lean on our own understanding but to trust in God in everything (Proverbs 3:5-6). It is tragic that we so often ignore the one true source of real help during troubling times or when faced with problems. We need to be constantly aware of Christ's loving presence and personal care, especially when we are in problem-solving mode. The Holy Spirit is especially attentive when our problems overwhelm us. He makes our needs clear to God even when are unable to even find the words (Romans 8:26-27).

216

Write down and keep this problem-solving formula[19] handy.

Single out real problems

Isolate the problems that are the most urgent

Find God's best solution

Take action as soon as a wise decision is reached

---

[19] Very special thanks to Pastor Troy Smith for this insightful and incredibly powerful tool!

DAILY PRACTICES	DAY 1	DAY 2	DAY 3	DAY 4	DAY 5	DAY 6	"REST" DAY
SATURATION VERSE ___	More ☐ 100 ☐ Less ☐	More ☐ 100 ☐ Less ☐	More ☐ 100 ☐ Less ☐	More ☐ 100 ☐ Less ☐	More ☐ 100 ☐ Less ☐	More ☐ 100 ☐ Less ☐	More ☐ 100 ☐ Less ☐
BIBLE READING	Chapters ___	Chapters ___	Chapters ___	Chapters ___	Chapters ___	Chapters ___	
STUDY MANUAL LESSON # ___	Read Today's Lesson Today Yes ☐ No ☐	Read Today's Lesson Today Yes ☐ No ☐	Read Today's Lesson Today Yes ☐ No ☐	Read Today's Lesson Today Yes ☐ No ☐	Read Today's Lesson Today Yes ☐ No ☐	Read Today's Lesson Today Yes ☐ No ☐	
DAILY REFLECTION	Completed Today's Lesson Today Yes ☐ No ☐	Completed Today's Lesson Today Yes ☐ No ☐	Completed Today's Lesson Today Yes ☐ No ☐	Completed Today's Lesson Today Yes ☐ No ☐	Completed Today's Lesson Today Yes ☐ No ☐	Completed Today's Lesson Today Yes ☐ No ☐	
USED "RESTORE" BOOK	Yes ☐ No ☐	Yes ☐ No ☐	Yes ☐ No ☐	Yes ☐ No ☐	Yes ☐ No ☐	Yes ☐ No ☐	Yes ☐ No ☐
PRE-MEAL SATURATION VERSE	Breakfast ☐ Lunch ☐ Dinner ☐	Breakfast ☐ Lunch ☐ Dinner ☐	Breakfast ☐ Lunch ☐ Dinner ☐	Breakfast ☐ Lunch ☐ Dinner ☐	Breakfast ☐ Lunch ☐ Dinner ☐	Breakfast ☐ Lunch ☐ Dinner ☐	Breakfast ☐ Lunch ☐ Dinner ☐
SPECIAL ITEMS	Yes ☐ No ☐	Yes ☐ No ☐	Yes ☐ No ☐	Yes ☐ No ☐	Yes ☐ No ☐	Yes ☐ No ☐	Yes ☐ No ☐
PRIVATE PRAYER	Time Spent ___	Time Spent ___	Time Spent ___	Time Spent ___	Time Spent ___	Time Spent ___	Time Spent ___
TODAY, I AM THANKFUL FOR...							

Lesson 16 Study Sheet

Each day review the lesson for that week.
Record one thing you are grateful for each day on your Progress Record.

This Lesson's Verse:

"So then, do not worry about tomorrow, for tomorrow will worry about itself. Today has enough trouble of its own. Matthew 6:34 (NET)

Day 1 Reflection

How have you normally dealt with problems in the past? How is that changing for you? *Additional study passages: Job 5:6-9; Psalm 10*

Day 2 Reflection

What is your emotional state when faced with a difficult situation? What does it need to be if you are going to face it and handle it with God's best solution? *Additional study passages: Psalms 42:5; Psalm 91*

Day 3 Reflection

Explain some of the reasons why God would be unwilling to become involved in our anticipated or imagined problems. *Additional study passage: Philippians 4:6-7*

Day 4 Reflection

Tell how we, by being godly problem-solvers, can turn our problems into pluses in our lives and in the lives of others. *Additional study passages: 2 Corinthians 4:16-18; Philippians 4:9*

Day 5 Reflection

Explain how we harm those close to us when we do not deal wisely and responsibly with our problems. *Additional study passage: Jonah 1:1-12*

Day 6 Reflection

Describe a time when you believe you dealt with a difficult situation in a wise and responsible manner. Was there a sense of satisfaction at being a successful problem-solver? Explain. *Additional study passages: Psalm 27:1-3; Philippians 1:6*

Do not forsake
WISDOM,
and she will PROTECT you;
Love Her,
and she will GUARD you.

WISDOM IS SUPREME –
so develop WISDOM, and
whatever you acquire,
acquire UNDERSTANDING!

Proverbs 4:6-7 (NET)

LESSON SEVENTEEN
WISE LIVING

Real victory that buoys successful living is rooted in our ability to make wise choices and follow through with them. There is little hope or help for someone who persists in making bad choices or in making wise choices but not carrying them out.

You have probably heard this one: "The definition of insanity is doing the same thing over and over again and expecting different results."

While often attributed to Albert Einstein, the renowned physicist actually never said it. In fact, the earliest place where this is found is in an old piece of Narcotics Anonymous literature. As witty and as humorous as this little ditty sounds, it is also grossly inaccurate.[20] In fact, it is a well-suited definition not for "insanity," but for "stupid." Or perhaps we ought to tone that down a little and talk about "foolishness."

Fools lack wisdom and discernment. Fools lack good sense and good judgment. The foolish person does not pay attention to the details and realities of what is happening. Rather, they focus instead entirely on the desired outcomes *without regard for* the path taken. In fact, we might say that such a person lacks true focus. Such a person will always struggle to make wise decisions.

Why? Because wise decisions require knowledge, understanding, insight, and logical thought. By ignoring these things, the fool ignores wisdom.

For this lesson, we want to concern ourselves with putting-off foolishness and putting-on wisdom.

Our working definition of wisdom is as follows: "The ability to discover the best course of action and take it." Knowing what is best to do is of little good if we fail to act on that knowledge. So, if we plan on learning to live wisely, we need a great desire to *know* best and then to *do* best.

Sometimes, instead of focusing on what we want (to make a wise choice), we focus on what we do not want (to avoid making a *wrong* choice). We end up settling for less-than-best. While the choices we make are not

---

[20] "Insanity" is a legal term "mental illness of such a severe nature that a person cannot distinguish fantasy from reality, cannot conduct her/his affairs due to psychosis, or is subject to uncontrollable impulsive behavior."

completely *wrong*, they are not completely correct, either. When we say things like, "It isn't *that* bad," "I don't think God minds if I do this," or "Just show me in the Bible where it's wrong to do 'whatever'," we are in fact moving away from wisdom and into foolishness. We need boundaries. And we need margins *within* those boundaries.

Picture riding in a car on a mountain road — rock wall on the left, wide shoulder, and a guardrail on the right. Over the guardrail is a 300-foot drop. Now, if the driver stays between the lines in your lane, that is very good. But, if they cross over that white fog-line on the right side of the lane, the margin between sure safety and ultimate danger begins to disappear.

What if they start driving in the gravel and broken glass scattered along the shoulder area between the white line and the guardrail? Feeling safe now?

Question: How often have you found yourself scraping the whole right side of the car down the guardrail of life instead of staying within the safe margins *between* the boundaries?

People will look for cosigners wherever they can find them, but they especially like to find cosigners who are Christians. They will present some "questionable" practice they are, or want to be, involved in, and try to pressure that person into agreeing that it is okay. It's as if getting someone else to agree that their actions are acceptable will make it so. Of course, the real question is: What is *God's* opinion on the matter?

The fact that they (we) are seeking another's approval is evidence that they have doubts about their choices. If they do not get the answer they want, they then consider the naysayer an enemy, criticize them for being so "narrow-minded" — or accuse them of being "judgmental" — and do it anyway. Here lies the road of foolishness.

We need to ask God early and often, "Lord, what is Your best in this situation? What would You have me do?" This is what we call "Getting God in Front." Since so many outcomes depend on the quality of our choices, we need to get very proficient at making wise choices.

> ### God's "math" for wise living is simple:
> ## *Knowing Best + Doing Best = WISDOM*

Knowing: Jesus says, *"If you continue to follow my teaching, you are really my disciples and you will know the truth, and the truth will set you free"* (John 8:31-32, NET).

1. *Set a foundation for making wise choices by studying the wisdom in the Bible.* Reading a Proverb a day is a great discipline to engraft into your life. Each day read the chapter that corresponds to that day of the month (There are 31 chapters in Proverbs). Or, read a Psalm (or part of a Psalm for the longer ones). There is virtually nothing in the human experience *not* covered by Psalms and Proverbs (let alone the rest of the Bible).

2. *Seek out and listen to mature Christian counsel.* People who have been down the road we are on and have experienced victory in their own lives can be invaluable when we need honest and sound advice (2 Corinthians 1:3-5). The Bible tells us that God has given us mature believers, pastors, and teachers to help us discover and follow God's plan for our life.

3. *Always ask the question, "Lord, what is best right now?"* We need to ask that question in light of what God's Word teaches us and what His purpose for our lives is (as best we can understand it). **Anchor Point**: The #1 enemy of "best" is often "good." If we are willing to settle for good-enough, we have robbed ourselves of God's best.

Doing: *Knowing* is the easy part; *doing* is often the hard part. Most of us are driven by our emotions, which often has disastrous results. Here are some suggestions:

1. *Stay away from places and people who increase temptation or have an unhealthy influence on us.* In Psalm 1:1, God makes clear what His "best" formula is in order for us to experience His blessings in our life. The rest of the Psalm shows us what that is, and what the outcomes are for those who do not follow His best plan.

2. _Learn to lean into and cling to God in trying times._ Trials and temptations pass. We need to reach out and cling to God during those times, knowing that He will not allow anything to overtake us that He has not also provided a way of escape from (1 Corinthians 10:13). Look to Christ and focus on Him (Matthew 14:22-33). He has already been through it Himself and will walk through it with you (Hebrews 4:15).

3. _Make no provision for pursuing anything that is not God's best (Romans 13:14)._ We need to use the tools we have to do our best to push out of our mind any thinking that is not in keeping with "best." If we allow our minds to ponder it for very long — even though we may decide in the end not to do it — then we have passed through our safety margin and are running up against the final boundary separating us from destruction. James tells us that sinful choices begin with our thinking (James 1:13-15). If we settle too long on those thoughts, we will often crash through the guardrail. Do not be seduced into giving consideration to those things which are not best.

☙ • ❧

BLESSINGS OF SEEKING WISDOM

My child, if you receive my words, and store up my commands inside yourself, by making your ear attentive to wisdom, and by turning your heart to understanding, indeed, if you call out for discernment — shout loudly for understanding if you seek it like silver, and search for it like hidden treasure, then you will understand how to fear the Lord, and you will discover knowledge about God.

For the Lord gives wisdom, and from his mouth comes knowledge and understanding. He stores up effective counsel for the upright and is like a shield for those who live with integrity, to guard the paths of the righteous and to protect the way of his pious ones.

Then you will understand righteousness and justice and equity — every good way. For wisdom will enter your heart, and moral knowledge will be attractive to you.

Discretion will protect you, understanding will guard you, to deliver you from the way of the wicked, from those speaking perversity, who leave the upright paths to walk on the dark ways, who delight in doing evil, they rejoice in perverse evil; whose paths are morally crooked, and who are devious in their ways.

So you will walk in the way of good people and will keep on the paths of the righteous. For the upright will reside in the land, and those with integrity will remain in it, but the wicked will be removed from the land, and the treacherous will be torn away from it.

PROVERBS 2:1-15, 20-22 (NET)

DAILY PRACTICES	DAY 1	DAY 2	DAY 3	DAY 4	DAY 5	DAY 6	"REST" DAY
SATURATION VERSE ___	More ☐ 100 ☐ Less ☐	More ☐ 100 ☐ Less ☐	More ☐ 100 ☐ Less ☐	More ☐ 100 ☐ Less ☐	More ☐ 100 ☐ Less ☐	More ☐ 100 ☐ Less ☐	More ☐ 100 ☐ Less ☐
BIBLE READING	Chapters ___	Chapters ___	Chapters ___	Chapters ___	Chapters ___	Chapters ___	
STUDY MANUAL LESSON # ___	Read Today's Lesson Today Yes ☐ No ☐	Read Today's Lesson Today Yes ☐ No ☐	Read Today's Lesson Today Yes ☐ No ☐	Read Today's Lesson Today Yes ☐ No ☐	Read Today's Lesson Today Yes ☐ No ☐	Read Today's Lesson Today Yes ☐ No ☐	
DAILY REFLECTION	Completed Today's Lesson Today Yes ☐ No ☐	Completed Today's Lesson Today Yes ☐ No ☐	Completed Today's Lesson Today Yes ☐ No ☐	Completed Today's Lesson Today Yes ☐ No ☐	Completed Today's Lesson Today Yes ☐ No ☐	Completed Today's Lesson Today Yes ☐ No ☐	
USED "RESTORE" BOOK	Yes ☐ No ☐	Yes ☐ No ☐	Yes ☐ No ☐	Yes ☐ No ☐	Yes ☐ No ☐	Yes ☐ No ☐	Yes ☐ No ☐
PRE-MEAL SATURATION VERSE	Breakfast ☐ Lunch ☐ Dinner ☐	Breakfast ☐ Lunch ☐ Dinner ☐	Breakfast ☐ Lunch ☐ Dinner ☐	Breakfast ☐ Lunch ☐ Dinner ☐	Breakfast ☐ Lunch ☐ Dinner ☐	Breakfast ☐ Lunch ☐ Dinner ☐	Breakfast ☐ Lunch ☐ Dinner ☐
SPECIAL ITEMS	Yes ☐ No ☐	Yes ☐ No ☐	Yes ☐ No ☐	Yes ☐ No ☐	Yes ☐ No ☐	Yes ☐ No ☐	Yes ☐ No ☐
PRIVATE PRAYER	Time Spent ___	Time Spent ___	Time Spent ___	Time Spent ___	Time Spent ___	Time Spent ___	Time Spent ___
TODAY, I AM THANKFUL FOR...							

Lesson 17 Study Sheet

Each day review the lesson for that week.
Record one thing you are grateful for each day on your Progress Record.

This Lesson's Verse:

"Do not forsake wisdom, and she will protect you; love her, and she will guard you. Wisdom is supreme – so develop wisdom, and whatever you acquire, acquire understanding!" Proverbs 4:6-7

Day 1 Reflection

Which emotions most often cause you to make unwise choices? *Additional study passages: Proverbs 14:30; 15:28; 21:4*

Day 2 Reflection

Why do you think God gave humankind free-will? *Additional study passage: Deuteronomy 30:15-20*

Day 3 Reflection

How do you relate humanity's free-will to a person's freedom in Christ? *Additional study passage: John 15:1-16*

Day 4 Reflection

What do you consider the driving passions that led to Satan's disastrous choices in heaven? *Additional study passage: Isaiah 14:12-15*

Day 5 Reflection

Why is it so common for us to seek others to cosign and condone our actions when we know in our heart that we made the wrong (worst) choice? *Additional study passages: Job 15:34-35; Isaiah 1:23*

Day 6 Reflection

Since much of your life is shaped by the choices you make, what do you believe are the most significant things you can do to assure you make the best choices going forward? *Additional study passages: Joshua 1:8; Psalm 1*

GOAL

5

RESOLVE CONFLICTS

RESOLVE CONFLICTS

Every one of us is in relationships with other people. Trouble is, we are *selfish* and *rebellious* people, in relationship with *selfish* and *rebellious* people, and we live in a *selfish* and *rebellious* world. The results can often be *disastrous*. The ability to build good, healthy relationships is possibly the greatest struggle many of us face.

> **Anchor Point**: A healthy relationship is one that makes both parties better. A godly relationship is one that honors God and helps those in the relationship in their walk with God.

Unhealthy and/or ungodly relationships either need repair, if possible, or they must be shelved when repair is not possible. Since our horizontal relationships with people reflect the health of our vertical relationship with God, the key to having healthy relationships is having a healthy relationship with God in Christ. How we relate to Him has a profound effect on all other relationships. In this section, we will discover critical truths that will guide us as we seek to build and restore relationships with those in our life.

"No one has *Greater Love* than this –

that one lays down his life for his *friends*."

John 15:13 (NET)

LESSON EIGHTEEN
RELATIONSHIP CIRCLES

Understanding and employing the following diagram (Relationship Circles), with its explanation, may prove to be a powerful tool for you in discerning the health of the relationships you are in and then categorizing them properly.

As we discovered in Lesson 5, "Is God Faithful?", trustworthiness needs to be demonstrated before trust is given. This truth matters because trust is the key to vulnerability and emotional intimacy in relationships. Trust creates relationships that are not "transactional;" not a trading of "this-for-that." The closer into the center of this diagram a person is, the greater the level of trust, authenticity, safe vulnerability, and true bonding we share with them. The "Island of No" is for those who are unsafe for us to be in relationship with and who we therefore keep out of our life whenever possible.

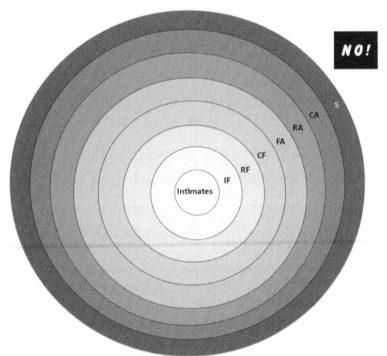

LEGEND: S = STRANGER, **CA** = CASUAL ASSOCIATE/ACQUAINTANCE,
RA = REGULAR ASSOC./ACQUAINT., **FA** = FRIENDLY ASSOC./ACQUAINT.,
CF = CASUAL FRIEND, **RF** = REGULAR FRIEND, **IF** = INTIMATE FRIEND,
INTIMATES = CLOSEST TO YOU, **NO!** = THE ISLAND OF "NO"

WORKING WITH THE DEFINITIONS

In order to make use of the above diagram, we need to first consider some working definitions for each identifier on a Relationship Circle. Then we want to take an inventory of the relationships we are involved in and see how our understanding matches the diagram.

Do I use the word "friend" in a manner consistent with this Relationship Circles diagram? Or do I characterize relationship terms (like "friend," or "intimate") in a manner remarkably different from this lesson? Where do my relationships actually belong according to this diagram?

Having observed myself and my relationships, it may be that I need to recategorize some that I have misinterpreted or misunderstood. Only by having an honest and accurate understanding of the trust and intimacy levels appropriate in each circle – i.e. in each relationship – can I best know how to steward those relationships.

Here is an example: Say you have someone that you have always considered as belonging in the RF, or "Regular Friend," Circle. Now, let us say that when you examine the relationship and the interactions the two of you have, you realize that it is pretty much a one-way relationship. You always do what the other person wants. Even when they say, "Let's do whatever you want to do this time," they rarely if ever follow through. They rarely agree to do what you want to do, and you end up doing what they want to do anyway.

A friendship like this example is not a healthy or authentic "friend" relationship based on what being a friend really is (see below). This is a relationship that is not "making both parties better." In fact, one person is simply "co-signing" and feeding the other person's self-absorption. Such a situation does not honor God, nor does it demonstrate a Biblical understanding and practice of love.

WORKING DEFINITIONS

Beginning with the outermost of the concentric circles in our diagram and working inward we have:

- **S:** "Stranger." Strangers are people we have not met and that we do not know. Just because we know "about" someone does not mean that we know *them*.

- **CA:** "Casual Acquaintance/Associate." These are people of passing familiarity with whom we have some level of casual contact, perhaps even ongoing contact. We might not even know their name and, if we do, we know little else. We do not even consider spending any unofficial time with folks in this circle.

- **RA:** "Regular Acquaintance/Associate." This may be someone you work with on a regular basis, but you do not have personal or beneath-the-surface conversations with. The lack of familiarity leaves little room for a history of trustworthiness to develop.

- **FA:** "Friendly Acquaintance/Associate." This is someone with whom we have developed a small level of familiarity. Our "surfacy" conversations have been light and not uncomfortable, but we have yet to share anything very personal with them. Folks in this circle are those we have observed over time. We've either seen nothing untoward in their attitude and behavior, or we have observed issues of concern and are wisely keeping the relationship cool and distant. We are not spending time with them away from "official" functions, except for some social gatherings that include a number of others.

- **CF:** This is the "Casual Friend" circle. Here we embrace those we have shared some level of personal information with and have developed at least a small level of trust in their ability to be discreet. These people have shown themselves to be somewhat "safe." We will spend time with them away from "official" functions, and we may even visit each other's homes on occasion.

- **RF:** "Regular Friends" are the people we tend to be more authentic and vulnerable with, feel more comfortable with, and whose company we enjoy. These relationships are the ones where we have learned to trust each other and rely on each other in deeper and more personal ways, far in contrast to the preceding circles. There may be a dozen or so people at this level (or perhaps not).

- **IF:** An "Intimate Friend" is the level where we have developed a mutual trust with, and reliance on, an exceedingly small number of people (1, 2, maybe 3 or 4 at most). With intimate friends we are quite authentic and very "real." These are the folks we accept and who accept us in spite of the things we know about each other. While neither they, nor we, co-sign each other's sin, we still love and support each other through the deepest struggles. The prerequisites for moving into this circle and remaining there are a passionate desire for God's best in the other person's life, even if it costs us dearly. Discretion and protection of privacy are normal here.

- **INTIMATES:** The people who can be most trusted with the deepest and most personal of all of your deepest truths. Very few will ever make this circle. This is the level of friendship referred to by Jesus in John 15:13, our verse for this week. A spouse is the most common person to find here.

Then there is the "Island of NO!" People banish *themselves* to the "Island of No" based on their being clearly unsafe and/or untrustworthy. They arrive here as a result of their own attitudes and behaviors. They may have severely mistreated us or someone else. They may be someone who is selfish, self-centered, self-absorbed, and disregarding of others; so much so that they cannot be trusted in a relationship.

People on the "Island of No" are those who we cannot safely be in relationship with, or those with whom we do not know how to be in healthy relationship. In one way or another they have broken trust, and restoration, if it is possible at all, remains a remote and distant possibility.

Think of it this way: Between the "Island of No" and the "Mainland of Relationships" lies a vast and difficult sea. There are specific things required of those banished to this far and distant place if they are to be welcomed back into relationship with us [refer to Lesson 14 on Forgiveness]. It is not that we condemn such persons, but rather that we acknowledge the truth of their own choices and decisions. Rather than try and relate in a way that is not commensurate with the truth, we instead extend "grace from a distance" to those on the "Island of No!"

(Note: Some family members, for the very same reasons noted above, may find themselves here in the "Island of

No!" just as much as those we are not related to. We need to be careful not to move them off the "Island of

No!" simply out of a sense of misplaced "loyalty."

It is important to keep four key things in mind:

1. <u>The lines between circles are like the lines on pavement.</u> Depending on the season a relationship is in, folks will move from one concentric circle to another. Be careful not to use ontological ("being") statements like, "She *is* my friend," casually or definitively. We have all had one or more people in our lives who have changed circles – friends who no longer are friends; casual acquaintances whom we have grown close to, and who now fit better in one of the circles closer to the center. A *close* relationship does not always equal a *good* relationship, and a *casual* relationship does not always equal a *bad* relationship.

2. <u>Be realistic about the nature and character of the other person</u> and the relationship you are in with them. Wishful thinking is not the same thing as hope. **Hope is confident assurance based on facts in evidence**. Wishful thinking is, well, wishful thinking - it is not based on any reality or truth.

3. While we are commanded by Jesus to "Love your neighbor as you love yourself" (Luke 10:27b), and to "turn the other cheek" (Matthew 5:39), <u>loving someone and not retaliating when they do us harm does not mean that these are "human doormat" verses</u>. On the contrary, these verses and the ones that surround them speak about an attitude of the heart, not about allowing others to do harm to us or to others. Allowing someone to continue to be oppressive or abusive is not showing love.

4. <u>The greatest debt we owe one another is to speak the truth and to do so in love</u> (Ephesians 4:15, 25). Love without truth is recklessness; truth without love is judgmental legalism.

Here is your opportunity to do an assessment of the key relationships in your life and recategorize them as you sense the Lord leading you to do.

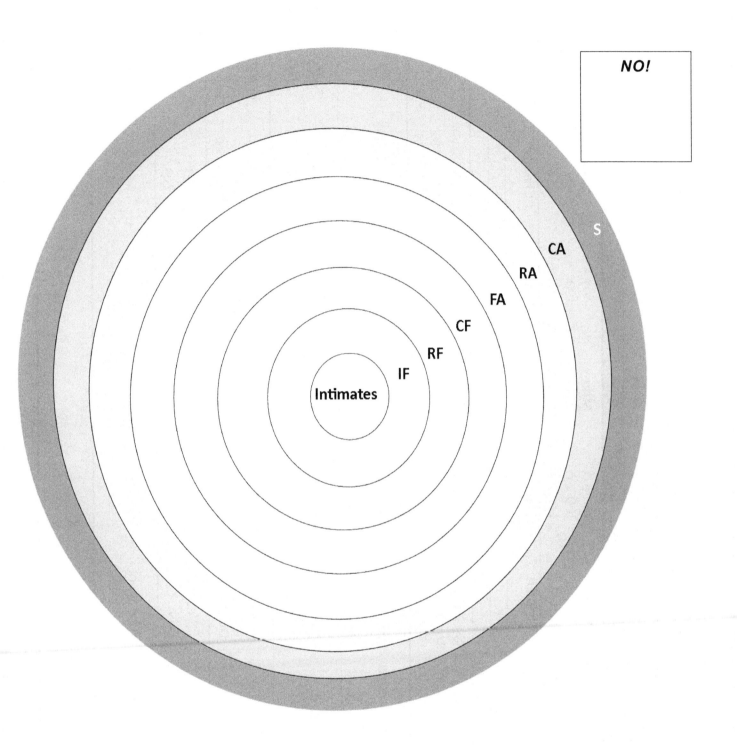

DAILY PRACTICES	DAY 1	DAY 2	DAY 3	DAY 4	DAY 5	DAY 6	"REST" DAY
SATURATION VERSE ____	More □ 100 □ Less □	More □ 100 □ Less □	More □ 100 □ Less □	More □ 100 □ Less □	More □ 100 □ Less □	More □ 100 □ Less □	More □ 100 □ Less □
BIBLE READING	Chapters ____	Chapters ____	Chapters ____	Chapters ____	Chapters ____	Chapters ____	
STUDY MANUAL LESSON # ____	Read Today's Lesson Today Yes □ No □	Read Today's Lesson Today Yes □ No □	Read Today's Lesson Today Yes □ No □	Read Today's Lesson Today Yes □ No □	Read Today's Lesson Today Yes □ No □	Read Today's Lesson Today Yes □ No □	
DAILY REFLECTION	Completed Today's Lesson Today Yes □ No □	Completed Today's Lesson Today Yes □ No □	Completed Today's Lesson Today Yes □ No □	Completed Today's Lesson Today Yes □ No □	Completed Today's Lesson Today Yes □ No □	Completed Today's Lesson Today Yes □ No □	
USED "RESTORE" BOOK	Yes □ No □	Yes □ No □	Yes □ No □	Yes □ No □	Yes □ No □	Yes □ No □	Yes □ No □
PRE-MEAL SATURATION VERSE	Breakfast □ Lunch □ Dinner □	Breakfast □ Lunch □ Dinner □	Breakfast □ Lunch □ Dinner □	Breakfast □ Lunch □ Dinner □	Breakfast □ Lunch □ Dinner □	Breakfast □ Lunch □ Dinner □	Breakfast □ Lunch □ Dinner □
SPECIAL ITEMS	Yes □ No □	Yes □ No □	Yes □ No □	Yes □ No □	Yes □ No □	Yes □ No □	Yes □ No □
PRIVATE PRAYER	Time Spent ____	Time Spent ____	Time Spent ____	Time Spent ____	Time Spent ____	Time Spent ____	Time Spent ____
TODAY, I AM THANKFUL FOR...							

Lesson 18 Study Sheet

Each day review the lesson for that week.
Record one thing you are grateful for each day on your Progress Record.

This Lesson's Verse:

"No one has greater love than this — that one lays down his life for his friends."
John 15:13

Day 1 Reflection

How did this lesson confirm your thinking or your experience in life? How did it shift what you previously thought? *Additional study passage: Deuteronomy 30:15-20*

Day 2 Reflection

When you think of the people you most often call friends, how many of those people fit the definition from this lesson? What do you plan to do with this conclusion? *Additional study passages: Proverbs 14:30; 15:28; 21:4*

Day 3 Reflection

When you consider the healthiest relationships you are in, what is it that makes them healthy? *Additional study passages: Proverbs 13:20; Romans 12:10; Colossians 3:12-14*

Day 4 Reflection

When you consider the unhealthiest relationships you are in, what plan of action do you have for dealing with those better going forward? *Additional study passages: Proverbs 12:26; 22:24-25; 1 Corinthians 15:33*

Day 5 Reflection

What was the greatest disappointment you experienced while going through this lesson? Explain. *Additional study passages: Proverbs 18:24; Job 16:20-21; James 4:1-4*

Day 6 Reflection

What was the greatest encouragement you experienced while going through this lesson? Explain. *Additional study passages: Proverbs 17:17; 19:20; Ecclesiastes 4:9-10*

"A NEW COMMANDMENT I GIVE YOU,

that you *Love one another*; even as I have loved you, so you must love one another.

By this all men will know that you are *My* disciples, if you love one another."

John 13:34-35 (NASB)

LESSON NINETEEN
RELATIONSHIPS THAT SHAPE US

In Matthew 22:34-40, Jesus gives us the baseline for all of our relationships: *"Jesus said to him, 'Love the Lord your God with all your heart, with all your soul, and with all your mind.' This is the first and greatest commandment. The second is like it: 'Love your neighbor as yourself.' All the law and the prophets depend on these two commandments."*

He later refines this baseline even more when He says to His disciples, *"I give you a new commandment – to love one another. Just as I have loved you, you also are to love one another. Everyone will know by this that you are my disciples — if you have love for one another."* (John 13:34-35)

From the moment we are born, we intuitively know that we were created to be in safe, caring, nurturing, and loving relationships with other people. In fact, it was discovered during the nineteenth century that children abandoned at birth and transferred to foundling homes died by the thousands. They literally wasted away, despite the fact that they were fed, kept clean, and protected from danger.

The condition, known as *marasmus* (from the Greek, meaning "wasting away"), claimed the lives of nearly 100 percent of the infants under the age of one-year in U.S. foundling hospitals as late as 1920. What these children lacked was physical contact. Infants raised normally in their own homes are cradled and fed at their mothers' breasts. These foundlings were not.

As the medical field began to understand this connection between life and touch, doctors and nurses in many institutions cooperated in a plan to supply "mothering" for these children.

Their efforts at surrogate mothering consisted of holding, stroking, speaking to the infant, and allowing significant periods of cuddling the child, especially at mealtimes. The results were dramatic and immediate. Infant mortality rates dropped within one year of adopting these touching practices.

The example of infants in foundling hospitals demonstrates a basic truth of human life: it is communal. We are meant to live in connection to and relationship with one another.

It is no wonder that our judicial system considers isolation – solitary confinement –in prison as one of the harshest forms of punishment. We have realized in America that loneliness is one of our most severe social problems we face, plaguing millions – in spite of social media. We cannot even measure accurately the avalanche of other problems our society faces that stem directly from loneliness.

The fact is, we need others and others need us. God created in us the basic human need to be loved and cared for. In Genesis 2, God said, *"It is not good for man to be alone,"* even though Adam had a perfectly good relationship with God all by himself.

Accordingly then, for better and for worse, we expend considerable time, energy, effort, and expense striving to gain and hold onto love and acceptance. Many a scoundrel has taken advantage of this need in others, devastating lives by holding out the promise of connection, only to withhold it in the end. Abusers manipulate their victims by enmeshing the fulfillment of a need for connection with the abuse. They often cause their victim to believe that true connection is not possible without the abuse.

Because there are so many powerful dynamics at work when we experience human connection, especially through touch, it is only normal that we try to satisfy this inherent need through physical means. Our tendency is to connect in relationships first through the five senses. Because sight, hearing, smell, taste, and touch make up the part of us that we are connected to most strongly, it is our "flesh" (as Scripture expresses it) that we seek to satisfy most.

1. **We want to LOOK good:** We will take on the latest diet craze or fashion fads, lock ourselves into the newest workout regimen, join the newest tanning salon, buy the most expensive make-up, and price-out an entire make-over, all to make ourselves more attractive to whomever. We want the world to see us being gorgeous – without spot, wrinkle, or blemish. Billions are spent annually for cosmetic surgeons, dental specialists, and make-over experts in an attempt to overcome genetics and the ravages of time; all

this in the interests of being known as "beautiful."

2. **We want to SOUND good:** Before an important conversation, we may rehearse over and over again what we are going to say. We will work tirelessly on vocabulary and pronunciation. When we hear someone who sounds better than we do, or who has the kind of following we would like to have, we will try to imitate them. We hear ourselves on a recording, hate it, and vow to never let ourselves be recorded again.

3. **We want to SMELL good:** We will spend multiple hundreds of dollars on soaps, powders, shampoos, oils, ointments, body washes, perfumes, aftershaves, and even laundry soap, just to try and smell good to other people...and, oh, horror of horrors if we forget to shower after work or a workout!

4. **We want things to TASTE good:** When you think about how many relationships and social interactions you have that revolve around food,

you can see how we have become enamored with the connection between good tasting food and emotional connection to others. Also, how many times have you knowingly chosen food because it tasted good over how healthy (or unhealthy) it was for you?

5. **We want to be TOUCHED good:** Our skin is the largest organ of our body, and it is always "on" and "open." There are thousands upon thousands of sensory nerves in our skin, and there are a multitude of chemical and other reactions that take place in our brains when someone (or something) activates these receptors. All of us have experienced the pleasant and soothing effects of a long hug. Ever wonder why a hug can feel so amazing, even from someone we do not really know very well? There are a number of emotional and physical benefits to healthy hugging, and it all flows from our need for human connection.

While we naturally use all of our senses in our attempt to achieve the social and personal connections and acceptance that we foundationally need, we have to understand that no connection through our physical senses alone will ever suffice for real life. Physical contact alone will never fill and satisfy our human need for relationship.

The Bible speaks about an overreliance on, or ungodly pursuit of, physicality — i.e. physical connection — when it speaks of "the flesh," or of "sensuality." Sensuality is about more than sexuality, although sexuality is the greatest opportunity for us to experience intense sensuality. Our captivation with connection through touch, or relationship through physicality, means that we often fall into the trap of thinking that sensual closeness to another person produces the intimacy we need and crave. Nothing could be more upside down or backwards than that.

You see, physical connection — especially sexual connection — is the ultimate *expression* of intimacy; it does not "produce" intimacy. In fact, sexual intimacy is at the far-end of the intimacy chain, not the front-end. When two people are truly bonded on a soul level in marriage, the ultimate God-ordained expression of that bonded intimacy is sexual intimacy.

If we get the intimacy chain "out of order," nothing works as God designed it to work and our relationships become more and more fragmented. More on this in a moment.

Relationships that fulfill our deepest needs will be the ones we develop on a soul level first and foremost. No other connection will truly satisfy. It is a glory of being created in the image of God that we actually can connect with another being on a soul level. In fact, we are the only creatures in all the universe that can connect to God — or each other, for that matter — on a spirit and soul level. Nothing else can truly satisfy our deepest need for deepest connection. We were made for fellowship with God who is fully spirit ("*God is Spirit,*" John 4:24a).

This spiritual relationship connection that we so desperately need we call **bonding.** It is deeper than mere connection, more than a demonstration of affection, and more necessary than friendly association. The importance of bonding is only highlighted by its loss.

For instance, an inability to bond with their mothers is the most serious problem related to caring for babies who are born addicted to drugs/alcohol (because their mothers abused drugs/alcohol). All too often such children are also unable to bond with anyone else either. Neurological processes have been hijacked by the drugs/alcohol, and their little brains have been mis-wired from before they were born. Beyond childhood, people with long-term addiction problems develop an ever-decreasing ability to bond with others.

Contrary to this negative example, for most babies bonding is a natural process that starts occurring with the mother before the child is even born. After birth, the first hour or so is crucial for healthy bonding and for important neurological development as the mother and child share their first face-to-face and skin-to-skin contacts. There are connections made — physically, mentally, emotionally, spiritually, even neurologically — that are critical to the child's ability to connect with others on those same levels. In fact, studies show that this lack of bonding with the birth mother usually underlies the brokenness of sociopaths.

Now, here's the great news about bonding: God created it...God is eager to bond with us...and God has an answer to all our brokenness in bonding! God's design for us bonding — with Him and with others — begins with developing a close, personal relationship with Him through Jesus Christ. This is where true bonding begins; bonding that we experience not primarily as emotions, but rather as a matter of soul and spirit. Bonding of any sort, including with other human beings, is essentially a spiritual matter of the soul. It is important to note here that since bonding takes place on a soul and spiritual level, the impediments to bonding also occur on a spiritual level.

If we experience problems relating to others, there is definitely a spiritual reason contributing to the issue.

As was mentioned a few moments ago, we often seek to artificially create the intimate bonds of real relationship through a sensory/sensual connection, the most intense (and seemingly meaningful) being a sexual connection. Too often this effort becomes a tragic expression of "bonding gone bad" in sin.

Rightly understood, sexual intimacy is the ultimate physical expression of the God-honoring bonding that happens between a man and a woman as they become "one flesh" in marriage. Therefore, we need to understand that for every sexually intimate relationship we have had outside of marriage, we have experienced an "out-of-God's-order bonding" with another person.

This "out-of-God's-order bonding" creates significant damage on a heart/mind/soul level; damage that confuses and distorts our ability to bond well with others, especially those God intends for us to intimately bond with on the deepest levels.

 Anchor Point: The health of our horizontal relationships reflects the health of our vertical relationship with God. Put another way, the health of our vertical relationship with God will be reflected in the health of our horizontal relationships with others.

SHIELDING[21]

"Shielding" is a term we use to describe the process of shutting others out and protecting ourselves from being emotionally vulnerable. Lack of vulnerability works two ways: it helps to protect us, and yet it also insulates us from healthy connection.

People often speak of "putting up walls" in a relationship, but "walls" implies something solid and permanent. The reality is we are able to raise and lower our shields at will. We raise our shields to keep others at bay, and we lower our shields to allow others to get in close. Whether we do so foolishly or wisely is not the issue right now. Rather, the idea (and reality) of shielding is what we need to understand.

When we lower our shields, we become vulnerable and open to both help and harm equally. In order to bond on a spiritual level, we have to lower our "shields" and become authentically vulnerable with another person.

Think of this idea of shielding by imagining a fight between two people who have bonded and grown close (whether as friends or as a married couple). They have bonded by repeatedly lowering their shields and becoming vulnerable with one another. Their shields stay down as they begin to fight, if for no other reason than the fact that one cannot lob a personal insult or accusation from behind a raised shield. Without realizing it, both have their shields down as they battle it out. This is how they each get hurt in the process of trying to "defend" themselves.

For this battling couple, or for any of us, the problem becomes even worse when they, or we, suddenly realize the pain of battle and instinctively raise our shields once again. In doing so, we wind up trapping heart-hurt *behind* the shield itself. As the hurt ricochets around, and we keep our shield up, it stays trapped, causing more and more injury and damage. By staying "shielded," we give the hurt fresh life. We live rehearsing our pain and "saturating" on our injury.

The only way to get rid of the hurt is to lower our shield and allow the hurt

---

[21] Thanks again go to Pastor Troy for articulating this concept so helpfully in the original S.A.F.E. Program.

to escape by sharing it with someone we trust. When we do that with the person who injured us in the first place, open and vulnerable to attack once again. It is not a surprise that we find ourselves reluctant to take such a step. True bonding has suffered and so has our relationship with the other person. Yet, despite this reluctance, sometimes lowering the shield and becoming vulnerable once again is exactly what we need to do in order to "work it out."

The dynamic described above is why we experience the deepest heart-hurts in our closest relationships. We have to lower our shields in order to bond and that makes us vulnerable. Because being vulnerable is critical to true bonding, it is not at all uncommon for us to experience strong and conflicting emotions, both good and bad at the same time, about our closest relationships. This is known as "ambivalence."

Before we are ready to have healthy relationships (or to experience renewed health in the relationships we are in), we need to find out how well we relate to those who are closest to us already. If there are problems that hinder those relationships in some way, we need to discover what those problems are and discern how God views them. Then we repair what can be repaired and shelve what remains unfixable.

1. **We need to make a list of the relationships that are the greatest influences in our life today.** Start with those that have the greatest impact on you right now — father, mother, siblings, spouse, children, employer, etc. Even if a person is no longer alive, if they nonetheless wield a significant influence on you, it is important to still do an inventory on that relationship (see the worksheet below).

2. **We need to pay attention to, and make note of, problems and difficulties in those relationships.** This will take prayerful honesty to avoid minimizing or magnifying. Ask God to help you see what is true about the relationship, no matter how that truth makes you "feel."

3. **We need to take an inventory of the emotions we experience when we contemplate our relationship with that person.** Remember:

emotions (feelings) are not right or wrong, they simply "are."

4. **Finally, we need to assess whether or not what we feel about that person and the relationship is reasonable and why.** This will help us determine the best course of action for dealing with that relationship in a way consistent with what God has said to us about relationships already (think Lesson 18): *We are to speak the truth in love, to love others as much as we love ourselves, and to be wise without being vengeful.*

Make as many copies of the following "Relationship Inventory Worksheet" as you need to adequately assess the relationships in your life that are the most influential at this time. As you use the worksheet, be prayerful, asking God to help you see the relationship from His viewpoint as much as possible. The clearer your perspective and the more honestly balanced your evaluation is, the more powerful this exercise will be.

৪০ • ୯୫

Relationship Inventory Worksheet

Please fill out a "Relationship Inventory Worksheet" for your most significant relationships, *in order of influence*, beginning with Number 1. (**MAKE AS MANY COPIES AS YOU NEED**)

Relationship with _____

1. I have had a relationship with this person for _____ years or months.

2. I would classify my relationship with this person as (circle one):

    1 – Very Good   2 – Good   3 – Fair   4 – Poor   5 – Very Poor   6 – Love/Hate

The emotions I most generally feel when I think of this person are: (Circle all that apply)

Spectrum of Emotions

MAD	SAD	GLAD	AFRAID	CONFUSED	ASHAMED	LONELY
Bothered	Down	Comfortable	Uneasy	Uncertain	Awkward	Out-of-place
Irritated	Blue	Relaxed	Apprehensive	Ambivalent	Self-conscious	Left out
Displeased	Disappointed	Content	Tense	Unsettled	Embarrassed	Disconnected
Annoyed	Melancholy	Satisfied	Anxious	Tentative	Flustered	Insecure
Steamed	Unhappy	Grateful	Nervous	Perplexed	Apologetic	Invisible
Perturbed	Dissatisfied	Warm	Distressed	Puzzled	Guilty	Unwelcome
Frustrated	Gloomy	Happy	Scared	Distracted	Regretful	Discounted
Angry	Mournful	Encouraged	Frightened	Flustered	Remorseful	Excluded
Fed-up	Grieved	Fulfilled	Vulnerable	Jumbled	Shamed	Insignificant
Disgusted	Depressed	Hopeful	Repulsed	Unfocused	Disgusted	Ignored
Indignant	Crushed	Cheerful	Agitated	Fragmented	Belittled	Neglected
Resentful	Miserable	Thrilled	Shocked	Disheartened	Humiliated	Disregarded
Fuming	Defeated	Delighted	Alarmed	Insecure	Disregarded	Isolated
Explosive	Worthless	Joyful	Overwhelmed	Bewildered	Violated	Unwanted
Enraged	Shameful	Elated	Frantic	Lost	Dirty	Rejected
Irate	Dejected	Exhilarated	Horrified	Stunned	Mortified	Deserted
Outraged	Empty	Overjoyed	Terrified	Torn	Defiled	Outcast
Furious	Devastated	Ecstatic	Numb	Baffled	Devastated	Abandoned
Raging	Embittered	Euphoric	Dead Inside	Speechless	Degraded	Forsaken

Are my feelings toward this person realistic? Yes _____ No _____ Why or why not?

DAILY PRACTICES	DAY 1	DAY 2	DAY 3	DAY 4	DAY 5	DAY 6	"REST" DAY
SATURATION VERSE ____	More ☐ 100 ☐ Less ☐	More ☐ 100 ☐ Less ☐	More ☐ 100 ☐ Less ☐	More ☐ 100 ☐ Less ☐	More ☐ 100 ☐ Less ☐	More ☐ 100 ☐ Less ☐	More ☐ 100 ☐ Less ☐
BIBLE READING	Chapters ____	Chapters ____	Chapters ____	Chapters ____	Chapters ____	Chapters ____	
STUDY MANUAL LESSON # ____	Read Today's Lesson Today Yes ☐ No ☐	Read Today's Lesson Today Yes ☐ No ☐	Read Today's Lesson Today Yes ☐ No ☐	Read Today's Lesson Today Yes ☐ No ☐	Read Today's Lesson Today Yes ☐ No ☐	Read Today's Lesson Today Yes ☐ No ☐	
DAILY REFLECTION	Completed Today's Lesson Today Yes ☐ No ☐	Completed Today's Lesson Today Yes ☐ No ☐	Completed Today's Lesson Today Yes ☐ No ☐	Completed Today's Lesson Today Yes ☐ No ☐	Completed Today's Lesson Today Yes ☐ No ☐	Completed Today's Lesson Today Yes ☐ No ☐	
USED "RESTORE" BOOK	Yes ☐ No ☐	Yes ☐ No ☐	Yes ☐ No ☐	Yes ☐ No ☐	Yes ☐ No ☐	Yes ☐ No ☐	Yes ☐ No ☐
PRE-MEAL SATURATION VERSE	Breakfast ☐ Lunch ☐ Dinner ☐	Breakfast ☐ Lunch ☐ Dinner ☐	Breakfast ☐ Lunch ☐ Dinner ☐	Breakfast ☐ Lunch ☐ Dinner ☐	Breakfast ☐ Lunch ☐ Dinner ☐	Breakfast ☐ Lunch ☐ Dinner ☐	Breakfast ☐ Lunch ☐ Dinner ☐
SPECIAL ITEMS	Yes ☐ No ☐	Yes ☐ No ☐	Yes ☐ No ☐	Yes ☐ No ☐	Yes ☐ No ☐	Yes ☐ No ☐	Yes ☐ No ☐
PRIVATE PRAYER	Time Spent ____	Time Spent ____	Time Spent ____	Time Spent ____	Time Spent ____	Time Spent ____	Time Spent ____
TODAY, I AM THANKFUL FOR...							

Lesson 19 Study Sheet

Each day review the lesson for that week.
Record one thing you are grateful for each day on your Progress Record.

This Lesson's Verse:

"A new commandment I give you, that you love one another; even as I have loved you, so you must love one another. By this all men will know that you are My disciples, if you love one another." John 13:34-35

Day 1 Reflection

When entering relationships, what do you give the most consideration to and why? How important do you think these things are to God and why? *Additional study passage: 1 Corinthians 13:4-13*

Day 2 Reflection

In reference to Question 1, do those things you consider important require "bonding" as defined in the lesson? Explain. *Additional study passages: Proverbs 17:17; 18:24*

Day 3 Reflection

What are some harmful emotions that cause us to put up shields and hinder us from bonding and forming close relationships with God or others? *Additional study passage: James 4:4-8*

Day 4 Reflection

What person do you most desire to form a stronger bond and healthier relationship with right now? Do you have shields up in your life and, if so, why are you reluctant to make yourself more vulnerable to that person? *Additional study passage: Philippians 2:1-4*

Day 5 Reflection

In your relationship with Jesus Christ, do you have shields up to protect yourself from Him? Explain. *Additional study passage: John 17*

Day 6 Reflection

What spiritual victories are necessary in your life before close bonding with Christ and others becomes more complete? *Additional study passage: 2 Peter 1:2-8*

See to it that
NO ONE comes short

of the
grace of God,

that NO ONE be like a
bitter root
springing up and causing
trouble,

and through him
many become

defiled.

Hebrews 12:15 (NASB)

LESSON TWENTY
THE TRUTH ABOUT BITTERNESS

There are many applications for the Biblical declaration, *"Do not be deceived, God is not mocked; for whatever a man sows, that he will also reap"* (Galatians 6:7). Consider how this statement of the Apostle Paul relates to one of the most potentially destructive forces in our lives: bitterness.

The term "bitterness," as it is used in Hebrews 12:15, means "putrefy." Think about the influence of one moldy strawberry in a basketful. Get the idea? When we allow unforgiveness to take root in our heart, bitterness sprouts up and permeates every aspect of our lives. When we allow unforgiveness to grow, the person (or people) we are embittered against gets off scot-free. In the meantime, we allow ourselves to be emotionally controlled-by-remote.

Ironically, we suffer far more than those against whom we are bitter. In fact, they often have little if any idea that we are holding a grudge against them, or that we think they owe us something. Think of it as letting someone live "Rent-Free" in your head.

Often that person has gone their own way, never knowing or caring that we are bitter; or, in other cases, fully aware of our bitterness and actually enjoying our misery. While the person we despise is often unaware of that fact, we are slowly but quite certainly destroying ourselves and everything good in our lives.

Let's look at how we end up in a place of bitterness...

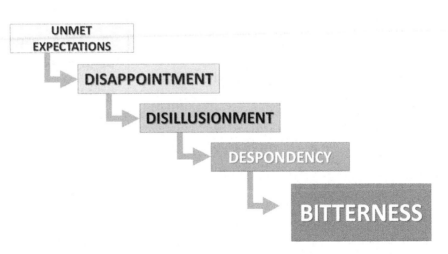

UNMET EXPECTATIONS

DISAPPOINTMENT

DISILLUSIONMENT

DESPONDENCY

BITTERNESS

Unmet Expectations: Expectations are like the ceiling; people can jump up and touch it, but they cannot live up there. So it is with the expectations we have of others. Often our expectations are rooted in a sense of entitlement (we believe we are entitled to have our wants and needs met when we want, the way we want). When our expectations go unmet, we experience...

Disappointment: Our hopes are dashed on the rocks and we feel sad that things did not go as we expected. Holding onto that disappointment quickly weights us down even lower and into...

Disillusionment: Now we are not just disappointed about a situation or with a person, now we are disappointed with relationships in general. The shiny picture we had of that person and the relationship is dark and dingy; we are losing hope. Remaining there long increases the dark burden and plunges us even lower and we fall into...

Despondency: This we call the "Eeyore Level." This is where we are pessimistic not only about relationships, we are pessimistic about our own worth and value.

"I'm leaving (if anybody cares)."

"Don't pay any attention to me — I don't really matter."

"Of *course* this fell apart — I'm stuck with the same idiots I'm *always* stuck with?!"

"What did I *expect*? That things would magically be different than they always are?"

We do not have to live here long before our persistent and unrelenting anger and hopelessness about how long we have been mistreated this way results in...

Bitterness:[22] Bitterness is rooted in deep-seated, long-term unforgiveness — usually, unforgiveness over someone (or multiple someones) not living up to our expectations. We may feel justified in those expectations, but they are expectations we feel entitled to, nonetheless.[23]

---

[22] Resentment is like a half-step between Despondency and Bitterness. Think of resentment as a slow-burning anger, a low-grade bitterness.

[23] In the "Restore" section, you will find "Weapons Against a Sense of Entitlement" (pg. 371) that can be quite helpful.

Depression: The only difference between **Bitterness** and **Depression** is the orientation of our anger. Which way is it facing? Who is it directed at? **Bitterness** has an *outward* focus. **Depression** has an *inward* focus. Both are the result of deep-seated, long-term unforgiveness. **Bitterness** says, "S/he is the problem." **Depression** says, "*I* am the problem."

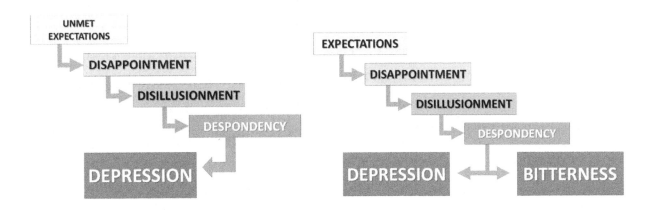

Again, we need to remember that bitterness harms us far more than it harms the one we are embittered toward. And it will corrupt every other relationship we are part of.

Let's look at the devastating consequences of bitterness in our lives:

1. *It will harm our health.*
2. *It will enslave us.*
3. *Bitterness poisons (putrefies) every relationship in our lives.*
4. *It is a sin that will keep us from experiencing God's forgiveness.*

FIRST, **bitterness harms our health.** The negative health effects of bitterness/unforgiveness have been well-documented, with research showing a link between prolonged anger or resentment and a host of heightened medical risks. Because of the ways in which resentment and unforgiveness interact with the brain, the body's reactions can lead to chronic — and sometimes serious — physical ailments. In fact, prolonged bitterness can make people 500% more likely to die before the age of 50. And, over time, we even show the effects of this stress in our faces: We begin to look "hard."

SECOND, we become enslaved. We are enslaved by our bitterness. We are emotionally tied to the person we are bitter toward. Everything they do or don't do affects us, whether we want it to or not. We spend so much time nursing our animosity that we hinder our ability to have a useful and productive life. Someone has said that "Unforgiveness is like drinking poison and waiting for the other person to die."

THIRD, bitterness poisons (putrefies) every relationship in our lives. Carefully read Hebrews 12:15 (and its referent, Deuteronomy 29:18). In both places, it speaks about a "root of bitterness." A bitter spirit toward one person will contaminate every relationship in our lives. We become the root of bitterness that putrefies almost every other relationship we are in. It is like the rotten apple that spoils the whole barrel. It is like a cancer that, unchecked, eats away at and destroys us from within.

FOURTH, unforgiveness is sin and it keeps us from experiencing God's forgiveness. Read carefully Jesus' instruction on prayer in Matthew 6:9-15. Especially note versus 14 and 15. An unforgiving spirit keeps us from God's forgiveness (see Lesson 14). After all, why would God forgive us if we are unwilling to forgive someone else? It will also serve well here if you study Jesus' parable in Matthew 18:21-35.

THE ANTIDOTE

So, what is the antidote to the descent from **Expectation** to **Bitterness/Depression**?

Anticipate that since you are a rebellious human being in relationship with rebellious human beings, all living in a rebellious world, chances are that things will go wrong — sometimes, often. When they do *not*, you experience...

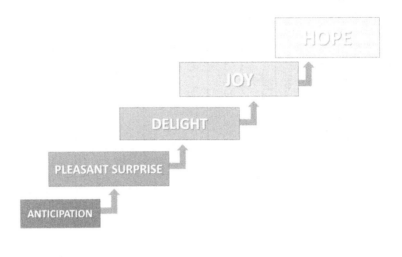

Pleasant Surprise that things went well. As you experience pleasant surprise more and more, you find yourself living in a place of...

Delight. And the more delight you experience as you recognize how often things go well, you experience a sense of...

Joy. Long-term joy gives us a sense of...

Hope; and it is hope that is the antidote to the hopelessness of **Depression & Bitterness!** Keep in mind that hope is "a confident assurance based on facts in evidence," not wishful or magical thinking.

℘ • ℭ

DAILY PRACTICES	DAY 1	DAY 2	DAY 3	DAY 4	DAY 5	DAY 6	"REST" DAY
SATURATION VERSE ___	More ☐ 100 ☐ Less ☐	More ☐ 100 ☐ Less ☐	More ☐ 100 ☐ Less ☐	More ☐ 100 ☐ Less ☐	More ☐ 100 ☐ Less ☐	More ☐ 100 ☐ Less ☐	More ☐ 100 ☐ Less ☐
BIBLE READING	Chapters ___	Chapters ___	Chapters ___	Chapters ___	Chapters ___	Chapters ___	
STUDY MANUAL LESSON # ___	Read Today's Lesson Today Yes ☐ No ☐	Read Today's Lesson Today Yes ☐ No ☐	Read Today's Lesson Today Yes ☐ No ☐	Read Today's Lesson Today Yes ☐ No ☐	Read Today's Lesson Today Yes ☐ No ☐	Read Today's Lesson Today Yes ☐ No ☐	
DAILY REFLECTION	Completed Today's Lesson Today Yes ☐ No ☐	Completed Today's Lesson Today Yes ☐ No ☐	Completed Today's Lesson Today Yes ☐ No ☐	Completed Today's Lesson Today Yes ☐ No ☐	Completed Today's Lesson Today Yes ☐ No ☐	Completed Today's Lesson Today Yes ☐ No ☐	
USED "RESTORE" BOOK	Yes ☐ No ☐	Yes ☐ No ☐	Yes ☐ No ☐	Yes ☐ No ☐	Yes ☐ No ☐	Yes ☐ No ☐	Yes ☐ No ☐
PRE-MEAL SATURATION VERSE	Breakfast ☐ Lunch ☐ Dinner ☐	Breakfast ☐ Lunch ☐ Dinner ☐	Breakfast ☐ Lunch ☐ Dinner ☐	Breakfast ☐ Lunch ☐ Dinner ☐	Breakfast ☐ Lunch ☐ Dinner ☐	Breakfast ☐ Lunch ☐ Dinner ☐	Breakfast ☐ Lunch ☐ Dinner ☐
SPECIAL ITEMS	Yes ☐ No ☐	Yes ☐ No ☐	Yes ☐ No ☐	Yes ☐ No ☐	Yes ☐ No ☐	Yes ☐ No ☐	Yes ☐ No ☐
PRIVATE PRAYER	Time Spent ___	Time Spent ___	Time Spent ___	Time Spent ___	Time Spent ___	Time Spent ___	Time Spent ___
TODAY, I AM THANKFUL FOR...							

Lesson 20 Study Sheet

Each day review the lesson for that week.
Record one thing you are grateful for each day on your Progress Record.

This Lesson's Verse:

"See to it that no one comes short of the grace of God, that no one be like a bitter root springing up and causing trouble, and through him many become defiled." Hebrews 12:15

Day 1 Reflection

Do you see a correlation between any health problems and the way you have dealt with the problem relationships in your life? *Additional study passage: Psalm 6*

Day 2 Reflection

Explain why bitterness and anger can be detrimental to our spiritual as well as our physical health. *Additional study passages: Job 7:1-11*

Day 3 Reflection

Is there one person you have a relationship with that, were it to be made healthy, your own emotional health would improve? Who is it and what is standing in the way? *Additional study passage: Psalm 64:10; Proverbs 24:16-18*

Day 4 Reflection

Explain how our approach to unhealthy relationships here on earth impacts our relationship with God and our eternity. *Additional study passages: Matthew 6:14-15; 20-21; 18:3-4*

Day 5 Reflection

Christ came to set us free and reconcile us in our relationship with God. Consider why a person who has poor relationships cannot be truly free. *Additional study passages: Galatians 5:1-2; 1 John 2:3-11*

Day 6 Reflection

What one attitude is most important in our relationships with others? Describe this attitude and how you are doing with developing it. *Additional study passage: 1 Corinthians 13: 1, 4-8*

"DO NOT AVENGE YOURSELVES,

Dear Friends,

but give place to **GOD's** wrath; for it is written,

'VENGEANCE IS MINE, I WILL REPAY,' SAYS THE LORD."

Romans 12:19 (NASB)

LESSON TWENTY-ONE
AND THEN THERE'S ANGER

The Bible has a great deal to say about anger. Here are just a few verses:

"He who is slow to anger has great understanding, but he who is quick-tempered exalts folly." (Proverbs 14:29)

"A hot-tempered man stirs up strife, but the slow to anger calms a dispute." (Proverbs 15:18)

"He who is slow to anger is better than the mighty, and he who rules his spirit, than he who captures a city." (Proverbs 16:32)

"A man's discretion makes him slow to anger, and it is his glory to overlook a transgression." (Proverbs 19:11)

"This you know, my beloved brethren. But everyone must be quick to hear, slow to speak and slow to anger; for the anger of man does not achieve the righteousness of God." (James 1:19)

We have all heard stories of the devastation left in the wake of someone who has "lost his temper," whose raging anger has caused destruction of property or harm to another person.

Uncontrolled anger is wicked and is never satisfied. It is a consuming fire that continues to be fueled by sinful emotions, primarily fear and unforgiveness. The Bible tells us to be angry, yet to not sin (Ephesians 4:26). The difference between righteous and unrighteous anger is this: Righteous anger has no personal component (it is not about us) and it compels us to seek change for the good of others. Personal anger seeks change for personal benefit.

We also need to realize that anger is like an umbrella. Anger usually serves as a cover for fear, pain, loss, or fear of pain or loss. When we are experiencing anger, that anger is like emotional acne. Just as with acne, the pimple is only the surface sign of a deeper problem. So is the anger that rises to the surface from our hearts.

This remains true regardless of which type of anger we think of; the "cold-as-dry-ice" sort (which we dealt with in our "The Truth about Bitterness" lesson), or the "red-hot-and-raging" anger we are working on now. Both burn us up, burn us out, and burn those around us...it is just a different kind of burn.

Let's be clear; anger itself is not a sin, but anger that is not dealt with and relinquished becomes bitterness, which *is* sin. As we learned in the last lesson, bitterness putrefies every meaningful relationship we are in and robs us of what is good and decent in our lives. Anger is harmful when it remains unresolved. Anger does not simply disappear when we choose to ignore it. It is highly caustic and corrosive on every aspect of our life, including on our sense of self, our general emotional state, our ability to feel safe or free, and our ability to connect with others in a healthy, vibrant, and God-honoring way.

The negative effects of unresolved anger even harm our physical health. It puts us under a state of constant stress, which often results in increased fatigue, insomnia, nightmares, interrupted sleep, excessive muscle tension, clenched jaws, grinding teeth during sleep, joint pain and stiffness, and sore, tense muscles.

Unresolved anger causes elevated blood pressure known as hypertension, as well as prolonged hyperarousal that taxes the heart and increases the risk of heart disease fivefold. On top of that, it lowers immune response important in cancer and disease prevention. Chronic hyperarousal from anger tends to suppress our immune system, leading to poorer overall health.

So, now that we have seen how unresolved and uncontrolled anger is sin, hampering our relationships with God and others, and also seen how it is harmful to us personally, how do we deal with it?

We can choose God's way, or the world's way. Let's consider the world's way first. The world has two ways of dealing with anger. The **first** approach is through suppression, internalizing it and holding it in; the **second** is venting — not letting it go, doing or saying whatever we feel we need to do or say to release the anger.

LET US CONSIDER WHAT IS WRONG WITH THESE TWO APPROACHES

FIRST, we have already seen what suppressed anger or bitterness does to our physical and mental health, to say nothing of our relationship with God. Because of the destructive nature of unrighteous anger, we cannot afford to try to suppress it and keep it bottled up inside. Nothing is solved or resolved as long as we hold the anger in; it simply continues to roil around inside of us, waiting to explode. If we hold it in too long, that explosion can cause us to harm ourselves or someone else.

SECOND, the practice of venting our anger is actually both sinful *and* counterproductive. On the opposite side of suppressing anger and holding it in (with that set of deep and harmful effects), we have been taught that it is better to just "get it off your chest."

While this may give some immediate, temporary relief, it solves nothing. The root cause of the anger is still unresolved, so the anger continues to burn. Also, others are usually hurt, both emotionally and physically, when we selfishly vent. It is a very short step from a man punching a pillow to punching his wife. And the ongoing damage we do to ourselves does not end.

Both approaches are equally defective and sinful. We can be grateful that we are not left to the world's way of "managing" our anger, something Scripture *never* directs us to do!

GOD'S REMEDY IS FOR US TO SURRENDER OUR ANGER TO HIM

So, bet you are wondering, "How do we do this?" It begins with an honest conversation with God, asking Him to help us identify what it is we are actually angry about. Is it fear, pain, loss, or fear of pain or loss? What is really going on in our heart? What is it that is making us so fearful that attacking the source of the threat seems to be the best answer (You see, what you often fear most is that the worst thing you believe about yourself is what will prove to be most true. Anyone or anything that triggers or feeds this fear becomes a threat and we feel compelled to destroy it!).

Confess to God: "This anger is based in some lie I believe. Help me see and surrender my fear and stop believing the lie." This is a helpful place to start. Such confession can help us become calm enough to surrender and release to God whatever we are holding onto. He is the only One who can effectively deal with it.

The Lord says, *"Vengeance is mine."* By implication then, vengeance is not ours! God very much wants us to give our anger to Him, to let go of whatever expectation we think we are entitled to, and to trust that He will handle it in His best manner and in the proper time according to His will.

God warns us not to let the sun go down on our anger. The key words for dealing with anger are "Forgive" and "Trust." Release every sense of wanting retribution, and trust God to work His best will in that person's life.

The KEY is to 1) FORGIVE; and 2) TRUST

1. **Forgive [Internal Forgiveness from Lesson 14]**. When we look at Jesus' example, know that He had done nothing to harm those who spat in His face, slapped Him, pulled out His beard, mocked Him, beat Him, and nailed Him to the cross. Then remember that these men were convinced they were in the right, so they had nothing to confess and ask forgiveness for.

Yet, Jesus Christ not only forgave them, He also asked His Heavenly Father to forgive them as well. It is not that they were innocent, but that He was trusting the father's righteous justice (Matthew 26:62-68; Luke 23:34; 1 Peter 2:22-23).

In the book of Acts, Stephen followed Jesus' example when he was being stoned to death by many of the same men who had crucified Christ.

We need not wait for someone to ask our forgiveness before we internally forgive. One thing we must remember is that forgiving does not let them off the hook with God. Rather, it lets *us* surrender the burden of their sin and leaves it between them and God to sort out. Once we have truly forgiven in our heart, the lifting of the burden that comes is the evidence that we are of the same mind as God.

Anchor Point: <u>a grudge is the heaviest man-made burden a person can ever carry.</u>

2. Trust. What do we do with the refrain we often shout, "I'll forgive, but I will *not* forget!" The Bible tells us that when God forgives, He also "remembers no more" (Isaiah 43:25). This does not mean that God develops "divine amnesia." If He were to ever forget or not know something, He would not be God (remember about God's Omniscience?). What it means is that God does not bring it up again, does not revisit it, and does not re-accuse us of what He has forgiven.

There is a very good reason why we need to learn to trust God to bring about His best will in the life of a person against whom we are tempted to sinful anger. If we do not trust God to work with them in His way and His time, then we continue to live life as if the offense is fresh and new. We continue to suffer the same wrong in our mind and heart, over-and-over again.

God promises to justly avenge sin (Romans 12:19). If someone who has wronged us comes to repentance, then great! If not, God will address it at their "Exit Interview." If we continue to hold onto the evil done to us, keeping it fresh in our minds and thriving in our hearts, we hold tightly to being wronged, keeping it alive and continuing to carry it. It becomes a grudge, and a grudge is the heaviest man-made burden a person can ever carry.

When we keep track of a wrong that has been done to us, our mind not only brings up the memory of the wrong, but the emotions associated with the memory are just as fresh as if it had just happened. <u>Emotionally-charged memories</u> place us back where we started, repeatedly fighting the same useless battles. This is not where we find "freedom," and this is surely not God's will for us.

DAILY PRACTICES	DAY 1	DAY 2	DAY 3	DAY 4	DAY 5	DAY 6	"REST" DAY
SATURATION VERSE ___	More ☐ 100 ☐ Less ☐	More ☐ 100 ☐ Less ☐	More ☐ 100 ☐ Less ☐	More ☐ 100 ☐ Less ☐	More ☐ 100 ☐ Less ☐	More ☐ 100 ☐ Less ☐	More ☐ 100 ☐ Less ☐
BIBLE READING	Chapters ___	Chapters ___	Chapters ___	Chapters ___	Chapters ___	Chapters ___	
STUDY MANUAL LESSON # ___	Read Today's Lesson Today Yes ☐ No ☐	Read Today's Lesson Today Yes ☐ No ☐	Read Today's Lesson Today Yes ☐ No ☐	Read Today's Lesson Today Yes ☐ No ☐	Read Today's Lesson Today Yes ☐ No ☐	Read Today's Lesson Today Yes ☐ No ☐	
DAILY REFLECTION	Completed Today's Lesson Today Yes ☐ No ☐	Completed Today's Lesson Today Yes ☐ No ☐	Completed Today's Lesson Today Yes ☐ No ☐	Completed Today's Lesson Today Yes ☐ No ☐	Completed Today's Lesson Today Yes ☐ No ☐	Completed Today's Lesson Today Yes ☐ No ☐	
USED "RESTORE" BOOK	Yes ☐ No ☐	Yes ☐ No ☐	Yes ☐ No ☐	Yes ☐ No ☐	Yes ☐ No ☐	Yes ☐ No ☐	Yes ☐ No ☐
PRE-MEAL SATURATION VERSE	Breakfast ☐ Lunch ☐ Dinner ☐	Breakfast ☐ Lunch ☐ Dinner ☐	Breakfast ☐ Lunch ☐ Dinner ☐	Breakfast ☐ Lunch ☐ Dinner ☐	Breakfast ☐ Lunch ☐ Dinner ☐	Breakfast ☐ Lunch ☐ Dinner ☐	Breakfast ☐ Lunch ☐ Dinner ☐
SPECIAL ITEMS	Yes ☐ No ☐	Yes ☐ No ☐	Yes ☐ No ☐	Yes ☐ No ☐	Yes ☐ No ☐	Yes ☐ No ☐	Yes ☐ No ☐
PRIVATE PRAYER	Time Spent ___	Time Spent ___	Time Spent ___	Time Spent ___	Time Spent ___	Time Spent ___	Time Spent ___
TODAY, I AM THANKFUL FOR...							

Lesson 21 *Study Sheet*

Each day review the lesson for that week.
Record one thing you are grateful for each day on your Progress Record.

This Lesson's Verse:

"Do not avenge yourselves, dear friends, but give place to God's wrath; for it is written, 'Vengeance is Mine, I will repay,' says the Lord." Romans 12:19

Day 1 Reflection

List some of the ways you try to punish those at whom you are angry. *Additional study passage: James 4:1-7*

Day 2 Reflection

Tying this lesson together with the concept of "shielding" from Lesson 19, why do you think so many couples say that their relationship improves after a fight? Some believe that "making-up" afterward makes the quarrel worthwhile. Do you agree or disagree? Why? *Additional study passages: Colossians 2:8; 3:8*

Day 3 Reflection

Explain how pridefulness and anger are interrelated and what you have learned so far about God's remedy. *Additional study passages: Psalm 10:2-4; James 4:6-10*

Day 4 Reflection

Picture a person controlled by anger, raging inside. What impact does that person and their anger have on others in their life? How likely are they to be someone others will want to follow? *Additional study passage: Colossians 3:8-10, 12-13*

Day 5 Reflection

Explain how unrighteous anger enslaves us and how it so easily makes us an object of shame and disgrace. *Additional study passages: Proverbs 12:16; 15:1; 19:19; 27:4*

Day 6 Reflection

What does God mean when He says, "Be slow to anger?" What do we need to "put on" in order to reflect this aspect of godly character? *Additional study passage: James 1:19-20*

"Shared joy is a double joy; shared sorrow is half a sorrow."
— **Swedish Proverb**

"Your own soul is nourished when you are kind, but you destroy yourself when you are cruel."
— **Proverbs 11:17**

"Friendship is stronger than kinship."
— **Yiddish Proverb**

"Fire goes out for lack of fuel, and quarrels disappear when gossip stops. A quarrelsome person starts fights as easily as hot embers light charcoal or fire lights wood."
— **Proverbs 26:20-21**

"Even from a foe a man may learn wisdom."
— **Greek proverb**

Get all the advice and instruction you can and be wise the rest of your life. You can make many plans, but the LORD's purpose will prevail.
— **Proverbs 19:20-21**

Be angry; do not sin...

GOAL

UNSHAKEABLE CONFIDENCE

UNSHAKABLE CONFIDENCE

When we lack confidence, it results from having a poor self-image. Having a poor self-image comes from not seeing ourselves as we really are and not seeing ourselves as God sees us. This poor self-image creates deep and lasting doubt, robbing us of confidence — confidence in our worth, our value, and our potential to become what God has created us to be. Confidence in God's view of us is a must if we are to build a healthy self-image and have a God-centered confidence. We are not referring to self-confidence here, but rather confidence that God loves us and places great value on us as a person, confidence that He will bring about the full completion of what He has begun in us (Philippians 1:6), and confidence that He will enable us to be successful as long as we work with Him. We will only find satisfaction and fulfillment in life as we become familiar with and practice *His* principles for success.

"I am able
to do
all things
⟨ THAT GOD ASKS OF ME ⟩
through the
one who
strengthens me."

PHILIPPIANS 4:13
CLARIFICATION ADDED
NET

mariah·hatfield
2020

LESSON TWENTY-TWO
THE FRUITFUL LIFE

There is an enormous difference between a life focused on being "successful" and a life focused on being "fruitful." "Success" builds SELF-esteem, "fruitful" esteems and builds up OTHER people. The success-oriented life is grounded in personal gain, often at the cost of personal integrity. The fruitful-oriented life is grounded in Christian character and faithfulness.

There are many in our society who suffer from something called "low self-esteem." The experts see this as the root cause of every misfortune and "illness" imaginable: social, physical, mental, personal, relational, and even spiritual. They often say that low self-esteem drives "mental illness." Our culture frequently promotes the idea that, in order to be truly successful or fulfilled, a person must have a staggering amount of self-esteem. We need to feel good about ourselves and live up to our potential. There are no longer "winners" and "losers." We do not keep score and every child gets a trophy.

We may tell a person – child, or adult – that they are "special" and "unique" and that they can do anything they set their mind to. What if the reality is that they (or we) are not that remarkable, not that much different than most others, or that they (or we) have a deeply selfish and sinful character that no one likes? What are we to say *then*?

The drive for success is often greedy and voracious, demanding more and more of us (and others) to feed the always-empty belly of self-esteem. Being content in our identity in Christ, in desiring God's best for others more than we desire it for ourselves, underlies the desire for a fruitful life. Success is to benefit *me*; fruitfulness is to benefit *others*.

An accurate and authentic self-image rooted in our understanding and belief in our inherent worth as God's image-bearers <u>is the prerequisite</u> for a fruitful life.

In order to live a fruitful life, two things are necessary:

1. *We have must understand and accept our* actual ***worth and value*** *as defined by God.*

2. *We must know that what we are accomplishing with our lives is truly* ***worthy of God's name.***

---

1. What is our *actual* worth and value?

God created us in His image, and it is He who sets the true worth of man. Jesus asked the symbolic question, *"What does it profit a man if he gains the whole world [created universe] and loses his soul?"* (Matthew 16:26). The implication is that Christ sees each of us as worth more than the entire created universe (the English word "world" translates a Greek word, "cosmos," which refers to all of creation, not just the Earth). **Christ demonstrated our true worth to Him when He willingly gave His life to redeem us and restore us to a right relationship with God.**

<u>Remember what we learned in Lesson 1</u>: We have inherent worth as image bearers of God. Yet the fact remains that, as long as we are spiritually dead (the state of a person without Christ), we are of little *functional value*. But, once we have been made alive in Christ Jesus (Ephesians 2:4-8), we are *priceless* to God (Ephesians 2:10). We are fully justified in having a positive self-image because of that renewed value through Jesus Christ.

2. We need to know our lives are invested in something that is truly worthy of God's name.

As His "image bearers," we are to "bear fruit" of eternal value (John 15:8; 16). We need to be invested in something that is larger and greater than ourselves; something that honors Him and brings to light His nature and character, maybe even something that we could not accomplish apart from Him. This can only happen when we know that what we are doing has eternal significance (Colossians 3:2). And we need to understand that the greatest eternal investment we can make in this world is to impact the souls of people for eternity.

Every human being is an everlasting being. We will continue to exist somewhere for the rest of eternity; either with God in the place He has prepared for those who have received Christ, or, for those who have rejected Him, in that place of eternal separation from God out of which there is no return [Luke 16:19-21 (see 26); Revelation 20:6, et.al.]. Anything that is truly worthy of God's name must be motivated – directly or indirectly – by the desire to expose people to the truth of their need for Christ. We must learn to ask ourselves, "How does what I am doing right now relate to the Gospel?" We have been made ambassadors of Christ, carrying with us the message that it is only through Christ that anyone can be reconciled to God (2 Corinthians 5:20ff), and that they *can indeed* be so reconciled.

The more we invest our life in those things that have eternal value, then the more our life makes sense, the more fruitful our life is in actuality, and the more we can legitimately feel good about ourselves. Certainly we know that what we do on earth has a bearing on our position and rewards in heaven, but preparing for eternity also has a tremendous effect on how we regard ourselves in the here and now.

> **If we want to make doing what is worthy of God's name a priority in our lives, there are some areas that will need special attention.**

1. **We need to begin with an investment in knowing God as best we can.** Sixty-seven times in the book of Ezekiel, God says, *"By this you will know/they will know that I am the LORD."* God wants us to *know* Him, and He has revealed Himself to us through His Word. He has preserved it through the centuries to ensure that we would have it available to us. Without it, no one can know the Gospel. It is that important. Is filling your mind with God's Word a priority in your life?

287

God also encourages us by assuring us that knowing Him is not only possible, but the most preferable thing for our lives. In Jeremiah 9:23-24, we read, *"The Lord says, 'Wise people should not boast that they are wise. Powerful people should not boast that they are powerful. Rich people should not boast that they are rich. If people want to boast, they should boast about this: They should boast that they understand and know me. They should boast that they know and understand that I, the Lord, act out of faithfulness, fairness, and justice in the earth and that I desire people to do these things,' says the Lord."*

2. **We need to pay close attention to what we fill our minds with.** We have visited this truth repeatedly in this program: What we saturate our lives with is what we live out (Romans 8:5-6). Saturating our minds with what is good and what is true will help us accomplish what is truly worthy of His name (Philippians 4:8; 2 Timothy 3:16-17).

3. **We need to pay close attention to what we invest ourselves in.** In Matthew 6:21, Jesus tells us that what we treasure reveals what our heart is devoted to. He also has left us the gravest of responsibilities for this life: To be and make disciples of Jesus Christ (Matthew 28:18-20).

Proclaiming the Kingdom of God is the greatest investment we could ever make. And we do this not so much with words as with how we live our life. God's Word tells us that the eternal investments we make today will be rewarded when we get "home" (2 Timothy 4:6-8).

Eternal investments are things that money cannot buy: love, grace, mercy, forgiveness, sacrifice, service, kindness, justice, lives impacted by the Gospel we have shared, and other priceless treasures of that kind. Can you think of anything of greater value than these?

80 • 03

DAILY PRACTICES	DAY 1	DAY 2	DAY 3	DAY 4	DAY 5	DAY 6	"REST" DAY
SATURATION VERSE ___	More ☐ 100 ☐ Less ☐	More ☐ 100 ☐ Less ☐	More ☐ 100 ☐ Less ☐	More ☐ 100 ☐ Less ☐	More ☐ 100 ☐ Less ☐	More ☐ 100 ☐ Less ☐	More ☐ 100 ☐ Less ☐
BIBLE READING	Chapters ___	Chapters ___	Chapters ___	Chapters ___	Chapters ___	Chapters ___	
STUDY MANUAL LESSON # ___	Read Today's Lesson Today Yes ☐ No ☐	Read Today's Lesson Today Yes ☐ No ☐	Read Today's Lesson Today Yes ☐ No ☐	Read Today's Lesson Today Yes ☐ No ☐	Read Today's Lesson Today Yes ☐ No ☐	Read Today's Lesson Today Yes ☐ No ☐	
DAILY REFLECTION	Completed Today's Lesson Today Yes ☐ No ☐	Completed Today's Lesson Today Yes ☐ No ☐	Completed Today's Lesson Today Yes ☐ No ☐	Completed Today's Lesson Today Yes ☐ No ☐	Completed Today's Lesson Today Yes ☐ No ☐	Completed Today's Lesson Today Yes ☐ No ☐	
USED "RESTORE" BOOK	Yes ☐ No ☐	Yes ☐ No ☐	Yes ☐ No ☐	Yes ☐ No ☐	Yes ☐ No ☐	Yes ☐ No ☐	Yes ☐ No ☐
PRE-MEAL SATURATION VERSE	Breakfast ☐ Lunch ☐ Dinner ☐	Breakfast ☐ Lunch ☐ Dinner ☐	Breakfast ☐ Lunch ☐ Dinner ☐	Breakfast ☐ Lunch ☐ Dinner ☐	Breakfast ☐ Lunch ☐ Dinner ☐	Breakfast ☐ Lunch ☐ Dinner ☐	Breakfast ☐ Lunch ☐ Dinner ☐
SPECIAL ITEMS	Yes ☐ No ☐	Yes ☐ No ☐	Yes ☐ No ☐	Yes ☐ No ☐	Yes ☐ No ☐	Yes ☐ No ☐	Yes ☐ No ☐
PRIVATE PRAYER	Time Spent ___	Time Spent ___	Time Spent ___	Time Spent ___	Time Spent ___	Time Spent ___	Time Spent ___
TODAY, I AM THANKFUL FOR...							

Lesson 22 Study Sheet

Each day review the lesson for that week.
Record one thing you are grateful for each day on your Progress Record.

This Lesson's Verse:

"I am able to do all things [that God asks of me] through the one who strengthens me." (Philippians 4:13; clarification added.)

Day 1 Reflection

Do you see yourself as focused on being successful or on being fruitful? Explain. *Additional study passage: Colossians 3:2-3*

Day 2 Reflection

What accomplishments and flops in your life have contributed most to the value you place on yourself as a person? Additional study passages: *1 Samuel 16:7; John 7:24; 8:15-16*

Day 3 Reflection

What person has most shaped your self-image? Why is that person's assessment of you so important in your life? What is the best thing you can do with what you see right now? *Additional study passage: John 15:1-17*

Day 4 Reflection

When you look at the "fruit-bearing" you are doing so far on this journey, what do you see? What would you like to see changed? *Additional study passage: Ephesians 4:25-32*

Day 5 Reflection

What new goals have you set for yourself as a result of this lesson? Where do you think you need to get started? *Additional study passages: 2 Thessalonians 1:11-12; Colossians 3:17*

Day 6 Reflection

In order of priority, what do you consider the two or three most important things you could focus on to cooperate with Christ in accomplishing His purpose in the world? *Additional study passages: 2 Peter 3:9; Romans 2:4*

Therefore
BE VERY CAREFUL
HOW YOU LIVE -
not as unwise
BUT AS WISE,
TAKING ADVANTAGE OF
EVERY OPPORTUNITY,
because the days are **evil**.
For this reason,
do not be **foolish**,
but be WISE by
UNDERSTANDING
what the LORD'S WILL is.

Ephesians 5:15-17 (NET)

LESSON TWENTY-THREE

WE *CAN* KNOW GOD'S WILL

The Bible says, *"For this reason do not be foolish, but be wise by understanding what the Lord's will is"* (Ephesians 5:17). That would seem to indicate that we can and need to know God's will, yes?

To find and fulfill God's will is the key to a strong, healthy, and fruitful life. Of course, if we are to *do* His will, we must first *know* His will. Since God instructs us in His Word to know His will, we can assume that He (being the God that He is) will most certainly make the knowledge of His will available to all of His children. The question then becomes: "How can I know the will of the Lord?"

The first key to knowing God's will is for us <u>to be regularly, consistently reading and studying the Bible</u>. The Bible is God's Word to all of humankind and is the primary source of knowledge about both God *and* His will.

God is changeless, as is His will; so also his Word. Only the Word of God is fully authoritative and unchanging regarding all matters of faith and life (2 Timothy 3:16-17; 2 Peter 1:3-4). Only God's Word can be depended on to rightly communicate God's nature, character, will, and ways.[24] Jesus tells us that not even the smallest word, or the smallest part of any letter of God's Word, will change until His plan for our world is complete (Matthew 5:17-19). To be successful in knowing and understanding God's will, it is essential for us to have a growing knowledge of, and familiarity with, God's Word.

Often when a person first receives Christ, they have a passionate desire to know more about Him and about His plan for their life. They will invest a great deal of time reading the Bible, praying, being involved with church, and speaking with other believers to make sure they are on the right track. Yet, too frequently though, something happens and that new believer's passion for

---

[24] You may have heard someone refer to the Bible as God's "Love Letter." Perhaps a more fitting word picture would be to see the Bible like "God's Resumé." When we consider what a well-written resumé provides, perhaps you will agree.

God's Word diminishes. Life's troubles can become distracting and overwhelming. The very thing that believer needs is the very thing they have let go of.

Despite our tendency toward fickleness with respect to Scripture, the Bible remains essential to our walk with Jesus. The more a person saturates with and absorbs the Scriptures, the easier it becomes to solidly know God's will. God will never lead us to violate the truths or purposes that are spelled out in His Word.

We ought to note here that it is important to recognize that there are many approaches to interpreting God's Word. Some are rock-solid and consistent with what believers have understood from the beginning of Christianity, all the way back to the disciples of the Apostles themselves. Others, however, are not. Finding a fellowship where the Bible is taught clearly, accurately, systematically, and historically-consistent is also an important part of knowing and understanding God's Word and will.

Many people, especially in American Christianity, put more confidence in events, personal experiences, dreams, visions, emotions, human reasoning, and the like, than they do in the Bible. If their personal experience, revelation, dream, or emotional episode disagrees with the Bible (or if they can "make" the Bible agree with their "new" interpretation) then it is too bad for God's Word. Any person or any group that takes and encourages this approach is dangerous indeed.

Read carefully Revelation 22:19. Jesus' words in Matthew 5:17-19 also make it plain that God intends for us to pay attention to *all* of His Word. He cares about what He has written, and He cares that we hear it well. Thus, it is no stretch to conclude that the warning of Revelation 22:19 also pertains to *all* of Scripture. The point, ultimately, is this: Your success at knowing and following God's will for your life relates directly to your ability to accept and absorb the truths in His properly-interpreted Word (Matthew 4:4).

Consider this: Through your exposure to God's Word in *Unbound*, you have probably already experienced a great deal of theological recalibration since beginning this program. Your understanding of who God is, what He has done, why He has done it, how He has done it, and what He intends for you to do with that understanding has grown and flourished, hasn't it? In short, solid hermeneutics (Biblical interpretation) underlies solid belief.

Solid belief underlies a godly and fruitful life.

The second key to knowing God's will <u>is found in Jesus Christ Himself</u>. In John 14:6, Jesus says, *"I am the way, and the truth, and the life. No one comes to the Father except through me."* Jesus *is* the truth; He does not just "speak" the truth. Later in John's Gospel, when Jesus is standing before Pontius Pilate, He says, *"For this reason I was born, and for this reason I came into the world – to testify to the truth. Everyone who belongs to the truth listens to my voice"* (John 18:37). To be a lover and pursuer of Jesus Christ is to be a lover and a pursuer of the truth — no matter where it leads, and no matter the cost. The Truth and Jesus Christ are inseparable because He is the Truth personified.

God's perfect will for our lives is not found in a place or a thing, but in a person — Jesus Christ. We cannot walk in God's will unless we are walking with Jesus. Entering into God's perfect will begins when we surrender our life to Jesus Christ, and then live surrendered to Him more and more each day. That means we give Him control of our lives, holding nothing back (Revisit Lesson 2 for a reminder).

Giving Jesus control places us in the center of God's will for our lives. The more we surrender, the more we are in His will. Any act of rebellion against Him takes us out of the center of God's will, and life starts to go back along the path we have been working so faithfully to forsake. The old grave-clothes start getting rewound around us and our freedom is lost (See Galatians 5:1-2).

The third key to walking in God's will <u>is to understand the person and work of our Perfect Counselor and Helper—the Holy Spirit</u>. When He lives within us, we have His voice to nudge us when we get off track (Isaiah 30:21). If we have His calm and confident peace, then we know we are keeping in step with Him and doing what He would have us do. This peace is the key to walking in God's will. When we do not have God's peace, it is certain that we have ceased to walk in God's will (John 14:27).

During the Last Supper, Jesus encouraged and prepared His disciples for His rapidly approaching death and all that followed. He wanted them to have the peace of knowing He was not abandoning them. He assured them that the Holy Spirit would be their Helper and their Counselor. The Spirit would, Jesus promised, guide them in their knowledge and understanding of all that Jesus had Himself taught them, so they could carry on what He had begun (John 14:25-27; 15:26; 16:7-15).

Now that same Holy Spirit — He who guided the writers of Scripture (Acts 4:24-26; 2 Peter 1:20-21; et.al.) and whom Jesus promised and sent to the disciples on the day of Pentecost (Acts 1:5; 2:4; 4:8; et.al.) — abides in every true believer in Jesus Christ (Romans 5:5; 15:13; 1 Corinthians 6:19; Ephesians 1:13; 2 Timothy 1:14; et.al.).

As you study and saturate on the Word of God, and as you surrender more and more to Jesus Christ, you will know, understand, and walk in the center of His will more fully and more successfully as time goes on. The goals you set for yourself when you began this program — goals to live and walk free in Christ and out of bondage to the lies and sins that were besetting you — will be realized and tangible in your life.

DAILY PRACTICES	DAY 1	DAY 2	DAY 3	DAY 4	DAY 5	DAY 6	"REST" DAY
SATURATION VERSE ___	More □ 100 □ Less □	More □ 100 □ Less □	More □ 100 □ Less □	More □ 100 □ Less □	More □ 100 □ Less □	More □ 100 □ Less □	More □ 100 □ Less □
BIBLE READING	Chapters ___	Chapters ___	Chapters ___	Chapters ___	Chapters ___	Chapters ___	
STUDY MANUAL LESSON # ___	Read Today's Lesson Today Yes □ No □	Read Today's Lesson Today Yes □ No □	Read Today's Lesson Today Yes □ No □	Read Today's Lesson Today Yes □ No □	Read Today's Lesson Today Yes □ No □	Read Today's Lesson Today Yes □ No □	
DAILY REFLECTION	Completed Today's Lesson Today Yes □ No □	Completed Today's Lesson Today Yes □ No □	Completed Today's Lesson Today Yes □ No □	Completed Today's Lesson Today Yes □ No □	Completed Today's Lesson Today Yes □ No □	Completed Today's Lesson Today Yes □ No □	
USED "RESTORE" BOOK	Yes □ No □	Yes □ No □	Yes □ No □	Yes □ No □	Yes □ No □	Yes □ No □	Yes □ No □
PRE-MEAL SATURATION VERSE	Breakfast □ Lunch □ Dinner □	Breakfast □ Lunch □ Dinner □	Breakfast □ Lunch □ Dinner □	Breakfast □ Lunch □ Dinner □	Breakfast □ Lunch □ Dinner □	Breakfast □ Lunch □ Dinner □	Breakfast □ Lunch □ Dinner □
SPECIAL ITEMS	Yes □ No □	Yes □ No □	Yes □ No □	Yes □ No □	Yes □ No □	Yes □ No □	Yes □ No □
PRIVATE PRAYER	Time Spent ___	Time Spent ___	Time Spent ___	Time Spent ___	Time Spent ___	Time Spent ___	Time Spent ___
TODAY, I AM THANKFUL FOR...							

Lesson 23 Study Sheet

Each day review the lesson for that week.
Record one thing you are grateful for each day on your Progress Record.

This Lesson's Verse:

"Therefore be very careful how you live – not as unwise but as wise, taking advantage of every opportunity, because the days are evil. For this reason do not be foolish, but be wise by understanding what the Lord's will is." Ephesians 5:15-17 (NET)

Day 1 Reflection

Give at least two solid reasons why a person with a poor knowledge of God's Word will have trouble finding and following God's will. *Additional study passages: Psalm 119:89-96; 97-104; 105-107*

Day 2 Reflection

When you look at the list of the priorities of your life, where does the Bible fall? Is this verified by your faithfulness to read and study it? *Additional study passages: Joshua 1:8; Psalm 1*

Day 3 Reflection

Explain why knowing God's will and complete surrender to Christ are equally vital to a godly and fruitful life. *Additional study passages: John 5:24; 8:31-32; 14:23*

Day 4 Reflection

List any attitudes or influences in your life that hinder you from being at peace with Christ. What do you plan to do about those? *Additional study passage: Isaiah 48:17-18, 22*

Day 5 Reflection

The Holy Spirit already knows God's will for your life. If you are a child of God, the Holy Spirit lives within you. What is a sure sign that you are in the center of God's will for your life? *Additional study passage: Galatians 5:14-26*

Day 6 Reflection

Is there anything in your life you have been unwilling or felt unable to fully surrender to Christ? Is there something He is asking you to do that you have not done? Explain. *Additional study passages: Micah 6:6-8; Hosea 6:6*

COME TO ME,

all who are **weary** and **heavy-laden**, and I will give you *Rest*.

Take MY yoke upon you and learn from Me, for I am *gentle* and *humble* in heart, and YOU WILL FIND REST FOR YOUR SOULS.

For MY yoke is *easy* and MY burden is *light."*

Matthew 11:28-30 (NASB)

LESSON TWENTY-FOUR
BURNING OUT

We each have an "energy tank" that holds our emotional, physical, and spiritual energy for the day. We start every day with a certain level in the tank, and we draw from it all day long. This energy fuels our mind and our bodies, providing us with the vitality we need to function.

As we fill our hearts and minds with God's Word and other things of God (like personal worship and "one-anothering"), we keep those stores at optimum levels. When we allow our minds to wander into dark places and allow negative emotions to run rampant, our reservoir rapidly empties. We cannot pour anything out of an empty bucket.

Once we have depleted our reserves, our ability to function wisely and well is impaired, even extinguished. The simplest tasks become difficult, interpersonal relationships deteriorate, and our walk with God becomes fragmented or interrupted. Life gets overwhelming.

EMOTIONAL BURN-OUT

Strong emotions like anxiety, fear, anger, entitlement, unforgiveness, and lust are a few of the fast-burning emotions that rapidly drain our reserves. They short-circuit our ability to be reasonable and rational. They impede our walk with Christ. Others, such as unresolved guilt, toxic-shame, bitterness, and the like, are a constant drain. Once these unhealthy emotions gain control, they strip us of the mental, emotional, physical, and spiritual energy that we need to live healthy, productive, godly lives.

Man-made medications like stimulants, depressants, anti-depressants, anti-anxiety medications, psychotropics, street drugs, and alcohol all have the same disastrous effect on those energy stores as do sin-driven emotions. When we depend on these substances, we rely on the created instead of the Creator.

We must learn to conserve and replenish our energy stores and use them in productive undertakings if we are to be the man/woman God created us to be. Here are a few suggestions on how we can make the best of this emotional energy.

I.   ***We must learn to conserve our emotional energy.*** Energy drained by toxic emotions (fearfulness, lust, anger, guilt, shame, worry, etc.) rob us of the ability to think and do our best. This leads to bogging down in pits of gloom and despair (Lessons 6 & 7) and we end up exhausted. **The remedy** is to remind ourselves, "This is how I feel, but this (i.e. God's perspective and reality) is what's true." We then intentionally saturate our minds on what is good and true (Philippians 4:8).

II.   ***Learn to draw strength and energy from the Holy Spirit.*** God says, "Not by power or by might but my Spirit, says the Lord of hosts" (Zechariah 4:6). When we are working *with* God to accomplish His purpose, we can draw from and lean on the Holy Spirit and on Jesus Himself (Matthew 11:28-30; John 14:6; 16). We can always accomplish more following and cooperating with God than we ever could on our own. In fact, we easily cross into selfish, sinful choices when we work and plan without Him (Isaiah 30:1).

III.   ***We need to maintain a list of legitimate priorities.*** We must invest our energy in things that are truly worthwhile and that count in the larger scheme of life (the Lord, family, ministry, work, etc.). We must not waste this precious energy on things that destroy our mental and emotional health and harm our intimate connection to God. One key **preventative measure** is making sure that we are in (or return to) our "Safe Zone." We commit to not making key decisions and not having important conversations when we are not in our "Safe Zone."

It is also important to make sure that we get God involved on the "front end" when making plans. "Lord, what would you have me do with this?" is a far better question to ask than making plans and then asking God to come in after-the-fact and "bless" (read that "cosign") the plans we have made. It is also important to not give God "multiple-choice" or "either/or" options. God's best ideas often will not show up on any list we offer Him.

WORKING <u>WITH</u> GOD, NOT <u>FOR</u> GOD

The wisest way to keep our energy reserves filled is to learn to work *with* God. When we are working *for* God, we focus on getting things done; on rules and check lists, and on looking good to others. We think the responsibility for the outcomes is ours. We work in an effort to please Him or to earn His favor. When working *with* God, the **relationship** is the primary focus. We are partnered with Christ (Matthew 11:28-30), the outcomes are His, and the load is not wearying (Galatians 6:9-10).

We need to understand that Jesus is more interested and invested in what He can do *in and through* us than He ever would be in what *we* can do for *Him*. All we do grows out of a devotion to Him and is due to the reality that we abide in Him and He in us (John 15:4-8). All that we do, then, is simply (and beautifully) what He is doing in and through us.

DAILY PRACTICES	DAY 1	DAY 2	DAY 3	DAY 4	DAY 5	DAY 6	"REST" DAY
SATURATION VERSE ___	More □ 100 □ Less □	More □ 100 □ Less □	More □ 100 □ Less □	More □ 100 □ Less □	More □ 100 □ Less □	More □ 100 □ Less □	More □ 100 □ Less □
BIBLE READING	Chapters ___	Chapters ___	Chapters ___	Chapters ___	Chapters ___	Chapters ___	
STUDY MANUAL LESSON # ___	Read Today's Lesson Today Yes □ No □	Read Today's Lesson Today Yes □ No □	Read Today's Lesson Today Yes □ No □	Read Today's Lesson Today Yes □ No □	Read Today's Lesson Today Yes □ No □	Read Today's Lesson Today Yes □ No □	
DAILY REFLECTION	Completed Today's Lesson Today Yes □ No □	Completed Today's Lesson Today Yes □ No □	Completed Today's Lesson Today Yes □ No □	Completed Today's Lesson Today Yes □ No □	Completed Today's Lesson Today Yes □ No □	Completed Today's Lesson Today Yes □ No □	
USED "RESTORE" BOOK	Yes □ No □	Yes □ No □	Yes □ No □	Yes □ No □	Yes □ No □	Yes □ No □	Yes □ No □
PRE-MEAL SATURATION VERSE	Breakfast □ Lunch □ Dinner □	Breakfast □ Lunch □ Dinner □	Breakfast □ Lunch □ Dinner □	Breakfast □ Lunch □ Dinner □	Breakfast □ Lunch □ Dinner □	Breakfast □ Lunch □ Dinner □	Breakfast □ Lunch □ Dinner □
SPECIAL ITEMS	Yes □ No □	Yes □ No □	Yes □ No □	Yes □ No □	Yes □ No □	Yes □ No □	Yes □ No □
PRIVATE PRAYER	Time Spent ___	Time Spent ___	Time Spent ___	Time Spent ___	Time Spent ___	Time Spent ___	Time Spent ___
TODAY, I AM THANKFUL FOR...							

This Lesson's Verse:

"Come to Me, all who are weary and heavy-laden, and I will give you rest. Take My yoke upon you and learn from Me, for I am gentle and humble in heart, and YOU WILL FIND REST FOR YOUR SOULS. For My yoke is easy and My burden is light." Matthew 11:28-30

Day 1 Reflection

List the major emotions you expend the most emotional energy on most often. Is this emotional "investment" healthy, unhealthy, productive, unproductive, helpful, or hurtful? Explain. *Additional study passages: Psalm 37:7-8; Matthew 6:19-21*

Day 2 Reflection

List some of the godly goals you have for your life. How do you think mastering this lesson will help you reach those goals? *Additional study passages: Psalm 37; 1 Timothy 6:6-11*

Day 3 Reflection

List some activities in your life that cause an unhealthy drain on your emotional reserves. What could you change about your lifestyle to help stop this waste of emotional energy? *Additional study passage: Galatians 5:19-21*

Day 4 Reflection

In developing a close personal relationship with Christ, which activities are you finding require the expenditure of the most emotional energy? *Additional study passage: Psalm 15*

Day 5 Reflection

How do we inadvertently promote an unhealthy drain of emotional energy in others? What can you do to help others conserve emotional energy? *Additional study passage: Ecclesiastes 2:24-26*

Day 6 Reflection

Explain why leaving the outcomes of our efforts in God's hands would help us not grow weary in doing good, even when it would be draining otherwise. *Additional study passage: Galatians 6:1-10*

LAST THINGS

CONCLUSION
LAST THINGS

LAST THINGS

Having a poor self-image comes from not seeing ourselves as God sees us —which is who we really are. This poor self-image creates deep and lasting doubt, robbing us of confidence; confidence in our worth, our value, and our potential to become what God has created us to be. Confidence in God's view of us is a *must* if we are to build a healthy self-image and have a God-centered confidence.

We are not referring to *self*-confidence here, but rather confidence that God loves us and places great value on us as a person; confidence that He will bring about the full completion of what He has begun in us (Philippians 1:6); and confidence that He will enable us to be successful as long as we work with Him. We will only find satisfaction and fulfillment in life as we become familiar with and practice *His* principles for success.

Every Good and Perfect Gift

is from above,
coming down from

the Father of Lights,

with whom there is NO VARIATION
or the slightest hint of change.
By His SOVEREIGN plan
He gave us NEW BIRTH
through the message of TRUTH,
so that we would be a kind of
FIRST FRUITS of all He created."

James 1:17-18 (Lamb)

LESSON TWENTY-FIVE
UNDERSTANDING SELF-SABOTAGE

We have all seen it in our lives — getting to the place where things are going well for us and then we do something that demolishes the progress we have made. For a while, our minds are clearer, our behaviors are less selfish, and our relationships are healthier; we are doing pretty well.

Then, all of a sudden, we find ourselves sliding back into old patterns of thinking, feeling, and believing. We dabble in our old ways of behaving and surrender to old ways of poorly treating ourselves and others. The ground we gained is lost — or starting to become so — and we cannot seem to hold on to the ground we have taken back from the Enemy. We have started wrapping ourselves again in the decay-ridden grave-clothes God has been unbinding us from all this time. It is as if we have joined the opposing side of this battle, become allies with our own enemy, and are working against God's best for our lives. We start to engage in **self-sabotage**. The question is, *"Why?"*

THERE ARE FOUR MAIN CULPRITS, ALL BASED ON LIES WE BELIEVE:

1. *"I'm no good. I don't deserve this better life Christ is offering me."*

2. *"I haven't earned the good that I'm receiving. It isn't right for me to accept this."*

3. *"I know how to live the old life. I don't have any idea how to live this new one."*

4. *"I'm going to blow it sooner or later. I may as well just get it over with."*

Let's look at these, one at a time, to diagnose the often non-conscious reasoning that causes us to self-sabotage and sends us back into the bondage that Christ has been setting us free from. Once we identify the convoluted reasoning, we can take those thoughts captive, bring them into surrender to Christ, and work through a robust **RMC** to get back on the freedom track.

REASON #1:

I'm no good. I don't deserve this better life Christ is offering me.

The culprit is A POOR SELF-IMAGE.

While it is true that within ourselves we are not good ("...*there is none good but God...*" Matthew 19:17), Christ's goodness and righteousness are provided to us when we surrender our lives to Him (Philippians 3:9, et.al.). He created us to be with Him. He paid the penalty for our rebellion so that we could be reconciled to God and restored to a right relationship with Him.

When we do not see ourselves as God sees us, the image we have is defective and all we see are flaws. We must develop the attitude that we are complete and good enough in Him — declared righteous in fact (Romans 5:1-2). We have value and purpose. We are fully worthy of His best because that is how He created us. Satan would steal from us our joy, our peace, our confidence, and our hope. But we do not have to cooperate with him, and we surely do not have to let him have that victory.

316

REASON #2:

I have not earned the good that I am receiving. It is not right for me to accept this.

The culprit is PRIDE.

While we are *deserving* of no good thing, we are fully *worthy* of every good and perfect gift that He has for us (James 1:17). If we are "in Christ," God pours His best into our lives in big ways and in small ways because He loves us!

If you offer me a gift out of friendship, and I refuse to accept what you offer unless I pay you for it, haven't I just offended you? Basically what I am saying is, "I will define the value that this has, and I will give that to you in exchange. You do not get to give a gift to me. Unless I am invested in the exchange, I won't be a part of it."

For us to feel like we have to invest something of our own in order to gain, keep, maintain, or preserve God's gift is to turn it into something other than a gift. Gifts are given out of affection, not out of "earned." Satan loves to twist things so that we cannot enjoy the good things God so freely gives His children. When Christ blesses, His motive is not to make us feel guilty because we have not earned it. His purpose is that we enjoy those blessings.

We can never earn even the smallest of God's blessings. He knows that. He does not expect it out of us. He simply wants us to love Him, thank Him, and do our best to be obedient to Him because it is in our best interest to do so. It really is prideful to think we could add any value to the priceless blessings of God.

REASON #3

I know how to live the old life.
I do not have any idea how to live this new one.

The culprit is FEAR.

It is normal for us to resist change. After all, we are created in God's image and He never changes. It is also normal for us to experience at least a little fearfulness over the unknown. This new life, and what the future holds, is full of unknowns.

We tend to fall into life-patterns and get stuck there. We easily get comfortable and entrenched in what is most familiar. We are "creatures of habit." It is hard for us to quit old habits, and equally hard to form new ones, because we have to put-off the old to put-on the new.

However, as we discipline ourselves into following a new pattern of thinking and behaving, and as we accept the blessings of a new way of living, the strange becomes familiar, the unknown becomes every-day, and soon we are just as rooted in our new pattern of living as we were in our old. Given enough time and enough success, we lose our desire to give up and go back. The new habits we form today become the old habits of tomorrow.

REASON #4

I am going to blow it sooner or later.
I may as well just get it over with.

The culprit is SELF-LOATHING.

To loathe is to experience a strong dislike or disgust – an intense aversion to someone or something. Self-loathing is a strong dislike or disgust toward oneself. Self-loathing is a thought pattern where individuals believe they are inferior, bad, worthless, unlovable, or incompetent. We can believe that God loves everybody in the whole, wide world—except **us**! The best we can expect of ourselves is more failure and more reasons for shame.

The truth of the matter is we are no less created in the image of God than the next person. In fact, if we have accepted Christ as Savior, we are nothing less than the adopted children of God (John 1:12; Romans 8:14-17). Seeing ourselves with this new identity is the antidote to this lie. As we saturate on this truth, we learn to see ourselves as God sees us and to live our lives with joyful freedom in Christ. We begin to understand that, because of who we are in Christ, we have nothing to prove, nothing to justify, and nothing to defend for He has already proven and justified us (Romans 5:1-2), and He ongoingly defends us before the Father (1 John 2:1).

So, what do we do? We stay with it, surrendering to and trusting the process until we become comfortable in the new life that our Savior has prepared for us.

DON'T GIVE UP, AND DON'T TURN BACK!

Each and every day, you will see the fruit of your faithfulness in yielding your life to Christ and saturating with His Word. Even in spite of difficulties, you will find that life grows ever better with Him. You've already started to learn to enjoy and appreciate your wonderful new life in Christ. This is His gift and plan for you, and He is working right alongside you to help you grow into the noble man or woman of God He created you to be.

೮ • ೞ

DAILY PRACTICES	DAY 1	DAY 2	DAY 3	DAY 4	DAY 5	DAY 6	"REST" DAY
SATURATION VERSE ___	More ☐ 100 ☐ Less ☐	More ☐ 100 ☐ Less ☐	More ☐ 100 ☐ Less ☐	More ☐ 100 ☐ Less ☐	More ☐ 100 ☐ Less ☐	More ☐ 100 ☐ Less ☐	More ☐ 100 ☐ Less ☐
BIBLE READING	Chapters ___	Chapters ___	Chapters ___	Chapters ___	Chapters ___	Chapters ___	
STUDY MANUAL LESSON # ___	Read Today's Lesson Today Yes ☐ No ☐	Read Today's Lesson Today Yes ☐ No ☐	Read Today's Lesson Today Yes ☐ No ☐	Read Today's Lesson Today Yes ☐ No ☐	Read Today's Lesson Today Yes ☐ No ☐	Read Today's Lesson Today Yes ☐ No ☐	
DAILY REFLECTION	Completed Today's Lesson Today Yes ☐ No ☐	Completed Today's Lesson Today Yes ☐ No ☐	Completed Today's Lesson Today Yes ☐ No ☐	Completed Today's Lesson Today Yes ☐ No ☐	Completed Today's Lesson Today Yes ☐ No ☐	Completed Today's Lesson Today Yes ☐ No ☐	
USED "RESTORE" BOOK	Yes ☐ No ☐	Yes ☐ No ☐	Yes ☐ No ☐	Yes ☐ No ☐	Yes ☐ No ☐	Yes ☐ No ☐	Yes ☐ No ☐
PRE-MEAL SATURATION VERSE	Breakfast ☐ Lunch ☐ Dinner ☐	Breakfast ☐ Lunch ☐ Dinner ☐	Breakfast ☐ Lunch ☐ Dinner ☐	Breakfast ☐ Lunch ☐ Dinner ☐	Breakfast ☐ Lunch ☐ Dinner ☐	Breakfast ☐ Lunch ☐ Dinner ☐	Breakfast ☐ Lunch ☐ Dinner ☐
SPECIAL ITEMS	Yes ☐ No ☐	Yes ☐ No ☐	Yes ☐ No ☐	Yes ☐ No ☐	Yes ☐ No ☐	Yes ☐ No ☐	Yes ☐ No ☐
PRIVATE PRAYER	Time Spent ___	Time Spent ___	Time Spent ___	Time Spent ___	Time Spent ___	Time Spent ___	Time Spent ___
TODAY, I AM THANKFUL FOR...							

Lesson 25 Study Sheet
Each day review the lesson for that week.
Record one thing you are grateful for each day on your Progress Record.

This Lesson's Verse:

"Every good and perfect gift is from above, coming down from the Father of lights, with whom there is no variation or the slightest hint of change. By His sovereign plan He gave us new birth through the message of truth, so that we would be a kind of firstfruits of all He created." James 1:17-18 (Lamb)

Day 1 Reflection

Why would *you* deliberately sabotage your life when you are doing well? Why would *you* feel drawn to return to the life you had before? *Additional study passages: Galatians 1:6-9; 5:1; 2 Peter 2:20-22*

Day 2 Reflection

What do you think God requires of you that you are unable to give Him or do for Him? *Additional study passage: Micah 6:8; Galatians 2:20*

Day 3 Reflection

List ways that you self-sabotage and make your own life difficult. What do you think your reasons are for doing so? *Additional study passages: Romans 8:5-8; 1 Thessalonians 5:9-10*

Day 4 Reflection

Do you have trouble receiving gifts? When someone gives you a gift simply because they care for you or pays you a compliment, how do you respond? *Additional study passage: Hebrews 13:15-16*

Day 5 Reflection

Looking back at the major changes in your life — both voluntary and involuntary — how long did it take and how difficult was it for you to adapt and become accustomed to those changes? The changes you've been experiencing in this program are ones you took on willingly. What are your thoughts on adapting to these changes? *Additional study passages: Psalm 55:16-19; Malachi 3:6*

Day 6 Reflection

When you consider the amazing purpose God has for your life, how willing are you to stick with His plan as He works it all out? What can you do to be more cooperative? *Additional study passages: Colossians 2:6-8; Colossians 3*

LOVE THE LORD YOUR GOD

with all your *Heart,*
with all your *Soul,*
with all your *Mind,*
and with all your *Strength.*
The second is:
Love your neighbor as yourself.
There is no other commandment greater than these."

Mark 12:30-31 (NET)

LESSON TWENTY-SIX
LOVE - GOD'S WAY

Love is probably the most sought-after and least understood aspect of the human experience. We long for it, we hunger for it, we actually *need* it, and yet these things are at the very root of our inability to love God's way.

Given the daily battle with sin, our longing, hunger, and need often become catalysts that drive our love toward self-serving idolatry of self, instead of leading us into an others-serving love of God.

So, how do we learn to surrender and walk in Christ-like love? That question lies at the heart of this final lesson in our journey to freedom.

The most famous passage in all of Scripture regarding love is 1 Corinthians 13:4-8a: *"Love is patient, love is kind, and it is not envious. Love does not brag; it is not puffed up. It is not rude, it is not self-serving, and it is not easily angered or resentful. It is not glad about injustice, but rejoices in the truth. It bears all things, believes all things, hopes all things, endures all things. Love never ends."*

Nice thoughts; great words; lovely sentiments. You have seen them on greeting cards, plaques on the wall, even hundreds of times on Facebook. What do they mean, and who are they for?

The Greek word for "love" in this passage of Scripture is *agapē* (ah-**gah**-pey). It does not refer to brotherly love, familial love, or even romantic love. Agapē is unique and quite distinctive from our usual understanding and use of the word "love."

Agapē is rooted in the very nature and character of God (1 John 4:8, 16b). Agapē is self-sacrificial (see Philippians 2:5-8). The verb form of this word means to love, highly value, honor, greatly esteem, manifest lavish concern for, be faithful towards, to delight in, and to emphasize the importance and value of another.

AGAPĒ EQUALS GIVE

To love God's way is to *give*; there is no "take" in love (although there is a "receive" aspect to it which we will discuss in a moment).

- John 3:16: *"For this is the way God loved [agapaō, the verb form of agapē] the world: He **gave** [abandoned and delivered up for] His one and only Son, so that everyone who believes in him will not perish but have everlasting life."*

- Galatians 2:20: *"I have been crucified with Christ, and it is no longer I who live, but Christ lives in me. So the life I now live in the body, I live because of the faithfulness of the Son of God, who loved [agapaō] me and **gave** Himself for me."*

- Ephesians 5:25: *"Husbands, love [agapaō] your wives just as Christ loved the church and **gave** himself for her."*

To "love" someone with any expectation at all of anything coming back in return is NOT love — it is a business deal, not relationship. *Quid pro quo* (this for that) is not love because it is not sacrificial; it is self-serving and self-seeking. This is not how God has loved us and not how we are to love others.

A relationship marked by love is a "give-and-receive" relationship, not a "give-and-take" relationship. We lovingly receive what is lovingly given (Matthew 13:20; John 1:12, 16; John 3:20; Philippians 4:15; Colossians 2:16; Hebrews 4:16; et. al.). The idea of "taking" carries a sense of entitlement to it; a grabbing and grasping flavor to it; an attitude of, "This is *mine!*" Receiving, on the other hand, caries a sense of kindness, gentleness, tenderness, and sharing.

Consider how you feel when you do a kindness for, or pay a compliment to, or give a gift to someone. How does it feel when they push back against that? How does it feel if they minimize the compliment or try to pay you for the gift? It feels cheapened, somehow, doesn't it? It doesn't feel very loving, does it?

Jesus emphatically establishes a brand-new economy in relationships for all those who are His true disciples (more than just followers). **Three times** in John 13:34-35, He uses the same words to express His command to them (and to us): *"I give you a new commandment—to **love one another** [agapaō]. Just as I have loved you, you also are to **love one another**. Everyone will know by this that* *you are my disciples — if you **have love for one another**."*

Repetition in Scripture is a device used to add emphasis to what is being said. Since the New Testament writers did not have exclamation marks, did not italicize or use all upper case for words, and didn't have a way to **bold** the letters; they used repetition. Repeating something once meant it was highly significant. Repeating twice (saying it three times) was like using all upper-case letters AND underlining-italicizing-bolding and adding *several* exclamation marks!!! The point is this: Jesus **_emphatically_** establishes love as the foundation of relationship for those who follow him.

Loving God's Way cannot be faked, pretended, or counterfeited for long. This is because loving like God loves (even with our human limitations) is about much more than just behavior. To *agapaō* someone is to have a higher regard for them than you do for yourself (Philippians 2:3-4). It is to have a passionate desire for God's best for them, even at great expense or sacrifice to yourself. It is to live the Old Testament command that Jesus retaught in his own earthly ministry: "Love your neighbor as you love yourself" (Mark 12:31a). This is something that happens on a heart level, not just with a bunch of words and some temporary actions.

Consider that Jesus' Word to us in John 13 includes the command to "love one another, just as I have loved you." How has He loved us?

Paul answers that question in Romans: "And hope does not disappoint, because <u>the love of God</u> has been poured out in our hearts through the Holy Spirit who was given to us. For while <u>we were still helpless</u>, at the right time Christ died for the <u>ungodly</u>...But <u>God demonstrates his own love for us</u>, in that <u>while we were still sinners</u>, Christ

died for us...For if <u>while we were enemies</u> we were reconciled to God through the death of his Son, how much more, since we have been reconciled, will we be saved by his life" (From Romans 5:5-6, 8, 10).

Jesus loved us by self-sacrificially giving himself, even unto death, out of a passionate desire for our good. *That* is what it means to love like God loves!

Contrary to this exemplar of Christ-like love is our tendency toward *quid pro quo* love – "loving" to get something in return. When we give to another with the expectation of receiving something back, we have just dehumanized and objectified that individual. Rather than view them in our hearts as a fellow image-bearer of God, we make them into a resource bent to meet our own perceived needs. Again, that is not relationship; that is using.

The *quid pro quo* trap can be especially pernicious in a marriage relationship. Most people get married because of needs they think the other person can meet, or emotions they experience when connected with their intended spouse. That is not a Biblical or a Christian model. To "love another" is to passionately desire God's best for *them — even at great cost to you.* It is _not_ to first passionately desire God's best for you (though, in the beautiful wisdom of God, desiring the best for another person _is_ what it means to ultimately desire His best for oneself as well!).

Another important "love" idea to grasp is the truth that our brothers and sisters in Christ are the "one another's" mentioned throughout Scripture. We are to love them first and love them best. It is from a solid "one anothering" love that the Body of Christ is able to love the lost.

Finally, one last point for our consideration of love: God also instructs us to **love our enemies** with the same love with which we love our fellow believers. This is an even more difficult kind of love. If you read **Luke 6:35**, you will find that Jesus explains love with these instructions:

> *"But love your enemies, do good to them, and lend to them without expecting to get anything back. Then your reward will be great, and you will be children of the Most High, because he is kind to the ungrateful and wicked."*

Matthew has a different quote from Jesus along these same lines (**5:43-47**):

> *"You have heard that it was said, 'Love your neighbor' and 'hate your enemy.' But I say to you, love your enemy and pray for those who persecute you, so that you may be like your Father in heaven, since he causes the sun to rise on the evil and the good, and sends*

> *rain on the righteous and the unrighteous. For if you love those who love you, what reward do you have? Even the tax collectors do the same, don't they? And if you only greet your brothers, what more do you do? Even the Gentiles do the same, don't they?"*

Paul picks up this theme in **Romans, Chapter 5** (verses **6, 8, and 10**), and gives us the baseline from which to love others – even our enemies:

- "For while we were still **helpless**, at the right time Christ died for the **ungodly**. (Verse 6)

- But God demonstrates his own love for us, in that while we were still **sinners**, Christ died for us. (Verse 8)

- For if while we were **enemies** we were reconciled to God through the death of his Son, how much more, since we have been reconciled, will we be saved by his life? (Verse 10)

Anchor Point: <u>Let us not forget that, just as God has loved us in Christ, so we are to love others. His love is not conditional, and so neither should ours be so.</u>

DAILY PRACTICES	DAY 1	DAY 2	DAY 3	DAY 4	DAY 5	DAY 6	"REST" DAY
SATURATION VERSE ___	More ☐ 100 ☐ Less ☐	More ☐ 100 ☐ Less ☐	More ☐ 100 ☐ Less ☐	More ☐ 100 ☐ Less ☐	More ☐ 100 ☐ Less ☐	More ☐ 100 ☐ Less ☐	More ☐ 100 ☐ Less ☐
BIBLE READING	Chapters ___	Chapters ___	Chapters ___	Chapters ___	Chapters ___	Chapters ___	
STUDY MANUAL LESSON # ___	Read Today's Lesson Today Yes ☐ No ☐	Read Today's Lesson Today Yes ☐ No ☐	Read Today's Lesson Today Yes ☐ No ☐	Read Today's Lesson Today Yes ☐ No ☐	Read Today's Lesson Today Yes ☐ No ☐	Read Today's Lesson Today Yes ☐ No ☐	
DAILY REFLECTION	Completed Today's Lesson Today Yes ☐ No ☐	Completed Today's Lesson Today Yes ☐ No ☐	Completed Today's Lesson Today Yes ☐ No ☐	Completed Today's Lesson Today Yes ☐ No ☐	Completed Today's Lesson Today Yes ☐ No ☐	Completed Today's Lesson Today Yes ☐ No ☐	
USED "RESTORE" BOOK	Yes ☐ No ☐	Yes ☐ No ☐	Yes ☐ No ☐	Yes ☐ No ☐	Yes ☐ No ☐	Yes ☐ No ☐	Yes ☐ No ☐
PRE-MEAL SATURATION VERSE	Breakfast ☐ Lunch ☐ Dinner ☐	Breakfast ☐ Lunch ☐ Dinner ☐	Breakfast ☐ Lunch ☐ Dinner ☐	Breakfast ☐ Lunch ☐ Dinner ☐	Breakfast ☐ Lunch ☐ Dinner ☐	Breakfast ☐ Lunch ☐ Dinner ☐	Breakfast ☐ Lunch ☐ Dinner ☐
SPECIAL ITEMS	Yes ☐ No ☐	Yes ☐ No ☐	Yes ☐ No ☐	Yes ☐ No ☐	Yes ☐ No ☐	Yes ☐ No ☐	Yes ☐ No ☐
PRIVATE PRAYER	Time Spent ___	Time Spent ___	Time Spent ___	Time Spent ___	Time Spent ___	Time Spent ___	Time Spent ___
TODAY, I AM THANKFUL FOR...							

Lesson 26 Study Sheet
Each day review the lesson for that week.
Record one thing you are grateful for each day on your Progress Record.

This Lesson's Verse:

"'Love the Lord your God with all your heart, with all your soul, with all your mind, and with all your strength. The second is: 'Love your neighbor as yourself. There is no other commandment greater than these.'" Mark 12:30-31 (NET)

Day 1 Reflection

How was your understanding of "love" impacted by this lesson? What effect do you think this might have going forward? *Additional study passages: Luke 6:35; John 13:34-35; Romans 12:9-21*

Day 2 Reflection

What do you think God expects from you now? What you are going to have the greatest trouble being obedient to and why? *Additional study passages: John 14:15; Ephesians 4:32; 1 John 4:7*

Day 3 Reflection

Consider what the lesson taught about love in the marriage relationship. What are your thoughts about this? *Additional study passages: Romans 13:8; Ephesians 4:2-3; 5:25, 33*

Day 4 Reflection

When you consider the people who are most difficult-to-love in your life, what do you think God wants you to do about that? How willing are you? *Additional study passages: 1 Peter 1:22; 1 John 2:9-11; 3:1, 16-18*

Day 5 Reflection

Who in your life has shown you the most authentic love when you were most undeserving of it? What are your thoughts on that now? *Additional study passages: Psalm 55:16-19; Malachi 3:6*

Day 6 Reflection

Thinking about God's love for you and your love for Him, what changes do you believe you need to make in your relationship with Him and why? *Additional study passages: Psalm 31:16; 63:3; John 15:9-17*

SUPPLEMENTAL

MATERIALS

A PATTERN FOR DEVELOPING YOUR PRAYER-LIFE

Jesus taught His disciples to pray by His own prayer life. There are several examples of Jesus' prayers in the Gospels, and they all seem to have somewhat similar patterns. One of those patterns is often called the Lord's Prayer [or, the Disciples' Prayer] and is found in *Matthew 6.9-14*. This simple acronym captures a pattern suggested by that prayer that you can follow in your own personal prayer time.

The acronym is **PRAISE**:

P - Praise is the beginning of all prayer. Start out praising God for what He has already done, grateful that He never changes.

> *Psalm 100:4*

R - Repent of and ask forgiveness for the sins you have committed, agreeing with God on the nature and character of those sins. In doing so, know that God will forgive you and cleanse you and give you a clean start.

> *1 John 1:9*

A - Ask for the things that you need knowing that God hears, and He will answer your prayers in accordance with His best will for you.

> *1 John 5:14-15*

I - Intercede (pray) on behalf of others. A huge part of the privilege of prayer is interceding for and praying on behalf of others.

> *1 Timothy 2:1-6*

S - Stand on His Word. Be in agreement with what His Word declares to be true and pray back to Him what His Word says about your situation.

> *Hebrews 4:12*

E - Enjoy just being in the presence of a good and loving God. Quietly **Worship** Him for who He is; rest in His company. This is often the most powerful part of prayer.

> *Psalm 16.11*

Use this Space to practice prayer-journaling[25]

---

[25] Prayer journaling is simply writing out your prayer, allowing the words to flow naturally. It takes a little practice, but it does not take very long before your prayers flow pretty freely. The reason this can be so effective is because, as you journal your thoughts and feelings, struggles and triumphs, hopes and disappointments, you are also surrendering them to God as you do. Give it a try...

LADDER-BRIDGE OF FAITH

A Supplemental Saturation Tool For
"Unbound: Growing Ever-freer in Christ"

This section goes with **Lessons Six and Seven**. If you would like a pocket-size version to carry with you and use, we would love to send you one. Simply request your free copy by sending an email to admin@tilbcc.com

ജ • ങ

"We urge you, brethren, admonish the unruly, encourage the fainthearted, help the weak, be patient with everyone."
1 Thessalonians 5:14

TRUTH IN LOVE
BIBLICAL COUNSELING ™

An Auxiliary Ministry of
Truth in Love Fellowship
Vancouver, WA
TILBCC.com
AuthenticBiblicalCounseling.com

Printed and bound in
The United States of America

338

THE LADDER-BRIDGE OF FAITH

God's Word teaches us that mankind is born into a fallen and troubled world. We are given to rebellious sin-choices and so is everyone else in the world. This means we can count on trouble in this life. We all know that life is never without difficulties, large and small, and they can become overwhelming. There are too many things we simply *cannot* control.

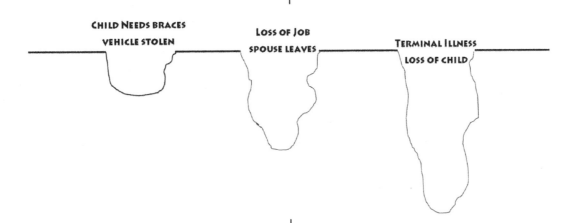

CHILD NEEDS BRACES
VEHICLE STOLEN

LOSS OF JOB
SPOUSE LEAVES

TERMINAL ILLNESS
LOSS OF CHILD

We know that life has "Pits of Gloom" with varying degrees of depth and darkness—and we very often find ourselves in the bottom of one with little or no warning.

God has a "Ladder-Bridge" we can use to both climb out of and cross over these Pits. We stand it on end and climb out when we are unable to avoid the Pits; we lay it down and cross over the Pits when we see ourselves coming up on one. Since we are more accustomed to finding ourselves in the "Pits," we first need to learn to climb out of them. Once we have that down a bit, we'll turn to working on avoiding them.

If we are unprepared when trouble comes - as we know it will—we can easily end up feeling fearfulness, anxiety, anger, misery, and find ourselves in bleak despair.

Hopelessness often follows. If we don't know how to climb out of those Pits of Gloom, we can end up stuck there for years.

As we will learn later in this program, when we are depressed and hopeless, our likelihood of making wise decisions is doubtful, at best.

It is also important to understand that it is during these times of trouble and difficulty that we need to make the wisest choices. So, we need something that can get us out of those dark places when we have nose-dived into them.

Unfortunately for many of us, the pattern that we have best perfected is the one of making our most important, life-impacting decisions when we are in the Pit of Gloom. Emotions are not truth, so

339

emotion-driven decisions are often defective and counterproductive.

The enemy of our souls (Satan) makes a shovel readily available to us in the form of doubt about God. We grab hold of that shovel with both hands, and we dig the Pit even deeper.

We all know that there is no real escape from having to face troubles in this life. Even if we could somehow create a trouble-free life, it would not even be in our best interest (James 1:2-4). It is vital that we learn to navigate through life's problems in wise, healthy, and godly ways.

It is in this place of struggle that we begin to become mature in dealing with life's troubles; that we begin to grow strong emotionally and spiritually. God knows that our ability to deal well with problems is important in shaping a healthy and abundant life, but He never intended that we deal with these difficulties alone (Matthew 11:28-30).

This leads us to two key questions: 1) how do we climb out of "Pits of Gloom" we so often find ourselves in? And 2) how do we learn to cross over those pits and avoid falling into them in the first place?

ASSEMBLING OUR "LADDER-BRIDGE OF FAITH"

The two main supports for our Ladder-Bridge of Faith are:

God's Word. There is nothing in the human experience that God's Word does not address (2 Peter 1:2-4);

Prayer. Openly and authentically surrendering to God everything that is on our hearts and minds, no matter what it is (Philippians 4:6-7).

Once we have the main supports in place, we begin to lay down the treads that will make up the rungs of the Ladder and the deck of the Bridge. The rungs are what we climb; the deck is where we stand. In both cases, they are where we put one foot after the other as we climb out of, or cross over, the Pits of Gloom.

These rungs and planks match up with key attributes and characteristics of God - the significant aspects of His nature and character that specifically connect us to how He interacts and intercedes in our life.

If our Ladder-Bridge is to be strong, the rungs and planks must be strong. A rung or plank is strong if our faith and trust in that aspect of God's character is strong. If our faith and trust are weak, then that rung or plank will be weak.

We need to learn what these rungs and planks are. Then we need to assess which rungs and planks are the strongest, and which are the weakest in our life. Strengthening our "Ladder-Bridge of Faith" will require us, through saturation, to strengthen our weakest rung or plank first.

Look through your "Ladder-Bridge of Faith" booklet and read the descriptions of the aspects of God's character that constitute our rungs and planks. There is a "Faith Assessment" on the last page of the booklet that will show you where to begin your saturation work.

God's Timing & Trajectory: Ecclesiastes 3:11
God's Guidance: Isaiah 42:16
God's Deliverance: Isaiah 12:2
God's Protection: 2 Samuel 22:31-32
God's Providence: 1 Chronicles 29:11-13
God's Presence: Psalm 46:7, 11
God's Mercy: Psalm 103:3-5
God's Grace: Ephesians 2:4-9
God's Love: Romans 5:6, 8, 10
God's Omnipotence: Revelation 19:6
God's Omniscience: Psalm 139:1-16
God's Goodness: Psalm 106:1

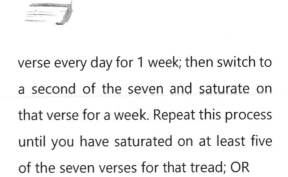

Each of the twelve **treads** has seven passages of Scripture that specifically relate to that particular attribute of God. The goal is to begin with the weakest tread first and use the verses corresponding to that tread to **saturate** on every day for several weeks until that tread becomes a great deal stronger than it was.

- Select one of the seven verses for that weak tread and **saturate** on that verse every day for 1 week; then switch to a second of the seven and saturate on that verse for a week. Repeat this process until you have saturated on at least five of the seven verses for that tread; OR

- Use a different verse each day for a week, making sure to use all seven verses for the week, and repeating this process for five to seven weeks;

At the end of the 5-7 weeks, retake the "Faith Assessment" and evaluate the strength of your faith and confidence in each of the twelve "treads."

Whichever one is the weakest, do as you did before and saturate with the Scriptures in this booklet (or others you find that fit) that relate specifically to the attribute and characteristic of God that you are doubting or struggling to see in your life.

This is how we take the weak parts of our Ladder-Bridge of Faith and make them strong. Once you have constructed a strong "Ladder-Bridge of Faith," you will find that your faith in God is now stronger and your life is now more settled, and your besetting sin patterns has weakened. You may even find that your life is now more stable than a person who has never been in the kind of bondage you were once in.

Keep in mind that we start with the bottom "rung" of the Ladder, because it is also the first plank in the Bridge, we will need to step out on to avoid the Pits of Gloom.

---

1. GOD'S GOODNESS

Hallelujah! Give thanks to the Lord, for He is good;
His faithful love endures forever.

Psalm 106:1

God is not only the Greatest of all beings, but the Good-est. When you think of someone who is a "good person," what do you think is true about them? They are kind; they are considerate of others; they are humble; they are joyful; they are never mean or unkind; they think of others first; they are never shady or dishonest in any way; they are dependable and trustworthy; that they have integrity; that they do all they can to stay away from evil.

Someone who is "good" is decent, ethical, upright, blameless, safe, benevolent, reliable, well-mannered, righteous, pleasant, able, competent, just, and helpful. Would you say that is a pretty good summary of "good?" That's a suitable place to start thinking about God's Goodness; but His goodness goes beyond that.

Apart from Him, nothing would be good; nothing could be good. The quality of His character and love is totally, completely, and fully good!

2. GOD'S OMNISCIENCE

Your eyes saw me when I was formless;

all my days were written in Your book and planned

before a single one of them began.

Psalm 139: (1-)16

Being "omniscient" means that He has always known everything and only what is true - including all true potentialities. By this it is meant that, even if something did not actually take place, He has always known the truth of whether or not it could take place and what the result would have been had it happened.

The reason this matters is that, instead of us having to be anxious about potentialities (those pesky not-now's and non-realities), we can fully surrender them to God because He knows (and has always known) whether or not they can or will take place, and He is fully prepared for whichever of those is true.

We can also always trust and depend on the fact that there is nothing in our heart, mind, or life—or in the heart, mind, and life of anyone else - that He is not and has not always known and been prepared for.

3. GOD'S OMNIPOTENCE

"I am the Alpha and the Omega," says the Lord God, "the One who is, who was, and who is coming, the Almighty."

Revelation 1:8

God is able in every respect for every action that is possible for Him. He has unlimited ability to be, and to do, all that He has said He is and will do. He is all-powerful; almighty. There is nothing God cannot do that is in keeping with His own nature and character.

For example, God cannot lie. He is Himself the Truth, so lying is not in His character or ability. If God could do anything contrary to His nature or character, He would cease to be God at that point, and He can never *not* be God!

This matters because it means that we can count on there being *nothing* that is impossible for God: nothing He has said He will do that He cannot and will not do; there is no promise He cannot and will not keep;

344

and there is no one and nothing stronger or mightier than He.

It also means that we can count on Him to provide us with everything we need to live as He has asked us to live and do all He has given us to do.

VERSES

Then I heard what sounded like the voice of a vast throng, like the roar of many waters and like loud crashes of thunder. They were shouting: "Hallelujah! For the Lord our God, the All-Powerful, reigns!" **Revelation 19:6**

I know that you can do all things; no purpose of yours can be thwarted. **Job 42:2**

I am able to do all things through the one who strengthens me. **Philippians 4:13**

Jesus looked at them and replied, "This is impossible for mere humans, but for God all things are possible." **Matthew 19:26**

Now to Him who by the power that is working within us is able to do far beyond all that we ask or think, to Him be the glory in the church and in Christ Jesus to all generations, forever and ever. Amen. **Ephesians 3:20**

This power He exercised in Christ when He raised Him from the dead and seated Him at His right hand in the heavenly realms far above every rule and authority and power and dominion and every name that is named, not only in this age but also in the one to come. **Ephesians 1:20-22**

And I will do whatever you ask in my name, so that the Father may be glorified in the Son. If you ask Me anything in My name, I will do it. **John 14:13-14**

---

4. GOD'S LOVE

While we were still helpless...ungodly...sinners [and] God's enemies, we were reconciled to God through the death of His Son...

Romans 5:6, 8, 10

Love — biblically — as it flows from God's nature and character, is "a passionate desire for God's best for someone else, even at great cost to oneself." The greatest example of this is spelled out in Philippians 2:5-8.

Here we see that Jesus, who is God just as much as God the Father is, loved us so much that He willingly laid aside everything

345

He was entitled to as God in order to take on human form, become obedient to the Father's will to the point that He bore God's wrath for human sin on the cross so that humankind would not have to.

God desires His best will for us and for everyone else. But He never forces us to accept His best - He always leaves that up to us to decide. And that too, is love. God is not some cosmic stalker, chasing us around, forcing us to "love" Him, because that isn't love at all, is it? In His Goodness, He cannot and will not do that.

Yet, God's love never ends and is far greater than any human love we can imagine. He extended His love to us when we were not only ignorant of Him and His love, but when we were in open rebellion against Him. For Him to seek and to save those who were His enemies truly *is* love! Now it is up to us to love others.

VERSES

But God demonstrates His own love for us in that, while we were still sinners, Christ died for us. **Romans 5:8**

For if while we were enemies we were reconciled to God through the death of His Son, how much more, since we have been reconciled, will we be saved by His life? **Romans 5:10**

For this is the way God loved the world: He gave His one and only Son, so that everyone who believes in Him will not perish but have eternal life. **John 3:16**

By this the love of God is revealed in us: that God has sent His one and only Son into the world so that we may live through Him. **1 John 4:9**

In this is love: not that we have loved God, but that He loved us and sent His Son to be the atoning sacrifice for our sins. **1 John 4:10**

Give thanks to the God of heaven, for His loyal love endures! **Psalm 136:26**

See what sort of love the Father has given to us: that we should be called God's children – and indeed we are! **1 John 3:1a.**

5. GOD'S GRACE

But God, who is rich in mercy, because of His great love that He had for us, made us alive with the Messiah even though we were dead in trespasses. You are saved by grace! Together with Christ Jesus He also raised us up and seated us in the heavens, so that in the coming ages He might display the immeasurable riches of His grace through His kindness to us in Christ Jesus. For you are saved by grace through faith, and this is not from yourselves; it is God's gift — not from works, so that no one can boast.

Ephesians 2:4-9

Grace is the undeserved kindness, support, and help God extends to all - especially His Children. Apart from God's grace, no one would stand a chance. But as it applies to those who are His by surrender to Christ, His Grace is an active and powerful force in our lives. Whenever we do not receive the punishment that we deserve for our willfulness and sin, THAT is "grace."

There is an old acronym that can be helpful to keep in mind: **G**od's **R**iches **A**t **C**hrist's **E**xpense. It is because of His grace that He asked Jesus to die in our place; it is because of His grace that Christ said, "Yes;" it is because of His grace that we have any hope at all, let alone a great hope.

VERSES

Now the Word became flesh and took up residence among us. We saw His glory – the glory of the one and only, full of grace and truth, who came from the Father.
John 1:14

For all have sinned and fall short of the glory of God. But they are justified freely by his grace through the redemption that is in Christ Jesus. **Romans 3:23-24**

For we have all received from His fullness one gracious gift after another. For the law was given through Moses, but grace and truth came about through Jesus Christ.
John 1:16-17

Therefore, since we have been declared righteous by faith, we have peace with God through our Lord Jesus Christ, through whom we have also obtained access by faith into this grace in which we stand, and we rejoice in the hope of God's glory.
Romans 5:1-2

> *And, after you have suffered for a little while, the God of all grace who called you to His eternal glory in Christ will Himself restore, confirm, strengthen, and establish you.*
> **1 Peter 5:10**

> *But He said to me, "My grace is enough for you, for My power is made perfect in weakness." So then, I will boast most gladly about my weaknesses, so that the power of Christ may reside in me.*
> **2 Corinthians 12:9**

> *For by grace you are saved through faith, and this is not from yourselves, it is the gift of God.* **Ephesians 2:8**

---

6. GOD'S MERCY

> He forgives all your sin; He heals all your diseases. He redeems your life from the Pit; He crowns you with faithful love and compassion. He satisfies you with goodness; your youth is renewed like the eagle.
> *Psalm 103:3-5*

Mercy means that God, in His Grace, instead of giving us what we do deserve - an immediate outpouring of His wrath on each and every sinner for each and every sin - in His Mercy, is patient and long-suffering, not wanting anyone to perish, but wanting instead for all to come to repentance (2 Peter 3:9).

Again, He will not force us, but He delays His punishment for our sins, giving us every possible opportunity to willingly turn from our sin and back to Him. If we do, Christ has taken our punishment in our place, and we will never have to bear it.

It is in God's Mercy that His forgiveness is found. While we are undeserving of any good thing, He created us worthy of His Love, His Grace, and His Mercy (Lesson One). It is through His Son Jesus that these have been bought for and made available to us (Lesson Two). This is where forgiveness and restoration to His Original Intent are to be found.

But You, O Lord , are a God merciful and gracious, Slow to anger and abundant in lovingkindness and truth. **Psalm 86:15**

He is the one who forgives all your sins, who heals all your diseases, who delivers your life from the Pit, who crowns you with His loyal love and compassion, who satisfies your life with good things, so your youth is renewed like an eagle's. **Psalm 103:3-5**

And the Lord said, "I will make all my goodness pass before your face, and I will proclaim the Lord by name before you; I will be gracious to whom I will be gracious, I will show mercy to whom I will show mercy." **Exodus 33:19**

However, due to your abundant mercy You did not do away with them altogether; You did not abandon them. For You are a merciful and compassionate God. **Nehemiah 9:31**

The Lord has heard my appeal for mercy; the Lord has accepted my prayer. **Psalm 6:9**

In all their affliction He was afflicted, and the angel of His presence saved them; in His love and in His mercy He redeemed them, and He lifted them and carried them all the days of old. **Isaiah 63:9**

If people want to boast, they should boast about this: They should boast that they understand and know me. They should boast that they know and understand that I, the Lord, act out of faithfulness, fairness, and justice in the earth and that I desire people to do these things," says the Lord. **Jeremiah 9:24**

<u>7. GOD'S PRESENCE</u>

The Lord of Hosts is with us; the God of Jacob is our stronghold. *Selah*

Yahweh of Hosts is with us; the God of Jacob is our stronghold. *Selah*

Psalm 46:7, 11

There is so much that happens in life that we don't understand, don't want to have to face, that we think is unfair, or that seems too difficult and too overwhelming.

First, we need to understand a principle known as God's Omnipresence. "Omnipresence" literally means "everywhere present." The literal meaning, however, does not really capture what the doctrine of God's Omnipresence entails. A better way to explain it is, "everywhere is in God's presence." This is because God is not in someone's cupboard, or inside someone ear, or in the back of a pickup truck.

If God is present, we ask, why does He let so many horrible things happen? This is, of course, the wrong question to be asking.

A better question to ask (building on the first six treads from the last lesson) would be, "Since God is Good, All-Knowing, All-Powerful, Faithfully Loving, Gracious, and Merciful, what does that tell me about where He is as I face this situation that has me in this Pit of Gloom?"

VERSES

Where can I go to escape Your Spirit? Where can I flee to escape Your presence?
Psalm 139:7

Even when I must walk through the darkest valley, I fear no danger, for You are with me; Your rod and Your staff reassure me. **Psalm 23:4**

The Lord who commands armies is on our side! The God of Jacob is our protector!
Psalm 46:7

The Lord is near all who cry out to Him, all who cry out to Him in truth. **Psalm 145:18**

For He has said, "I will never leave you and I will never abandon you." So we can say with confidence, "The Lord is my helper, and I will not be afraid. What can man do to me?" **Hebrews 13:5b-6**

The Lord is indeed going before you – He will be with you; He will not fail you or abandon you. Do not be afraid or discouraged! **Deuteronomy 31:8**

For I am convinced that neither death, nor life, nor angels, nor heavenly rulers, nor things that are present, nor things to come, nor powers, nor height, nor depth, nor anything else in creation will be able to separate us from the love of God in Christ Jesus our Lord. **Romans 8:38**

---

8. GOD'S PROVIDENCE

Yours, Lord, is the greatness and the power and the glory and the splendor and the majesty, for everything in the heavens and on earth belongs to You. Yours, Lord, is the kingdom, and You are exalted as head over all. Riches and honor come from You, and You are the ruler of everything. Power and might are in Your hand, and it is in Your hand to make great and to give strength to all. Now therefore, our God, we give You thanks and praise Your glorious name.

1 Chronicles 29:11-13

This word "providence,", derived from the word "provision" (which means "to see ahead"), refers to God's sovereign oversight of not only each one of our lives, but over all of time and creation as well. Think of settlers getting ready to head West in the wagon trains of long ago. They had to "see ahead," and make plans and "provision" for what they would need throughout the journey.

As this applies to the nature and character of God, since He has always known everything that is or could possibly be true (Psalm 33:13-15); He has always known everything you or I could ever need, every situation any and all of us would ever face, each and every choice every one of us would make, and He has always known what His best plan is for "providing" for those needs and what His best remedies for every situation will be (Psalm 139:4, 16); and even seemingly chance events are known by and involve God (Proverbs 16:33).

God's Providence also refers to His guiding hand being always involved in the affairs of His creation, even those things that are evil (Jeremiah 18:1-6).

This is not to say that God creates or causes evil; it simply means that in spite of evil, God's best will is going to be accomplished and He is always going to supply for our every true need, no matter what.

VERSES

You are the source of wealth and honor; You rule over all. You possess strength and might to magnify and give strength to all. **1 Chronicles 29:12**

For the Lord promotes justice, and never abandons His faithful followers. They are permanently secure, but the children of evil men are wiped out. **Psalm 37:28**

He provides rain for the earth; he sends water on the countryside. **Job 1:5**

Now to Him who by the power that is working within us is able to do far beyond all that we ask or think, to Him be the glory in the church and in Christ Jesus to all generations, forever and ever. Amen. **Ephesians 3:20-21**

"While the earth continues to exist, planting time and harvest, cold and heat, summer and winter, and day and night will not cease." **Genesis 8:22**

> *Everything looks to You in anticipation, and You provide them with food on a regular basis. You open Your hand, and fill every living thing with the food they desire.* **Psalm 145:15-16**
>
> *So do not be overly concerned about what you will eat and what you will drink, and do not worry about such things. For all the nations of the world pursue these things, and your Father knows that you need them. Instead, pursue His kingdom, and these things will be given to you as well.* **Luke 12:29-31**

9. GOD'S PROTECTION

God — His way is perfect; the word of the Lord is pure. He is a shield to all who take refuge in Him. For who is God besides the Lord? And who is a rock? Only our God.

2 Samuel 22:31-32

This is so closely related to the previous two treads that they are best understood together. Psalm 91 is perhaps one of the clearest expressions in all of Scripture by someone who knows and understands God's Protection in some of the direst of circumstances.

God' Protection is not always a protection *from*; it is often a protection *through*. God will always protect us through each and every circumstance, no matter how grim, no matter how difficult. NOTHING can befall you that will be too much for you—even if it seems too much at the time. God knows what you are made of, and He knows what it will take for Him to finish making you into Christ's image (Romans 8:28-29).

> ### VERSES
>
> *He will shelter you with his wings; you will find safety under His wings. His faithfulness is like a shield or a protective wall.* **Psalm 91:4**
>
> *"I have told you these things so that in me you may have peace. In the world you have trouble and suffering, but take courage – I have conquered the world."* **John 16:33**
>
> *The Lord will deliver me from every evil deed and will bring me safely into His heavenly kingdom. To Him be glory for ever and ever! Amen.* **2 Timothy 4:18**

But the Lord is faithful, and He will strengthen you and protect you from the evil one. **2 Thessalonians 3:3**

He who dwells in the shelter of the Most High will abide in the shadow of the Almighty. **Psalm 91:1**

No trial has overtaken you that is not faced by others. And God is faithful: He will not let you be tried beyond what you are able to bear, but with the trial will also provide a way of escape so that you may be able to endure it. **1 Corinthians 10:13**

Indeed, who is God besides the Lord? Who is a protector besides our God? The one true God is my mighty refuge; He removes the obstacles in my way. **2 Samuel 22:32-33**

---

10. GOD'S DELIVERANCE

Indeed, God is my salvation; I will trust Him and not be afraid, for Yah, the Lord, is my strength and my song. He has become my salvation.

Isaiah 12:2

Deliverance in the Bible is the acts of God whereby He rescues His people from peril. In the Old Testament, deliverance is focused primarily on God's removal of those who are in the midst of trouble or danger. He rescues His people from their enemies, and from the hand of the wicked. He preserves them from famine, death, and the grave.

The most striking example of deliverance is the exodus from Egypt. Here God is defined as the Deliverer of Israel who rescues His people, not because they deserve to be rescued, but as an expression of His mercy and love.

The descriptions of deliverance in the Old Testament serve as symbolic representations of the spiritual deliverance from sin which is available only through Christ. He offers deliverance from mankind's greatest peril—sin, evil, death and judgment.

By God's power, believers are delivered from this present evil age and from the power of Satan's reign. All aspects of deliverance are available only through the person and work of Jesus Christ.

11. GOD'S GUIDANCE

I will lead the blind by a way they did not know; I will guide them on paths they have not known. I will turn darkness to light in front of them and rough places into level ground.

This is what I will do for them, and I will not forsake them.

Isaiah 42:16

God knows what His best will is for each of us and He has provided us with everything we need to know how to live in harmony with His will. His Word is filled with all manner of descriptions about how He thinks about every aspect of the human condition and experience.

I will instruct and teach you about how you should live. **Psalm 32:8a**

Your Word is a lamp to walk by, and a light to illumine my path. **Psalm 119:105**

Make me understand Your ways, O Lord! Teach me your paths! Guide me into Your truth and teach me. For You are the God who delivers me; on You I rely all day long. **Psalm 25:4-5**

But if anyone is deficient in wisdom, he should ask God, who gives to all generously and without reprimand, and it will be given to him. **James 1:5**

Trust in the Lord with all your heart, and do not rely on your own understanding. Acknowledge Him in all your ways, and He will make your paths straight. **Proverbs 3:5-6**

12. GOD'S TIMING & TRAJECTORY

He has made everything appropriate in its time. He has also put eternity in their hearts, but man cannot discover the work God has done from beginning to end.

Ecclesiastes 3:11

These two go together; they are "two sides to the same coin," as it were. One of the best examples can be found in the first half of Jonah 2: "The Lord had arranged for a huge fish to swallow Jonah..." We see it once again in Jonah 4:6-8, where God "arranged for" a little plant to grow up and shade Jonah, then sent a worm to attack the plant so that it dried up, then ensured that Jonah experienced a hot east wind and scorching sun.

God has so ordered the universe and made provision for every choice every human being will ever make, that His best will is ultimately going to be accomplished, and His Timing & Trajectory that cause it all to flow together are *flawless*.

This is the same God who created you, who loves you, who sent His Son to take your eternal punishment in your place — and who created you for the purpose of loving you and one day inviting you to share in His glory.

Verses

You will keep in perfect peace and safety those who maintain their faith, because they trust in You. **Isaiah 26:3**

Wait for the Lord; be strong, and let your heart take courage; wait for the Lord!
Psalm 27:14

The Lord is not slow concerning his promise, as some regard slowness, but is being patient toward you, because he does not wish for any to perish but for all to come to repentance. **2 Peter 3:9**

For the message is a witness to what is decreed; it gives reliable testimony about how matters will turn out. Even if the message is not fulfilled right away, wait patiently; for it will certainly come to pass – it will not arrive late. **Habakkuk 2:3**

But those who wait for the Lord's help find renewed strength; they rise up as if they had eagles' wings, they run without growing weary, they walk without getting tired.
Isaiah 40:31

Remember what I accomplished in antiquity! Truly I am God, I have no peer; I am God, and there is none like Me, who announces the end from the beginning and reveals beforehand what has not yet occurred, who says, "My plan will be realized, I will accomplish what I desire." **Isaiah 46:9-10**

But when the appropriate time had come, God sent out His Son, born of a woman, born under the law, to redeem those who were under the law, so that we may be adopted as sons with full rights. **Galatians 4:4-5**

TREAD STRENGTH SELF-ASSESSMENT

↓ ATTRIBUTE | DATE →						
GOD'S GOODNESS						
GOD'S OMNISCIENCE						
GOD'S OMNIPOTENCE						
GOD'S LOVE						
GOD'S GRACE						
GOD'S MERCY						
GOD'S PRESENCE						
GOD'S PROVIDENCE						
GOD'S PROTECTION						
GOD'S DELIVERANCE						
GOD'S GUIDANCE						
GOD'S TIMING & TRAJECTORY						

SELF-ASSESSMENT: Score using 0 thru 5, then saturate (20x to 100x a day) with appropriate verses (lowest score) for that tread from the booklet (or other helpful verses you may find). Reassess every 6 to 8 weeks.

Restore

An Unbound
Supplemental Saturation Tool

TRUTH IN LOVE
BIBLICAL COUNSELING ™

AuthenticBiblicalCounseling.com

TILBCC.com

The following pages contain the materials found in the
"Restore" Supplemental Saturation Tool
used in conjunction with the "Unbound" curriculum of
Truth in Love Biblical Counseling Center, Vancouver, WA.

Copyright © 2002–2020, Truth in Love Fellowship
PO Box 5281, Vancouver, WA 98668
Truth in Love Biblical Counseling, Edition 5, 2020
TILBCC.com

℘ • ℭ

"We urge you, brethren, admonish the unruly, encourage the fainthearted, help the weak, be patient with everyone."
1 Thessalonians 5:14

TRUTH IN LOVE
BIBLICAL COUNSELING   T M

An Auxiliary Ministry of
Truth in Love Fellowship
Vancouver, WA
TILBCC.com
AuthenticBiblicalCounseling.com

Printed and bound in
The United States of America

RESTORE CONTENTS

RESTORE: ANTIDOTES FOR THE LIES

Surviving, enduring, getting by: we all know how to do that — we have managed to at least figure that out, right? (Even if only just barely sometimes, yes?) What would it be like to actually *thrive* in life? To feel alive, joyful, even happy sometimes?

Some of us cannot even imagine it; others of us can remember a time long ago when it was like that — for a minute, anyway. But so many bad things have happened, so many mistakes have been made, so many bad choices have been opted for, that our hearts and minds are saturated with the black, gooey, smelly sludge of guilt, shame, and a bevy of other toxic emotions.

Jesus, the Great Shepherd, declares in **John 10:10**, *"The thief comes only to steal and kill and destroy; I have come so that they may have life, and may have it abundantly."* Who is the "they" He speaks of? "They" is "we," His sheep.

All those who have surrendered their hearts and lives to God through Christ are sheep belonging to the Great Shepherd, Jesus Christ. He loves, cares for, provides for, protects, and defends those who are His. He provides strength and encouragement for us, as well as wisdom and insight for us to follow Him.

And what does He mean by "have it abundantly?" Abundant life means life that is far more than we would ever expect or anticipate. It is not a life filled with all of the earthly pleasures we can imagine, but a life filled with a sense of God's comforting and guiding presence no matter where we are or what we face.

God truly has prepared an abundant and fruitful life for us here — now. This abundant life is ours as we walk daily with Him. Very often, however, because of difficult and troubling circumstances in life or ongoing consequences of choices we have made in the past, we feel that the benefits of being the redeemed of God will have to wait until we get to Heaven. The ultimate experience of that will be ours once Christ returns. But there is abundant life for us to live now, even before that happens.

In order thrive in this abundant life Jesus provides us with — the life that is filled with far more than we would ever expect or anticipate — we need to learn to believe in (totally trust in, depend on, rely upon) Him and His truth-claims instead of the lies that seem always ready to take back over our minds and our hearts.

We do this by getting His Word into us by getting into His Word (**John 8:31-32**). To know God's best for our life, we must learn to replace our defective thinking with His thinking and search His Word to find the antidotes to the lies we believe and then live out those truths. It is then that we can effectively deal with our corrupted motives and destructive desires.

In order to experience the freedom that Christ promised when He said, *"So if the Son makes you free, you will be really free* (**John 8:36**)," and to keep from returning to our former way of life, there are battles we will

363

have to fight and win. ("For freedom Christ has set us free. Stand firm, then, and do not be subject again to the yoke of slavery." **Galatians 5:1**)

That battle is for our hearts and souls, but it begins with our minds. In order to be transformed from what we were to what we were created to be, we must renew our minds (**Romans 12:2**).

WEAPONS FOR
FIGHTING AND WINNING THE BATTLES

When we look honestly at our lives, we can see that we have lost many battles many times and that, on our own, we are powerless in this war. **Romans 12:2** reads, *"Do not be conformed to this present world but be transformed by the renewing of your mind, so that you may test and approve what is the will of God – what is good and well-pleasing and perfect."*

In order to renew our minds, we must saturate on the Scriptures; we must bring out the "Big Guns", so to speak. The Bible is the "Sword of the Spirit" (**Ephesians 6:17**) and is the most powerful weapon available to us to fight the blatant lies and subtle deceptions of the Enemy. Jesus used only the Scriptures in His head-to-head with Satan in the wilderness (**Matthew 4:4, 7, 10**). If He relied on the Word of God that way, we know that we can, too!

Hebrews 4:12 assures us that, *"For the word of God is living and active and sharper than any two-edged sword, and piercing as far as the division of soul and spirit, of both joints and marrow, and able to judge the thoughts and intentions of the heart."*

2 Timothy 3:16-17 tells us that, *"All Scripture is inspired by God* [literally, "God-breathed"] *and profitable for teaching, for reproof, for correction, for training in righteousness; so that the man* [human person] *of God may be adequate, equipped for every good work."*

Remember: there is a battle raging, and that battle is for our hearts and minds. The war is and always has been between God's truth-claims and the truth-claims of our adversary, the Devil — and the unbelieving world that prefers his ways to God's ways.

2 Corinthians 10:3-5 provides a very practical key to fighting and winning these battles with these words: *"For though we live as human beings, we do not wage war according to human standards, for the weapons of our warfare are not human weapons, but are made powerful by God for tearing down strongholds. We tear down arguments and every arrogant obstacle that is raised up against the knowledge of God, and we take every thought captive to make it obey Christ."*

Since Jesus Christ IS *"the way, the TRUTH, and the life"* (**John 14:6**), and because He came into the world for the express purpose of testifying TO the truth (His words, **John 18:37**), another powerful way to think of "make it (every thought) obey Christ" is to render that phrase this way: "Bring them (our thoughts) into surrender to the Truth."

364

Our enemy, the Devil, is a liar and a thief. He is called the Destroyer and the Accuser of God's people. He is the "thief" who comes only to "steal, and kill, and destroy" that Jesus referred to in **John 10:10** (previous page). Satan has made it his eternal mission to do everything in his power to destroy as many lives as possible before Jesus returns and brings the whole war to an end. Until that time, Satan (the Devil) will do all he can to gain control over your thought-life so he can gain control over your mind and the rest of your life — and your eternity, if he were able.

It is up to us to choose whether we will cooperate with him or fight against him; whether we will allow him to establish "strongholds," or tear down his strongholds with the weapons and power that God has given us.

In order to be successful in gaining godly control of our lives, we must learn to use this amazing weapon that God has provided called "The Bible." This program will assist you in reclaiming your mind for Christ and help you thrive in the life He died to give you.

The areas of warfare and the categories of weaponry we have that help us win the battles and cooperate with God's plan to completely transform our lives are:

- Our Minds = Scripture Saturation & Prayer

- Our Emotions = "Seat on the bus, but NOT the driver's seat""

- Our Body = Healthy-Living Choices

We say many times in this program that "The number one antidote for lies is the truth—God's truth." On the following pages, there are several groupings listed as "weapons" for defeating the Enemy at his own game. If we will regularly and faithfully apply God's specific antidotes to the Devil's specific lies, we win and he loses!

As you go through this "Supplemental Saturation Tool," Think of it as "An Emotional First-aid Kit." Read the material that precedes each collection of Scriptures for saturation. Getting a proper mindset before engaging your Adversary is powerfully helpful for your success.

I.   WEAPONS FOR ESTABLISHING
SELF-CONTROL

When our thoughts and emotions are out of control, our lives are out of control as well. God does not force us to walk surrendered to

Christ; He leaves the decision to do so up to us. If we resist the enemy by submitting to God and drawing near to Him, God will draw near to us and the enemy will flee (**James 4:7-8a**).

The main reason that we often surrender to unhealthy attitudes and behaviors is because we have become habituated to taking the easy road. We very often prefer pursuing those things that please our senses than those things that feed our souls.

We fight the battle for self-control by saturating on one or more of the following verses. They help us renew our minds and so it becomes easier to choose to surrender to God than to our flesh.

Therefore I exhort you, brothers and sisters by the mercies of God, to present your bodies as a sacrifice – alive, holy, and pleasing to God – which is your reasonable service. **Romans 12:1**

Do not be conformed to this present world but be transformed by the renewing of your mind, so that you may test and approve what is the will of God – what is good and well-pleasing and perfect. **Romans 12:2**

Encourage younger men likewise to be self-controlled, showing yourself to be an example of good works in every way. **Titus 2:6-7a**

Be sober-minded and alert. Your enemy the devil, like a roaring lion, is on the prowl looking for someone to devour. Resist him, strong in your faith, because you know that your brothers and sisters throughout the world are enduring the same kinds of suffering. **1 Peter 5:8-9**

But He answered, "It is written, 'Man does not live by bread alone, but by every word that comes from the mouth of God.'" **Matthew 4:4**

For the word of God is living and active and sharper than any double-edged sword, piercing even to the point of dividing soul from spirit, and joints from marrow; it is able to judge the desires and thoughts of the heart. **Hebrews 4:12**

For the weapons of our warfare are not human weapons, but are made powerful by God for tearing down strongholds. We tear down arguments and every arrogant obstacle that is raised up against the knowledge of God, and we take every thought captive to make it obey Christ. **2 Corinthians 10:4-5**

But the fruit of the Spirit is love, joy, peace, patience, kindness, goodness, faithfulness, gentleness, and self-control. Against such things there is no law. **Galatians 5:22-23**

For the grace of God has appeared, bringing salvation to all people. It trains us to reject godless ways and worldly desires and to live self-controlled, upright, and godly lives in the present age. **Titus 2:11-12**

Do you not know that all the runners in a stadium compete, but only one receives the prize? So run to win. Each competitor must exercise self-control in everything. They do it to receive a perishable crown, but we an imperishable one. **1 Corinthians 9:24-25**

"For the eyes of the LORD move to and fro throughout the earth that He may strongly support those whose heart is completely His." **2 Chronicles 16:9a**

Blessed is the one who endures testing, because when he has proven to be genuine, he will receive the crown of life that God promised to those who love him. **James 1:12**

For the culmination of all things is near. So be self-controlled and sober-minded for the sake of prayer. Above all keep your love for one another fervent, because love covers a multitude of sins. **1 Peter 4:7-8**

For God did not give us a Spirit of fear but of power and love and self-control. **2 Timothy 1:7**

Love is patient, love is kind, it is not envious. Love does not brag; it is not puffed up. It is not rude, it is not self-serving, it is not easily angered or resentful.
1 Corinthians 13:4-5

II. Weapons for
Repelling Temptation

Most of us have heard the saying, "I can resist anything but temptation." The truth of the matter is, if we are to have control in our lives, if there is to be hope for permanent change, we must not only resist temptation but also conquer it.

Prayer and saturating our minds with God's Word are the only effective weapons we have at our disposal when we come under attack. That trigger can come from within or without, but sin is "an inside job," so we have to be prepared to engage the battle on both fronts.

James 1:13-15 tells us clearly where the temptation we have to fight comes from –- sin is "an inside job":

"Let no one say when he is tempted, 'I am being tempted by God'; for God cannot be tempted by evil, and He Himself does not tempt anyone. But each one is tempted when he is lured and enticed by his own desires. Then when desire has conceived, it gives birth to sin; and when sin is full grown, it brings forth death."

Long-term victory over unbridled desires and unrighteous behaviors requires us to be in control of our thoughts and keep them in submission to Jesus Christ.

When we allow our thoughts to wander down old, dark paths, we already know the outcomes will be bad. When we fill our minds with Scripture, we change what we believe, replace selfish desires for godly one, and how we act and treat others is admirable instead of detestable.

To "renew the mind" does not mean to freshen up what is already there; it means to replace the thoughts we have with new thoughts — God's thoughts. Being transformed (think caterpillar-into-a-butterfly) is the outcome to our faithful investment in renewing our mind.

We must understand that every circumstance in our life is designed to bring ultimate benefit and that Christ has great plans for each one of us—no matter what we might believe. Think of temptation this way: Every temptation is the opportunity for us to choose between God's way and the Enemy's way — that simple.

Only by knowing what God says in His Word and by being in agreement with it do the things that enticed us and easily lured us into sin lose their power in our lives. We must have the mind of Christ in order to live the life He died to give us.

I am not saying this because I am in need, for I have learned to be content in whatever circumstance I find myself. I know what it is to be in want, and I know what it is to have an abundance. In any and every circumstance, I have learned the secret, whether I am well-fed or hungry, have plenty or am in need. I can do all things through Him who strengthens me. **Philippians 4:11-13**

Let no one say when he is tempted, "I am tempted by God," for God cannot be tempted by evil, and he himself tempts no one. But each one is tempted when he is lured and enticed by his own desires. **James 1:13-14**

But he gives greater grace. Therefore it says, "God opposes the proud, but he gives grace to the humble." 7 So submit to God. But resist the devil and he will flee from you. 8 Draw near to God and he will draw near to you. **James 4-6-8a**

"Stay awake and pray that you will not fall into temptation. The spirit is willing, but the flesh is weak." **Matthew 26:41**

No trial has overtaken you that is not faced by others. And God is faithful: He will not let you be tried beyond what you are able to bear, but with the trial will also provide a way out so that you may be able to endure it. **1 Corinthians 10:13**

For whatever is born of God overcomes the world; and this is the victory that has overcome the world--our faith. Who is the one who overcomes the world, but he who believes that Jesus is the Son of God? **1 John 5:4-5**

I can do all things through Him who strengthens me. **Philippians 4:13**

Be sober and alert. Your enemy the devil, like a roaring lion, is on the prowl looking for someone to devour. Resist him, strong in your faith, because you know that your brothers and sisters throughout the world are enduring the same kinds of suffering. **1 Peter 5:8-9**

Resist him, strong in your faith, because you know that your brothers and sisters throughout the world are enduring the same kinds of suffering. And, after you have suffered for a little while, the God of all grace who called you to his eternal glory in Christ will himself restore, confirm, strengthen, and establish you. **1 Peter 5:9-10**

My brothers and sisters, consider it nothing but joy when you fall into all sorts of trials, because you know that the testing of your faith produces endurance. And let endurance have its perfect effect, so that you will be perfect and complete, not deficient in anything. **James 1:2-4**

Blessed is the one who endures testing, because when he has proven to be genuine, he will receive the crown of life that God promised to those who love him. **James 1:12**

He said, "What comes out of a person defiles him. For from within, out of the human heart, come evil ideas, sexual immorality, theft, murder, adultery, greed, evil, deceit, debauchery, envy, slander, pride, and folly. All these evils come from within and defile a person." **Mark 7:20-23**

He has told you, O man, what is good, and what the Lord really wants from you: He wants you to promote justice, to be faithful, and to live obediently before your God. **Micah 6:8**

"But to this one I will look, to him who is humble and contrite of spirit, and who trembles at My word." **Isaiah 66:2b**

III. Weapons for
Breaking Free & Staying Free

It is far easier to resist a behavior pattern before it starts than it is to break it once it is firmly established in our lives. The Bible teaches us that it is nearly impossible for us to change the way we act without Christ once a pattern of behavior has been established (*"Can you ever change and do what's right? Can people change the color of their skin, or can a leopard remove its spots? If so, then maybe you can change and learn to do right."* **Jeremiah 13:23, CEV**).

This is why, for our own protection, we must cling to the freedom we have in Christ. We must fill our minds with as much of the Bible as we can, guarding the areas of weakness in our hearts and minds so Satan cannot gain a foothold. Once he has a foothold, a stronghold usually follows.

God relates these areas of weakness to lack of knowledge:

"My people are destroyed for lack of knowledge." **Hosea 4:6a**

Therefore My people go into exile for their lack of knowledge; And their honorable men are famished, and their multitude is parched with thirst. **Isaiah 5:13**

I shall delight in Your commandments, which I love. And I shall lift up my hands to Your commandments, Which I love; and I will meditate on Your statutes. **Psalm 119:47-48**

"So if the Son makes you free, you will be free indeed." **John 8:36**

True freedom lies in who we are in Christ, what He has done for us, and what He has called us to:

So Jesus was saying to those Jews who had believed Him, "If you continue in My word, then you are truly disciples of Mine; and you will know the truth, and the truth will make you free." **John 8:31-32**

Brethren, I do not regard myself as having laid hold of it yet; but one thing I do: forgetting what lies behind and reaching forward to what lies ahead, I press on toward the goal for the prize of the upward call of God in Christ Jesus. **Philippians 4:13-14**

So I gave my attention to the Lord God to seek Him by prayer and supplications, with fasting, sackcloth and ashes. **Daniel 9:3**

You will seek Me and find Me when you search for Me with all your heart. **Jeremiah 29:13**

"By your endurance you will gain your lives." **Luke 21:19**

For you have need of endurance, so that when you have done the will of God, you may receive what was promised. **Hebrews 10:36**

May the Lord direct your hearts into the love of God and into the steadfastness of Christ. **2 Thessalonians 3:5**

Do you not know that those who run in a race all run, but only one receives the prize? Run in such a way that you may win. **1 Corinthians 9:24**

Consider it all joy, my brethren, when you encounter various trials, knowing that the testing of your faith produces endurance. And let endurance have its perfect result, so that you may be perfect and complete, lacking in nothing. **James 1:2-4**

Blessed is a man who perseveres under trial; for once he has been approved, he will receive the crown of life which the Lord has promised to those who love Him. **James 1:12**

For you have not received a spirit of slavery leading to fear again, but you have received a spirit of adoption as sons by which we cry out, "Abba! Father!" The Spirit Himself testifies with our spirit that we are children of God, and if children, heirs also, heirs of God and fellow heirs with Christ, if indeed we suffer with Him so that we may also be glorified with Him. **Romans 8:15-17**

I pray that the eyes of your heart may be enlightened, so that you will know what is the hope of His calling, what are the riches of the glory of His inheritance in the saints, and what is the surpassing greatness of His power toward us who believe. **Ephesians 1:18-19a**

Therefore we do not lose heart, but though our outer man is decaying, yet our inner man is being renewed day by day. **2 Corinthians 4:16**

IV. WEAPONS FOR BATTLING A
SENSE OF ENTITLEMENT

There are times when may have the attitude, "I want what I want, and I want it *now*!"

That thinking is accompanied by a feeling that we have a right to expect our demands to be met. This is what is meant by a "sense of entitlement." We believe we have the right to expect the best of everything. The slightest inconvenience, delay, or restriction makes us angry—even resentful. We will go out of our way to satisfy whatever need or desire we have because, after all, we are entitled to have our wants and needs met when we want, the way we want—aren't we?

"Everybody else has...", "How come he got...?", "But, what about me?" These protests and others like them indicate a sense of entitlement. Envy and jealousy underlie this emotional cancer.

What is the difference between envy and jealousy? Envy is my burning desire to have what another has and I feel entitled to it; jealousy is my burning desire to have what

another has because it rightfully belongs to me instead of to them. Again, I feel entitled to it. Envy and jealousy are based in selfish pride and have to be gotten rid of if we are to be at peace with God, with ourselves, and with others in our life.

Our plans don't work out, people don't treat us the way we want them to, someone owes us something they aren't giving us, someone else gets what we have worked hard for—the list goes on and on. This is all normal living. What matters is how we feel about it and what we do with those feelings. A lack of contentment and a lack of trust in the full nature and character of God and His promises to provide for us are the root cause, and we have to know and believe the truth if we are to defeat our sense of entitlement.

God in His sovereignty has led us to the place where we are right now. He has given us what we have or denied us what we do not have. A sense of entitlement is based in an attitude of self-sovereignty. What that means is that we feel that God does not know what He is doing and we think we could do a better job. This is prideful.

But godliness actually is a means of great gain when accompanied by contentment. For we have brought nothing into the world, so we cannot take anything out of it either. If we have food and covering, with these we shall be content. 1 Timothy 6:6-8

Whatever you do, do your work heartily, as for the Lord rather than for men, knowing that from the Lord you will receive the reward of the inheritance. It is the Lord Christ whom you serve. Colossians 3:23-24

Every good thing given and every perfect gift is from above, coming down from the Father of lights, with whom there is no variation or shifting shadow. James 1:17

I know how to get along with humble means, and I also know how to live in prosperity; in any and every circumstance I have learned the secret of being filled and going hungry, both of having abundance and suffering need. Philippians 4:12

It is better to be humble in spirit with the lowly than to divide the spoil with the proud. Proverbs 16:19

A man's pride will bring him low, But a humble spirit will obtain honor. Proverbs 29:23

"But the greatest among you shall be your servant. Whoever exalts himself shall be humbled; and whoever humbles himself shall be exalted. Matthew 23:11-12

But He gives a greater grace. Therefore it says, "GOD IS OPPOSED TO THE PROUD, BUT GIVES GRACE TO THE HUMBLE." James 4:6

There is only one Lawgiver and Judge, the One who is able to save and to destroy; but who are you who judge your neighbor? James 4:12

Therefore humble yourselves under the mighty hand of God, that He may exalt you at the proper time, casting all your anxiety on Him, because He cares for you. 1 Peter 5:6-7

Now for this very reason also, applying all diligence, in your faith supply moral excellence, and in your moral excellence, knowledge, and in your knowledge, self-control, and in your self-control, perseverance, and in your perseverance, godliness, and in your godliness, brotherly kindness, and in your brotherly kindness, love. **2 Peter 1:5-7**

He has told you, O man, what is good; And what does the LORD require of you But to do justice, to love kindness, And to walk humbly with your God? **Micah 6:8**

"But to this one I will look, to him who is humble and contrite of spirit, and who trembles at My word." Isaiah **66:2b**

But the fruit of the Spirit is love, joy, peace, patience, kindness, goodness, faithfulness, gentleness, self-control; against such things there is no law. Galatians 5:22-23

V. Weapons for Battling
Toxic Shame

<u>There are two kinds of shame we experience in this life</u>.

<u>First</u>, there is "righteous" shame. This is the shame we feel when we have done something morally bad or ethically wrong. This is the shame that causes us to blush; to be remorseful over the wrong we have done and the harm we have caused; and it brings us to the place of confession, repentance, and restoration. Righteous shame is the right shame for us to feel when we are guilty of wrong.

<u>The second kind</u> of shame we experience is "toxic" shame. This is the shame that says "I am bad" instead of "I did badly" or "I am wrong" instead of "I did wrong." Toxic shame results from us taking the guilt that is someone else's to carry.

We believe we are guilty, so we beg and plead for forgiveness, but it never comes - because we cannot be forgiven for something that we are not guilty of! We feel unforgiven and unforgivable because, technically, we are - God does not provide forgiveness for sins we are not guilty of.

In addition, toxic shame hijacks every other emotion, thought, and perception, attaching itself to those things like the HIV virus attaches itself to healthy cells and camouflages itself, wreaking havoc throughout the immune system and eventually destroying the one infected. Toxic shame operates that same way on a person's emotions, thought processes, sense of worth, perceptions about God, others, and even themselves.

God does not expect us to seek forgiveness for anything we are not guilty of. He also does not want us to carry shame that is rightfully someone else's to carry. Learning to separate the two can be tricky sometimes, so keep this in mind: Righteous shame is not condemning, toxic shame is. If you're feeling condemned, that is not from God.

Don't be afraid, for you will not be put to shame! Don't be intimidated, for you will not be humiliated! You will forget about the shame you experienced in your youth; you will no longer remember the disgrace of your abandonment. **Isaiah 54:4**

Instead of shame, you will get a double portion; instead of humiliation, they will rejoice over the land they receive. Yes they will possess a double portion in their land and experience lasting joy. **Isaiah 61:7**

For the scripture says, "Everyone who believes in him will not be put to shame." **Romans 10:11**

Look, at that time I will deal with those who mistreated you. I will rescue the lame sheep and gather together the scattered sheep. I will take away their humiliation and make the whole earth admire and respect them. **Zephaniah 3:19**

The Lord watches over the innocent day by day and they possess a permanent inheritance. They will not be ashamed when hard times come; when famine comes they will have enough to eat. **Psalm 37:18-19**

There is therefore now no condemnation for those who are in Christ Jesus. **Romans 8:1**

Do not let the afflicted be turned back in shame! Let the oppressed and poor praise your name! **Psalm 74:21**

Look, all who were angry at you will be ashamed and humiliated; your adversaries will be reduced to nothing and perish. When you will look for your opponents, you will not find them; your enemies will be reduced to absolutely nothing. For I am the Lord your God, the one who takes hold of your right hand, who says to you, 'Don't be afraid, I am helping you.' **Isaiah 41:11-13**

VI. Weapons for Battling
LUST

Lust is a fast-burning, all-consuming emotional bondage that robs us of peace, stability, and intimacy. It fractures our relationship with God, and it pushes us away from those we want to be closest to. Simply defined, lust is the intense desire to satisfy God-given needs in an ungodly manner and/or to an ungodly degree.

God created us with the need to eat, to sleep, to be in relationship, to feel loved, to have intimate sexual union with another person, and the list goes on and on. It is natural for us to seek to satisfy these needs.

Difficulties arise when we seek to satisfy these needs in ways not in keeping with God's will.

Sexual lust is perhaps the most damaging and difficult lust to break free of because it strikes at the core of who we are. From our earliest days, we learn to identify ourselves and others through gender labels: him, her, his, hers, that boy, that girl, etc.

Our sexuality is a core identifier and it has been since God created Adam and Eve in the Garden: *"He created them male and female, and He blessed them and named them Man in the day when they were created."* **Genesis 5:2**

When we seek to satisfy these needs in an ungodly manner and/or to an ungodly degree, we tell God, "You are not meeting my needs well enough — I can do a much better job, and I am entitled to do so." This is sin. We all know the cycle: sin; broken intimacy with God; pain; manage & medicate=sin; more broken intimacy with God; more pain; more manage & medicate=sin — and on and on it goes.

To break this cycle in the area of lust and sexual sin, we have to repattern our thinking about this basic God-given desire. We do this by saturating with Scriptures and training ourselves to think God's thoughts after Him as they apply to our sexual needs and control of our bodies. We have to change what we believe if we are going to change how we live.

For WHO HAS KNOWN THE MIND OF THE LORD, THAT HE WILL INSTRUCT HIM? But we have the mind of Christ. **1 Corinthians 2:16**

But each one is tempted when he is carried away and enticed by his own lust. Then when lust has conceived, it gives birth to sin; and when sin is accomplished, it brings forth death. **James 1:14-15**

You lust and do not have; so you commit murder. You are envious and cannot obtain; so you fight and quarrel. You do not have because you do not ask. **James 4:2**

For all that is in the world, the lust of the flesh and the lust of the eyes and the boastful pride of life, is not from the Father, but is from the world. **1 John 2:16**

"You have heard that it was said, 'YOU SHALL NOT COMMIT ADULTERY'; but I say to you that everyone who looks at a woman with lust for her has already committed adultery with her in his heart. **Matthew 5:27-28**

I promised myself never to stare with desire at a young woman. **Job 31:1 (CEV)**

Flee immorality. Every other sin that a man commits is outside the body, but the immoral man sins against his own body. **1 Corinthians 6:18**

Do you not know that your bodies are members of Christ? Shall I then take away the members of Christ and make them members of a prostitute? May it never be! Or do you not know that the one who joins himself to a prostitute is one body with her? For He says, "THE TWO SHALL BECOME ONE FLESH." **1 Corinthians 6:15-16**

Now flee from youthful lusts and pursue righteousness, faith, love and peace, with those who call on the Lord from a pure heart. **2 Timothy 2:22**

Therefore I am well content with weaknesses, with insults, with distresses, with persecutions, with difficulties, for Christ's sake; for when I am weak, then I am strong. **2 Corinthians 12:10**

Food is for the stomach and the stomach is for food, but God will do away with both of them. Yet the body is not for immorality, but for the Lord, and the Lord is for the body. **1 Corinthians 6:13**

Or do you not know that the unrighteous will not inherit the kingdom of God? Do not be deceived; neither fornicators, nor idolaters, nor adulterers, nor effeminate, nor homosexuals, nor thieves, nor the covetous, nor drunkards, nor revilers, nor swindlers, will inherit the kingdom of God. Such were some of you; but you were washed, but you were sanctified, but you were justified in the name of the Lord Jesus Christ and in the Spirit of our God. **1 Corinthians 6:9-11**

VII. Weapons That Destroy a
Poor Self-Image

There is nothing that affects our lives more negatively than a lack of confidence, and there is nothing that destroys our confidence faster than a poor self-image. The world speaks of self-esteem, but we do not.

If we seek to esteem ourselves, we will always be in lack. But, if we seek our esteem in who we are in Christ, the resources available to us are limitless. Improvement of our self-image and our sense of worth starts when we begin to grasp how much God loves us. Our value is based on who we belong to. Belonging to God makes us priceless.

The following verses will help restore our confidence in God and His great love for us. These will help us begin to have a true and healthy self-image based in that unwavering truth.

By this the love of God was manifested in us, that God has sent His only begotten Son into the world so that we might live through Him. **1 John 4:9**

I will give thanks to You, for I am fearfully and wonderfully made; wonderful are Your works, and my soul knows it very well. **Psalm 139:14**

God created man in His own image, in the image of God He created him; male and female He created them ... God saw all that He had made, and behold, it was very good. And there was evening and there was morning, the sixth day. **Genesis 1:27, 31**

"Worthy are You, our Lord and our God, to receive glory and honor and power; for You created all things, and because of Your will they existed, and were created." **Revelation 4:11**

And we know that God causes all things to work together for good to those who love God, to those who are called according to His purpose. For those whom He foreknew,

He also predestined to become conformed to the image of His Son, so that He would be the firstborn among many brethren. **Romans 8:28-29**

For I am confident of this very thing, that He who began a good work in you will perfect it until the day of Christ Jesus. **Philippians 1:6**

Therefore, having been justified by faith, we have peace with God through our Lord Jesus Christ, through whom also we have obtained our introduction by faith into this grace in which we stand; and we exult in hope of the glory of God. **Romans 5:1-2**

For while we were still helpless, at the right time Christ died for the ungodly. **Romans 5:6**

But God demonstrates His own love toward us, in that while we were yet sinners, Christ died for us. **Romans 5:8**

For if while we were enemies we were reconciled to God through the death of His Son, much more, having been reconciled, we shall be saved by His life. **Romans 5:10**

Therefore there is now no condemnation for those who are in Christ Jesus. **Romans 8:1**

For I am convinced that neither death, nor life, nor angels, nor principalities, nor things present, nor things to come, nor powers, nor height, nor depth, nor any other created thing, will be able to separate us from the love of God, which is in Christ Jesus our Lord. **Romans 8:38-39**

"The LORD your God is in your midst, A victorious warrior. He will exult over you with joy, He will be quiet in His love, He will rejoice over you with shouts of joy." **Zephaniah 3:17**

He predestined us to adoption as sons through Jesus Christ to Himself, according to the kind intention of His will. **Ephesians 1:5**

VIII. WEAPONS AGAINST
UNFORGIVENESS

Unforgiveness is the root of many of our emotional bondages. Unforgiveness not only keeps us ties us to past hurts that we are trying to be healed of, it keeps us under the emotional control of someone other than God. It has been wisely said, "Unforgiveness is like drinking poison and waiting for the other person to die."

Unforgiveness is like picking up head-sized, jagged boulders and strapping them to our backs. Every time we do not forgive someone, we pick up another boulder and strap it on top of the others that we are carrying.

Jesus died to pay the price of all sin — ours and as well as the sins of those who have hurt or harmed us. Sin is His burden to carry, not ours. When we are unforgiving, we say, "Sorry, Jesus, but Your sacrifice was just not quite enough in this case. I can do a much better job of dealing with this than you can."

There are three types of forgiveness: Judicial Forgiveness, Internal Forgiveness, and Relational Forgiveness.

- Judicial forgiveness is the kind that only God can provide through the cross of Jesus Christ. We are not responsible for this kind of forgiveness.
- Internal forgiveness is the one that we are responsible for and that this section of this booklet addresses. We are responsible for this type of forgiveness.
- Relational forgiveness requires the confession, repentance, and the "bearing fruit in keeping with repentance" from the offending party. Without these elements, we are not required nor are we scripturally permitted to be relationally restored to the one who has wronged us.

Aside from the burden unforgiveness places on us, it is a sin and it fractures our relationship with God and others. In the fifth clause of the Lord's Prayer, we petition God, *"And forgive us our debts, as we also have forgiven our debtors."* **Matthew 6:12** <u>Jesus follows this model prayer with this admonition:</u>

"For if you forgive others for their transgressions, your heavenly Father will also forgive you. But if you do not forgive others, then your Father will not forgive your transgressions." **Matthew 6:14-15**

Be kind to one another, tender-hearted, forgiving each other, just as God in Christ also has forgiven you. **Ephesians 4:32**

So, as those who have been chosen of God, holy and beloved, put on a heart of compassion, kindness, humility, gentleness and patience; bearing with one another, and forgiving each other, whoever has a complaint against anyone; just as the Lord forgave you, so also should you. **Colossians 3:12-13**

Do nothing from selfishness or empty conceit, but with humility of mind regard one another as more important than yourselves; do not merely look out for your own personal interests, but also for the interests of others. **Philippians 2:3-4**

Walk in a manner worthy of the calling with which you have been called, with all humility and gentleness, with patience, showing tolerance for one another in love, being diligent to preserve the unity of the Spirit in the bond of peace. **Ephesians 4:1b-3**

There is only one Lawgiver and Judge, the One who is able to save and to destroy; but who are you who judge your neighbor? **James 4:12**

Bless those who persecute you; bless and do not curse. **Romans 12:14**

Never pay back evil for evil to anyone. Respect what is right in the sight of all men. If possible, so far as it depends on you, be at peace with all men. **Romans 12:17-18**

Never take your own revenge, beloved, but leave room for the wrath of God, for it is written, "VENGEANCE IS MINE, I WILL REPAY," says the Lord. **Romans 12:19**

Do not be overcome by evil, but overcome evil with good. **Romans 12:21**

To sum up, all of you be harmonious, sympathetic, brotherly, kindhearted, and humble in spirit; not returning evil for evil or insult for insult, but giving a blessing instead; for you were called for the very purpose that you might inherit a blessing. **1 Peter 3:8-9**

IX. Weapons Against
Anger

Anger is the most self-defeating and self-limiting of all the emotions because it is what is known as a "secondary emotion" or an "umbrella" emotion (it "covers up" other emotions). Anger is rooted in the primary emotions of fear, and/or pain, is fed by pride and selfishness, and is a reaction to them.

Anger is either righteous or unrighteous. How can we tell the difference? Righteous anger has no personal component to it: righteous anger is about what happened, not about who did it. Righteous anger is not about personal pain or loss. Righteous anger drove the changes in slavery laws, child-labor laws, and issues like that. Unrighteous anger, on the other hand, is all about us.

If we are honest, our anger is almost always of the unrighteous variety—we have a deep, personal and vested interest. Our anger seeks revenge for a wrong done us, not the resolution of a fundamental wrong.

We also must be aware that, when we experience deep wounding and anger arises in our life, two things are present: 1) there is an element of unforgiveness that we need to deal with (the previous section will help with that); and, 2) there is an underlying anger at God that we are either ignorant of or are unwilling to acknowledge.

Saturating on the following passages of Scripture will help us see what is real and true, and will defeat the anger in our life:

This you know, my beloved brethren. But everyone must be quick to hear, slow to speak and slow to anger; for the anger of man does not achieve the righteousness of God. **James 1:19-20**

Never take your own revenge, beloved, but leave room for the wrath of God, for it is written, "VENGEANCE IS MINE, I WILL REPAY," says the Lord. **Romans 12:19**

He who is slow to anger is better than the mighty, and he who rules his spirit, than he who captures a city. **Proverbs 16:32**

A man's discretion makes him slow to anger, and it is his glory to overlook a transgression. **Proverbs 19:11**

A gentle answer turns away wrath, but a harsh word stirs up anger. **Proverbs 15:1**

He who is slow to anger has great understanding, but he who is quick-tempered exalts folly. **Proverbs 14:29**

Scorners set a city aflame, but wise men turn away anger. **Proverbs 29:8**

Cease from anger and forsake wrath; Do not fret; it leads only to evildoing. **Psalm 37:8**

BE ANGRY, AND yet DO NOT SIN; do not let the sun go down on your anger. **Ephesians 4:26**

Therefore I want the men in every place to pray, lifting up holy hands, without wrath and dissension. **1 Timothy 2:8**

A fool's anger is known at once, but a prudent man conceals dishonor. **Proverbs 12:16**

He who despises his neighbor lacks sense, but a man of understanding keeps silent. **Proverbs 11:12**

X. Weapons Against
Fear of Failure

When we are convinced that we will fail anyway, we often either will not start something, or we will stop short before completing it. Faith in God and confidence in ourselves is the only healthy cure for the fear of failure.

First, we must keep I mind that nowhere in God's Word is "failure" used in reference to any human being. We fall short, but we never "fail."

Second, we must strengthen our faith by filling our mind with the Word of God. Then, as we take action on this truth with God's guiding, we begin to see our confidence grow (**Romans 10:17**: *"So faith comes from hearing, and hearing by the word of Christ."*)

Since our confidence is not based on ourselves but on Christ who lives in us (**Galatians 2:20**), and since we know that Jesus Christ cannot fail, we can have a new kind of confidence.

Confidence founded and built on Him will help us as we grow through times when we fall short, helping us realize that a temporary falling is not an abject failure — just a setback, a "missing the target."

"I have been crucified with Christ; and it is no longer I who live, but Christ lives in me; and the life which I now live in the flesh I live by faith in the Son of God, who loved me and gave Himself up for me." **Galatians 2:20**

For the weapons of our warfare are not of the flesh, but divinely powerful for the destruction of fortresses. We are destroying speculations and every lofty thing raised up against the knowledge of God, and we are taking every thought captive to the obedience of Christ. **2 Corinthians 10:4-5**

For I am confident of this very thing, that He who began a good work in you will perfect it until the day of Christ Jesus. **Philippians 1:6**

Brethren, I do not regard myself as having laid hold of it yet; but one thing I do: forgetting what lies behind and reaching forward to what lies ahead, I press on toward the goal for the prize of the upward call of God in Christ Jesus. **Philippians 3:13-14**

Now for this very reason also, applying all diligence, in your faith supply moral excellence, and in your moral excellence, knowledge, and in your knowledge, self-control, and in your self-control, perseverance, and in your perseverance, godliness, and in your godliness, brotherly kindness, and in your brotherly kindness, love.
2 Peter 1:5-7

But I say, walk by the Spirit, and you will not carry out the desire of the flesh. **Galatians 5:16**

But the fruit of the Spirit is love, joy, peace, patience, kindness, goodness, faithfulness, gentleness, self-control; against such things there is no law. **Galatians 5:22-23**

XI. Weapons for
Building Endurance

Staying the course will be the single most important factor for assuring success in the renewing of our minds and in the restorative work of God (see **Joel 2:25**).

Good intentions alone accomplish nothing. Only the one who finishes the race has a chance to win the prize. In order to be a finisher, we must keep our goal firmly in mind and not allow ourselves to be sidetracked. There is no prize for those who stop short of the goal.

It was for freedom that Christ set us free; therefore keep standing firm and do not be subject again to a yoke of slavery. **Galatians 5:1**

But whenever a person turns to the Lord, the veil is taken away. Now the Lord is the Spirit, and where the Spirit of the Lord is, there is liberty. **2 Corinthians 3:16-17**

[Jesus said] "Come to Me, all who are weary and heavy-laden, and I will give you rest. Take My yoke upon you and learn from Me, for I am gentle and humble in heart, and YOU WILL FIND REST FOR YOUR SOULS. For My yoke is easy and My burden is light." **Matthew 11:28-30**

But those who wait for the Lord's help[bf] find renewed strength; they rise up as if they had eagles' wings, they run without growing weary, they walk without getting tired. **Isaiah 40:31**

But one who looks intently at the perfect law, the law of liberty, and abides by it, not having become a forgetful hearer but an effectual doer, this man will be blessed in what he does. **James 1:25**

No soldier in active service entangles himself in the affairs of everyday life, so that he may please the one who enlisted him as a soldier. **2 Timothy 2:4**

"This book of the law shall not depart from your mouth, but you shall meditate on it day and night, so that you may be careful to do according to all that is written in it; for then you will make your way prosperous, and then you will have success. Have I not commanded you? Be strong and courageous! Do not tremble or be dismayed, for the LORD your God is with you wherever you go." **Joshua 1:7-8**

XII. Weapons for Overcoming "Emotional Orphaning"

God's original design, His created intent, was for each of us to be in safe, caring, loving, and nurturing relationships—first with our biological parents, then with our family of origin, then our extended family, and then continuing on through ever-expanding circles of relationship.

The closer in to the "center" and the earlier in life this original intent gets fractured or broken, the deeper and more significant the relational brokenness, the wounding of the heart, and the mangling of the soul a person experiences. We call this "emotional orphaning."

In battling besetting sin (including sexual sin all the way to unwanted SSA (Same-Sex Attraction), we need to understand the core reason for it and the internal battle that manifests itself. Neither sin nor sexuality define one's identity in Christ nor one's humanity. (<u>NOTE</u>: While this section speaks much to sexualized sin, the principles herein apply to all besetting sin patterns, sexual or otherwise.)

Besetting sin patterns are multi-tiered and multi-causal, especially sexual sin patterns . Yet there are also some elements that we find to be very common among those who experience deep bondage to any besetting sin problem.[25]

Proper restorative bonding leads the way to a healthy, God-designed humanity—including our sexuality. When one has suffered a major deficit in one's relationship with one's parent(s) (especially with the same gendered parent in the case of SSA), there is often a struggle to make good this deficit through relationships that are sexualized.

In cases where sexual abuse or early sexualization of a child takes place, intimacy-via-sex often becomes the counterfeit approach to experiencing true relational intimacy that each of us needs and longs for.

The deep hurt of unacceptance — real or perceived — that occurs when our relationships with one or more of our parents, with our family of origin, or with our peer group, this creates an intense drive to avoid attachment and connection to others on the one hand. Yet there is also the equally intense drive to fill the need that our detachment creates on the other hand. Our need for love, connection, and acceptance by our parents (which is foundational for us to learn about the love of God early in life) needs to be met, yet we both are not able to do so and we work to prevent ourselves from doing so at the same time. We have become "emotional orphans."[26]

Healthy relationships of children do not have a sexual component, even on the deepest levels of bonding. Adult relationships that are the most intimate of all are those of committed spouses. There is a sexual component not only present but also foundational to that deepest of all intimacy. Sexual intimacy is the ultimate expression of intimacy — it doesn't create intimacy.

Unfortunately, this often gets "out of order," and sexual intimacy is used as a substitute for or as a means to create godly, healthy intimacy. Hence, our drive for loving intimacy as adults (or near-adults) can easily become sexualized. It becomes a replacement for love, both as God defines it and as we truly need.

The key to healing this rift and meeting this love-deficit is to learn and accept the loving parenting of God Himself. Our Heavenly Father is not at all like our earthly parents. He cannot lie, He cannot abandon, He cannot be vicious, He cannot be selfish, and His love for us is so great that we can spend a lifetime trying to understand it and only grasp on a little of it.[27]

For [or "If"] my father and my mother have forsaken me, But the LORD will take me up.
Psalm 27:10

---

[25] (With regard to SSA, there are different degrees and levels of SSA that people experience, and there is a combination of factors that work together to create SSA in a person's life.

[26] For those who struggle with SSA, underlying all of this is our natural attraction to "other." They have not learned to be identified as "same" with their own gender. When a person does not identify with their own gender, they see members of their own gender as "other." The resulting attraction then seems "natural."

[27] Note: The root problem when dealing with unwanted SSA lies in the unmet emotional need to bond with the same gender parent and to feel welcomed as a member of that gender. This is also a common underlying component of other besetting sexual and non-sexual sin patterns.

"The LORD your God is in your midst, a victorious warrior. He will exult over you with joy, He will be quiet in His love, He will rejoice over you with shouts of joy." **Zephaniah 3:17**

But now, O LORD, You are our Father, We are the clay, and You our potter; And all of us are the work of Your hand. **Isaiah 64:8**

For You are our Father, though Abraham does not know us And Israel does not recognize us. You, O LORD, are our Father, Our Redeemer from of old is Your name. **Isaiah 63:16**

Because you are sons, God has sent forth the Spirit of His Son into our hearts, crying, "Abba! Father!" **Galatians 4:6**

For all who are being led by the Spirit of God, these are sons of God. **Romans 8:14**

For you have not received a spirit of slavery leading to fear again, but you have received a spirit of adoption as sons by which we cry out, "Abba! Father!" **Romans 8:15**

He predestined us to adoption as sons through Jesus Christ to Himself, according to the kind intention of His will. **Ephesians 1:5**

God created man in His own image, in the image of God He created him; male and female He created them...God saw all that He had made, and behold, it was very good. **Genesis 1:27, 31a**

A father of the fatherless and a judge for the widows, is God in His holy habitation. **Psalm 68:5**

The Spirit of the Lord GOD is upon me, Because the LORD has anointed me To bring good news to the afflicted; He has sent me to bind up the brokenhearted, To proclaim liberty to captives And freedom to prisoners. **Isaiah 61:1**

You have seen it, for You have beheld mischief and vexation to take it into Your hand. The unfortunate commits himself to You; You have been the helper of the orphan. **Psalm 10:14**

The LORD protects the strangers; He supports the fatherless and the widow, But He thwarts the way of the wicked. **Psalm 146:9**

He who dwells in the shelter of the Most High will abide in the shadow of the Almighty. I will say to the LORD, "My refuge and my fortress, My God, in whom I trust!" For it is He who delivers you from the snare of the trapper and from the deadly pestilence. He will cover you with His pinions, and under His wings you may seek refuge; His faithfulness is a shield and bulwark. **Psalm 91:1-4**

Do not move the ancient boundary or go into the fields of the fatherless, for their Redeemer is strong; He will plead their case against you. **Proverbs 23:10-11**

XIII. Weapons for Overcoming
DEPRESSION

Depression is an enduring sense of helpless hopelessness that is often accompanied by a deep sense of worthlessness. It is very hard to have a sense of purpose or a "point to all this" -- let alone the ability to be productive — when depression sets in.

Depression is a trap because it is "frozen rage." It is not a rage that explodes and consumes, but one that freezes and immobilizations everything it touches, burning a hole in the soul and sapping the very energy of life right out of the one suffering from it. (think dry ice) It is rooted in deep-seated, long-term unforgiveness — anger and bitterness turned inward.

Depression, boredom, a profound lack of motivation — all signs of a deeper, more serious problem that is deeply rooted in our heart and our beliefs about God, ourselves, and others — beliefs that are usually lies. Unmet expectations have resulted in disappointments that went unresolved; a series of disappointments left us disillusioned with people and relationships in general; disillusionment quickly led to a despondency over our worth and value; despondency results in depression and bitterness — one inwardly focused, the other outwardly focused.

We often do not give our disappointment with unmet expectations much thought. We *expect* to never suffer loss. We *expect* that everything is going to work out well. We *expect* that we will not get fired, that our romantic interest will not lose interest, and that our children will grow up wise and obedient to the Lord.

When these expectations go unmet, we suffer loss — and it saddens us. Scripture is *filled* with language like "grief," "sorrow," and "anguish of the soul." These are a normal part of the human experience.

Forgiveness is the key. Forgive the one who left, or the one who let us down, or even God (who somehow did not live up to what we expected Him to do). And realize that these things are not *because* of us; they are simply the normal result of living in a fallen and sin-suffering world.

Once the root of our unforgiveness has been isolated, we can attack it at its source by retraining our minds to view these things as God does, exercising Biblical forgiveness (See Section VII).

We do this by allowing the Scriptures to become our teacher. We find in the Bible the truth that exposes every lie that has taken us captive, bring it into surrender to the truth, and saturate our minds with that truth until our decisions are made based on the truth instead of the lies that have controlled us.

Finally, brethren, whatever is true, whatever is honorable, whatever is right, whatever is pure, whatever is lovely, whatever is of good repute, if there is any excellence and if anything worthy of praise, dwell on these things. **Philippians 4:8**

"Peace I leave with you; My peace I give to you; not as the world gives do I give to you. Do not let your heart be troubled, nor let it be fearful." **John 14:27**

I will lift up my eyes to the mountains; from where shall my help come? My help comes from the LORD, who made heaven and earth. **Psalm 112:1-2**

Rejoice in the Lord always; again I will say, rejoice! Let your gentle spirit be known to all men. The Lord is near. Be anxious for nothing, but in everything by prayer and supplication with thanksgiving let your requests be made known to God. And the peace of God, which surpasses all comprehension, will guard your hearts and your minds in Christ Jesus. **Philippians 4:4-7**

What then shall we say to these things? If God is for us, who is against us? **Romans 8:31**

Rejoice always; pray without ceasing; in everything give thanks; for this is God's will for you in Christ Jesus. **1 Thessalonians 5:16-18**

The godly cry out and the Lord hears; he saves them from all their troubles. **Psalm 34:17**

The Lord is near the brokenhearted; he delivers those who are discouraged. **Psalm 34:18**

Why are you depressed, O my soul? Why are you upset? Wait for God! For I will again give thanks to my God for his saving intervention. **Psalm 42:11**

Consequently the Lord provides safety for the oppressed; He provides safety in times of trouble. **Psalm 9:9**

God delivers me and exalts me; God is my strong protector and my shelter. Trust in Him at all times, you people! Pour out your hearts before him! God is our shelter! **Psalm 62:8-9**

XIV. WEAPONS FOR OVERCOMING
ANXIETY

Anxiety is unfocused fearfulness based on an unreal, imaginary, and intangible threat. Anxiety is fearfulness over potentialities, not realities. When we are faced with a real and tangible threat, the fight-or-flight responses God has hard-wired into our bodies gets activated, and everything we are focuses on getting us out of the unsafe situation and making us safe. This is fear.

The problem with anxiety is that it is fearfulness that treats an unreal or potential situation as if it is a real one. The same fight-or-flight responses get activated, but there is no real threat for those defenses to focus on and deal with. All of the physical and emotional energy is undirected and, as our imaginations continue to manufacture more and bigger potential threats, the processes become more and more intense as well. Fear becomes fearfulness and caution becomes anxiety.

In 2 Corinthians 10:3-5, Paul provides great encouragement to everyone who feels faced by enormous battles too big to win. One of the encouragements he provides is that we (the redeemed) don't do battle the way the world (the unredeemed) does battle—and the weapons we have available are not weapons of this earth.

When we add a saturation Scripture to the physical interruption techniques above, we rapidly get back into reality and back in control. If we don't do this, our imaginations can easily concoct multiple and varied potential scenarios, all of which are as unreal as the one that triggered the initial reaction.

The emotional distress related to worry piled upon worry and anxiety piled upon anxiety renders us mentally and emotionally incapable of effectively dealing with the legitimate problems that we face daily in our lives. Our entire focus becomes the anxiety we feel and how to get relief from it—even if only for a moment.

That is not how God intended for us to live. In fact, there is an enormous promise for us in 2 Timothy 1:7: "For God has not given us a spirit of fear, but of power and of love, and of a sound mind."

The way to understand this and apply it is to begin with the "not" statement the verse opens with: "God has not given us a spirit of fear." Fear here is better rendered "fearfulness." To be "full of fear" means to be driven by, gripped with, and focused on indefinable imagined dangers.

For God has not given us a spirit of fearfulness, but of power and of love, and of a sound mind. **2 Timothy 1:7**

When my anxious thoughts multiply within me, Your consolations delight my soul. **Psalm 94:19**

"Do not fear, for I am with you; Do not anxiously look about you, for I am your God. I will strengthen you, surely I will help you, Surely I will uphold you with My righteous right hand." **Isaiah 41:10**

Be anxious for nothing, but in everything by prayer and supplication with thanksgiving let your requests be made known to God. **Philippians 4:6**

Therefore humble yourselves under the mighty hand of God, that He may exalt you at the proper time, casting all your anxiety on Him, because He cares for you. **1 Peter 5:6-7**

"For this reason I say to you, [n]do not be worried about your [o]life, as to what you will eat or what you will drink; nor for your body, as to what you will put on. Is not life more than food, and the body more than clothing?" **Matthew 6:25**

"But above all pursue his kingdom and righteousness, and all these things will be given to you as well. So then, do not worry about tomorrow, for tomorrow will worry about itself. Today has enough trouble of its own. **Matthew 6:33-34**

The Ten Keys for Self-Control

I will purpose to have no desire above the Lord.

I will look to God's Word first and most for life's answers.

I will develop an awareness of God's blessings.

I will surrender ever more completely to the Lord my God.

I will focus on the solutions and not the problems.

I will renew my mind with Scripture saturation.

I will guard my mind against unhealthy thinking.

I will avoid situations and people that invite temptation.

I will review my past only to learn from it and heal.

I will not compare myself to others.

For this is God's will: that you become holy, that you keep away from sexual immorality, that each of you know how to possess his own body in holiness and honor.

1 Thessalonians 4:3-5

THE PLEDGE

1. I will not make it my main goal to improve my life, but to improve my relationship with Jesus Christ. As a result, I will enhance the total quality of my spiritual, emotional, and physical life.

2. I will eat healthily at least 80% of the time, and I will commit to getting the amount of rest I know is adequate for me to be fully rested.

3. I will make the necessary adjustments to the discretionary aspects of my schedule in order to do this.

4. I will read through "The Ten Keys for Self-Control" at the front of this booklet at least once each day and prayerfully seek to live by them for the duration of my involvement in this program.

5. I will saturate twelve times before breakfast with: "Therefore I exhort you, brothers and sisters, by the mercies of God, to present your bodies as a sacrifice – alive, holy, and pleasing to God – which is your reasonable service." Romans 12:1

6. I will saturate twelve times before lunch with: _____

    _____

    _____

7. I will saturate twelve times before dinner with: _____

    _____

    _____

8. I will complete the Unbound daily reading and saturation, realizing that it is only through strict adherence to what is prescribed in the program that my mind will truly be renewed and my life transformed.

9. I will set realistic goals and try to achieve them. I will share these goals with my Unbound group, my Unbound partner, and/or my counselor.

10. I will be accountable to my Lord, to my Unbound group, my Unbound partner, and/or my counselor.

Signed _____

Date _____

Made in the USA
Las Vegas, NV
26 September 2021